Theory of National Economic Planning

Theory of National Economic Planning

By CARL LANDAUER

UNIVERSITY OF CALIFORNIA PRESS

BERKELEY AND LOS ANGELES · 1947

UNIVERSITY OF CALIFORNIA PRESS
BERKELEY AND LOS ANGELES
CALIFORNIA

◇

CAMBRIDGE UNIVERSITY PRESS
LONDON, ENGLAND

Second Edition

PRINTED IN THE UNITED STATES OF AMERICA
BY THE UNIVERSITY OF CALIFORNIA PRESS

ACKNOWLEDGMENTS

THE READER of this little treatise will easily realize my indebtedness to several authors, so I consider it unnecessary to mention names, except one. My exchange of opinions with Eduard Heimann, professor in the Graduate Faculty of the New School of Social Research in New York, has stimulated my thought on economic planning to a far greater extent than I can document by quotations.

Upon the appearance of the first edition, several friends and colleagues assisted me in the further development of my thoughts through their comments on various passages of the book. They will find many of their arguments for agreement and dissent reflected by alterations in the original text.

I also wish to express my gratitude to Mrs. Mary Mosk, who has advised me in matters of grammar and style. If the English of this book is readable, the credit goes to her and to Mrs. Mary Anne Whipple and Miss Lucie E. N. Dobbie, both of the University of California Press, from whom I have received very valuable suggestions for changes in the form of presentation.

C. L.

Berkeley, California,
May, 1947.

CONTENTS

[vii]

Introduction

THIS ESSAY deals with change in the economic order. The particular kind of change it discusses, transition from an unplanned to a planned system, is a task for statesmen and practical reformers, who must apply considerations of practicability and political expediency to the problems of social transformation. They also need, whether they know it or not, a theoretical framework. It is with these theoretical aspects of change that this study is concerned, and the other problems involved will be discussed only so far as they cannot be isolated from the main topic.

Even with this restriction, the discussion necessarily cuts across many lines of approach to the core problems of human society—so many, indeed, that completeness in the reviewing of relevant facts and important literature proved unachievable. An author who would try to acquaint himself with all the books and articles touching upon one or another phase of the planning problem would have no time to think out his own ideas. Therefore the selection of the arguments for discussion in this essay had to some extent to be arbitrary, and it can only be hoped that no important type of argument, either for or against planning or any particular form of it, has been entirely overlooked.[1] It would be unwarranted to assume that this

---

[1] Alvin H. Hansen's *Economic Policy and Full Employment* (New York and London: Whittlesey House, 1947), appeared too late to be used in preparing the second edition.

writer has in every instance succeeded in singling out for controversy or assent those writings which represent their particular school of thought at its best.[2]

A place of special significance for our topic is held by recent theoretical writings on the theory of socialism. This literature, represented, for instance, by the writings of Lange, Pigou, and Dickinson, starts from the question: Is a rational economy possible if all the factors of production are communally owned and under communal control? The authors assume that for some reasons of justice or economic necessity private enterprise must be superseded by social enterprise. No such assumption is made in this essay, and the question to be investigated is: What form and degree of social control must be established as a remedy for the most irrational feature of the present system, economic instability? The two questions, of course, are interrelated, and the discussion will make it clear that the theoreticians of socialism have been trailblazers for the investigation of the problem of national planning. But their objective was to find the conditions under which a definite concept of society, representing, in a sense, a maximum of change, might be put into reality, whereas here we will discuss the minimum requisites of a program destined to accomplish a more limited purpose.

The last years have seen great changes in socioeconomic relations. Aside from the nationalization of key industries, which is in the process of execution in England and at least on the agenda almost everywhere on the European continent,

---

[2] Therefore no attempt has been made to compile a bibliography, although it might have been a convenience for some readers. A mere listing of books would have hardly been worth the space, for no student of the subject could profit much from moving within that ocean of literature without a guide. Any offer of guidance, however, would have required the establishment of an order of value, and this task seemed impossible of fulfillment at the present time.

many nations have greatly added to the protection of their citizens from economic hazards. Great Britain has introduced her "from cradle to grave" system. In the United States, the social security laws, enacted in one great sweep a few years before the outbreak of the war, are in operation and supplementary laws are proposed to fill out the gaps that still remain. These measures are necessary elements of any social order which endeavors to reduce human suffering to a minimum. No general policy can prevent accidents, of a physical or a social nature, which may deprive individuals of their incomes or may impose on them financial burdens for the restoration or preservation of their working ability. But insurance is primarily a means to protect the individual against harmful economic consequences of events in his personal life and has only a very limited remedial effect if economic hardships are rooted in general conditions. From the individual's point of view, insurance benefits are no adequate compensation for protracted unemployment. From a general viewpoint, it is true that unemployment benefits operate as a cushion against the drop of consumers' purchasing power in a depression, but the worst depression the world has even seen occurred at a time when society had made better provisions than ever before for the maintenance of those who lost their jobs. This experience is at least prima facie evidence that the cushioning effect of insurance benefits cannot substantially weaken the impact of those forces which make our economy unstable. In some countries the structure of social insurance crumbled when the depression caused extreme distress in public finance, and in one nation—the German Republic—the inability of the government to maintain insurance benefits on a decent level helped to undermine faith in democracy. Some economists might maintain that the insurance system would have withstood the effects of the depression better, or would have shortened the period of economic paralysis, if other methods of financing had been chosen, or if benefits had been more liberal, or if work relief had been offered more generally in place of cash relief. This author, for one, has not been able to convince himself that any such alterations would have made an essential difference in the outcome.

Social insurance, therefore, does not in itself guarantee stability of employment and avoidance of jerks in the price level. It cannot function properly in an economy which is not stabilized by the use of other techniques. The purpose of this book is to discuss some fundamental questions which must be answered before those techniques can be elaborated and applied.

I. The Function and Concept of Planning

IN THE ECONOMY of perfect competition, which we perhaps may better call the economy of the perfect market, all intra-marginal resources are used in the way best suited to satisfy effective demand. The slightest degree of idleness—whether of man power, equipment, or stocks of material—produces immediately a price drop great enough to cause the unemployed resources to be reabsorbed without delay into the productive process. Therefore, unemployment must be explained in terms of some of the many differences between the perfect market economy and the real economy.

One of these differences is the disregard of the element of time in the concept of the perfect market economy. It would not be correct to say that we abstract entirely from the lapse of time when we use the concept of the perfect market, for this concept includes, for instance, the phenomenon of interest. However, in two very essential respects the abstraction takes place. First, we assume that there are no frictions, and that, therefore, economic action and reaction—for instance, increase of supply, lowering of price, and increase of demand—are simultaneous, or nearly so. Second, by assuming that all persons have full knowledge of the consequences of their actions, we disregard the fact that this knowledge can only be obtained in the course of time. In a competitive economy, producers do not compare notes on their plans, and even under imperfect competition or monopoly few producers inform each other fully about all their designs. More often than not one entrepreneur learns of the intentions of his fellow entrepreneurs only when these intentions have been carried out to a point where the effects become visible. Frequently this occurs a considerable time after the action has been initiated. Entrepreneurs enter commitments for the execution of projects without knowing what commitments are accepted by other entrepreneurs at the same time, or what will be accepted before their own projects can be brought to fruition.

This is one of the major reasons why the price system cannot achieve perfect coördination of individual economic activities. Present prices reflect only the present relationship of supply and demand, with an entirely inadequate and haphazard correction through speculation. Most frequently, present prices are the basis of decisions for industrial expansion, not because entrepreneurs are foolish enough to think that prices cannot change, but because they rarely find any adequate source of information of the likelihood of change and, therefore, accept the possibility of price fluctuation as an inevitable risk in their economic ventures. Their actions, inadequately adjusted to conditions which are bound to arise, will aggravate instead of alleviate the price changes, and the resulting disturbances of the market will cause major fluctuations in employment. Economic stabilization, in the sense of a stable rate of growth without violent changes in the price level and without widespread interruption of employment, is unobtainable unless present actions are planned with a view to the supply-demand relations which they are bound to create, and not merely guided by the supply-demand relations existing at the start.

All business-cycle theories explain the change from prosperity to depression, in fact if not in terms, by reference to the inadequacy of the present prices as a guide for economic acts which are bound to exert an influence on the future. If the purely psychological theories are neglected, the various schools of business-cycle theory can be divided, broadly speaking, into two main groups, distinguished by their acceptance or rejection of Say's famous proposition that every additional supply creates an equal amount of additional demand. Those who do not believe in this proposition assume the possibility of a growing divergence of productive capacity and purchasers' incomes. They think that in periods of prosperity the entrepreneurs expand their plants so much that the development of purchasing power does not keep pace with the growth of the ability to produce. "Underconsumption theory" has become the accepted term for this kind of explanation. Evidently, if present prices reflected not merely the supply-demand relation which exists today, but offered any way to recognize that relation which present commitments, according to this theory, are bound to create, expansion would not reach the danger point, for no entrepreneur wants to create capacity which he cannot use.

The business-cycle theorists who accept Say's law also explain the origin of depressions by the exaggerated size and number of the expansion projects in prosperity. This type of thought is now commonly labeled "overinvestment theory," which is a very unsatisfactory term, since nearly all the theories of the business cycle refer somehow to the phenomenon of large investment during the boom. Yet terminological discussions are rarely fruitful, and thus the name may as well be accepted. The conception of the overinvestment theorists is not that the expansion projects are too large or numerous in relation to the prospective purchasing power, but rather that they are too large in relation to the resources available for their completion. Evidently, if the entrepreneurs had been warned in time, by a rising level of factor prices, of the impending shortage of resources, the collapse could have been avoided.[1]

There are two imaginable ways to remove the cause which both schools, from their different positions, regard as responsible for economic fluctuations. Either the mechanism of the price system must be so influenced that present prices reflect to a sufficient extent the future supply and demand situation; or the effects of commitments into which entrepreneurs plan to enter must be calculated in advance, and entrepreneurs must be induced to disobey present prices so far as these would lead them into commitments that cannot be carried out successfully.

A policy which attempts to correct the reactions of the price system in an otherwise unregulated economy must use credit

---

[1] The reader may find it difficult, perhaps, to fit the business-cycle theory of John Maynard Keynes into this scheme. As Haberler has convincingly shown, the general elements of Keynes's economic theory are compatible with almost any explanation of the phenomenon of depressions. See Gottfried von Haberler, *Prosperity and Depression* (Geneva, 1939), chap. 8, esp., p. 235.

Even his own explanation of slumps, which Keynes offers rather hesitatingly in his "Notes on the Trade Cycle" (chap. 22 of *The General Theory of Employment, Interest, and Money,* New York: Harcourt, Brace, 1936), is only a framework with room for different cycle theories. Keynes sees the main cause of a depression in the sudden collapse of the marginal efficiency of capital, that is, the expected yield of the last unit of money capital. A collapse of expectations may be due to one of two causes. Either conditions have changed, so that previous expectations have become unjustified, and this change is suddenly realized, or people change their mood without a change in underlying conditions—they were optimistic before and suddenly become sober or even pessimistic. If the latter change is assumed to be the cause of depressions, we have to deal with one of the purely psychological explanations.

Keynes mostly leans toward a psychological theory, but he does by no means exclude the possibility that objective conditions may have reduced the real prospects of making a profit. Since he assumes a secular decline in the trend of these prospects, it is not impossible that he thinks of depressions as periodical adjustments of capital values to this downward trend. There is a very similar conception in the thought of

as an instrument. Almost as long as there have been Central Banks of Issue, it has been their policy to curtail booms by restricting credit and to encourage economic activity in periods of depression by an abundant supply of "cheap money." More recently, aside from other refinements of this technique, support of Central Bank policy by adequate fiscal measures and by public works programs has become frequent. In this way the range of economic fluctuations has been reduced, not in comparison with previous epochs, but with the magnitude which it would probably have assumed without an attempt at regulation.

In a later place we shall try to summarize recent experience with credit policy and to show some of the reasons why it has not been more successful. Here it will suffice to state that credit policy can, at best, mitigate or shorten but not prevent depressions, and therefore, that it is not an effective means of economic stabilization at full employment. This statement, of

---

Karl Marx (*see Capital,* Vol. III, chap. 15)—not the only point of contact between Keynes and the great socialist thinker.

If we assume for a moment that Keynes really held a deterioration of objective conditions responsible for the collapse of expectations, the question arises why conditions should have so deteriorated. The overinvestment theorists would suggest that the strain on the resources had been too great, but it is certain that Keynes would not accept this explanation. There is a possibility that other technical factors, related to the tendency of diminishing returns from land and analogous phenomena, might be considered the cause of the decline, but it is difficult to see how this could explain depressions, since a characteristic feature of the latter is the depreciation of capital assets, whereas the lower return of new factor units would necessarily enhance the value of those already in existence. Therefore, the cause of deterioration would have to be found in a decline of marketing possibilities for products. This presupposes the belief that the disbursement of large sums, invested in industry during the prosperity period, has somehow failed to maintain consumers' purchasing power to an extent sufficient for the buying of all the products which the newly created capital goods are able to produce. Therefore, if Keynes followed this line of thought, he would be committed to the conception of a periodically growing discrepancy between capacity to produce and capacity to consume, and would thereby be placed where probably most of his followers stand, namely, among the underconsumption theorists.

course, refers to the role of credit regulation when it is considered the exclusive or principal instrument of economic stabilization. As an auxiliary measure to carry out a comprehensive production scheme, credit regulation is indispensable and far more likely to be effective.

The purpose can only be accomplished if the effects of the entrepreneurs' commitments are anticipated with respect to their kinds and magnitudes and if economic activities are then coördinated in a more perfect way than they would be under the exclusive guidance of the price mechanism. The agency charged with the task of anticipation will have to survey the entrepreneurs' projects and have to find out what processes of production they require and what quantities of the various production factors are necessary for these processes. It will have to estimate how the incomes of the various population groups will be affected by the contemplated changes in production and how consumers will react to the changes in supply and income. The agency may then work out modifications of the projects, so that they can be executed without major disturbances in the body economic. There is no reason why the agency should confine itself to the examination of the expansion projects which individual entrepreneurs have worked out. It may assume the initiative by proposing its own projects, either as a supplement to those contemplated by the entrepreneurs, or as the main scheme for the expansion. No matter where the initiative lies, or how it may be divided, there will emerge from the work of that agency a scheme of economic growth, comprising those expansion projects which in its opinion are mutually compatible and preferable to all alternatives. We are in accordance with general usage when we call this scheme a national economic plan, on the assumption that the agency—

the planning board—is operating on behalf of a national, not a regional or international, community.

It may be useful to consider some of the implications of this line of reasoning, which has led us to the concept of economic planning, before we attempt to work out a clear-cut definition. The interest in planning, as a permanent policy or institution, springs mainly from the desire to avoid depressions. Except for this interest, planning in the western countries might never have become the object of serious thought and widespread discussion. However, there is no reason why planning, once instituted, should not be made to serve other purposes as well. A plan shows the interdependence of all economic operations at any moment within the planning period, and such a demonstration is very important for the determination of policies in many fields. An especially important task of planning results from increased intensity of struggles over the distribution of the national income. If wages or farm prices are to be fixed for some period in advance, and if they are to be determined by some kind of rational consideration and not merely by the relative power of the interested parties, it will be necessary to estimate in advance the magnitude of the social product and the possible effects of changes in the cost of production upon that magnitude. Not even an approximately accurate estimate of that kind is possible without a production plan.

The problems which planning is intended to solve originate from the growth of the economy. This is immediately clear for the task of straightening out the business cycle, with which only growing economies are afflicted but in other respects too a task for planning exists merely because economic facts are subject to continuous change. The interdependence of economic processes offers serious problems of investigation only because the data are in flux, otherwise the effects of changes, for example, in the wage or interest rates, would be so clear that the services of the planner would hardly be required. More will be said later about the tasks of planning outside of the elimination of depressions.

When the planning board works out its suggestions for the future, its main task is to determine how the activities of the various business units must fit together to secure a full and balanced use of resources. Thus it takes over a function of the market, namely, coördination of individual activities. Planning is justified only if it can achieve a better coördination than the unregulated market. There is hope that the complete survey of resources and operations, extended by way of estimation into the future, will enable the planning board to avoid the pitfalls of the market mechanism. But the difference lies in the better fulfillment of the function, not in the function itself.

Planning means coördination through a conscious effort, instead of the automatic coördination which takes place in the market, and that conscious effort is to be made by an organ of society. Therefore, planning is an activity of a collectivistic character and is regulation of the activities of individuals by the community. This is true whether or not the plan is enforced by compulsion. Even if the plan is carried out through counsel voluntarily accepted, the weight is shifted from individual decisions to the deliberations of communal bodies.

The collectivistic nature of planning is so much in the public mind, that planning has quite frequently been identified with government interference. But history is full of examples of government interference, whereas the establishment of an economic plan (namely, a comprehensive scheme of expected economic processes), has rarely even been attempted. It seems a misuse to speak of planning when there is no plan; all planning is government control, but not all government control is planning.

A plan should be distinguished from a mere determination of policy, even if the latter is connected with an advance analysis of its probable effects, as it was in Alexander Hamilton's Report on Manufactures, which represented an effort to coördinate economic activities for an intended purpose, but did not draw up a scheme of economic processes in quantitative terms. Of course, it is by no means impossible to base the proposal of a tariff or a social welfare law or a measure to regulate domestic commerce or the stock exchange upon a quantitative anticipation of the economic processes as they will develop if the proposal is carried out, but that is tantamount to saying that a mere program of economic policy can be developed into an economic plan. A program may describe the desired processes merely in terms of their kind; it may, for instance, propose that a country should take up manufacturing industry or certain types of industry, or should, on the contrary, confine itself to agriculture. A plan adds quantitative determination. It provides for a definite volume and value of steel and machine output, wheat production, railroad service, and for a definite consumption of man power and material in each industry.

Planning can be defined as guidance of economic activities by a communal organ through a scheme which describes, in quantitative as well as qualitative terms, the productive processes that ought to be undertaken during a designated future period. To achieve the main purpose of planning, these processes must be so chosen and designed that they secure the full use of available resources and avoid contradictory requirements, making a stable rate of progress possible.

Planning must be carried out in two phases. First, a plan must be compiled, and second, it must be executed. It is necessary to emphasize this commonplace because an inadequate distinction between planmaking and plan execution has led to many misunderstandings. A very different degree of intensity or comprehensiveness may be required for these two spheres. In making the plan, we must take into account all the processes within the body economic, since each of them may influence the other. Once we have established the plan, we may well find that it is sufficient to apply special measures of inducement or compulsion in some fields only, whereas in others development is likely to follow the lines devised in the plan without any action by the organs of society. At any rate, thoroughness in the sphere of planmaking may be compatible with the application of mild means in the field of plan execution. That a plan is all-inclusive, as it should be, does not mean that it has to be carried out by compulsion, still less that it requires a dictator. A total plan may be put into effect by methods which are not totalitarian at all.

II. The Making of the Plan

DEFINITION OF the function of planning—our endeavor in the foregoing pages—is not the same as description of the purpose which a plan may be made to serve. Nearly all human purposes require material means for their achievement and are pursued over a period of time. The achievement will always be easier if the economy is more efficient in producing goods, the efficiency will always be greater if economic expansion goes on without interruption, and there will always be more likelihood for a continuous growth of production facilities if the expansion process is guided by a plan. Thus a tyrant may plan for the achievement of maximum power, a religious group for the building of a great church organization, a people in danger of foreign invasion for the organization and equipment of the most efficient army, a benevolent autocrat for providing the citizens with goods which, in his opinion, they ought to have, and a democratic government for the best satisfaction of the people's desires. Every one of these governments will wish to use the resources of the national economy as effectively as possible, and therefore the function of planning, economic stabilization at full employment, will be the same; but the purposes of the particular plan, and therefore the ways in which the resources of the economy are employed, will be very different.

In the western countries, aside from periods of emergency, planning for the satisfaction of consumers' desires is of greater significance than any other type, but it is also, for two reasons, a more complex undertaking. In the first place, planning for the sake of the consumers lacks that near-complete unity of ultimate purpose which we find, for instance, in war planning; consumers' preferences are proverbially different. Second, if the consumers are to be given what they want, machinery is needed to ascertain their desires. The planning board does not assume ultimate power to decide what should be produced, but lays down a framework for the decision of the consumers. As we shall see, this procedure raises some questions which would not become significant if the consumer were denied economic sovereignty.

It is easy, however, to exaggerate the sacrifice which the planning board will have to make in terms of effort and difficulty of operation if it puts itself at the service of the consumer. Even a despot can exert his rule only through human beings, and if he wants to use them he must take their wishes and needs into account. Thus the difference between planning for the satisfaction of consumers' desires and all the other types of planning is one of degree only. A despotic government, or a ruler who is convinced that he understands the real needs of the consumers better than the consumers themselves, may disregard their wishes in many respects, and may thereby simplify his economic policy, yet he cannot deprive them of every freedom of choice. His machinery for anticipation of what the consumers are going to choose will be cruder than that of a democratic planning board, but it cannot be spared entirely if disaffection and inefficiency are to be avoided.

Democratic planning requires full consumers' sovereignty, as distinguished from the narrower concept of "consumers' free choice." The latter term, in the language now generally used by economists, means merely that consumers do not draw fixed rations of individual commodities but can choose among all the commodities they find on the market; in other words, that incomes are paid out in money, usable in exchange for all sorts of wares, rather than in bread stamps, meat stamps, assignment certificates for rooms, and so on. Under this system the government still retains the right to decide what ought to be produced, without being bound by consumers' preferences. Consumers' sovereignty, however, means that consumers decide how each available unit of resources should be used. Therefore they can choose not merely among goods already produced but among all practicable objectives of production. The consumer, through the "pull" of his demand, steers production. Consumers' free choice is essentially a technical method of distributing goods; consumers' sovereignty is a principle of fundamental importance.

We have to beware of the error—which permeates Hayek's widely read book *The Road to Serfdom*[1] and is turned by him into an argument against planning—that consumers' sovereignty leads to innumerable conflicts which will put the planning board in the center of a continuous political struggle and thereby end every hope of making it a body of impartial experts. Consumers' desires are different, but they are not necessarily contradictory. Divergence of consumers' tastes does not

---

[1] Friedrich A. Hayek, *The Road to Serfdom*. Foreword by John Chamberlain. (Chicago: University of Chicago Press, 1944).

produce effects similar to the divergence of opinions between political parties, for the consumer wants only a proportional part of the available resources to be devoted to the purposes for which he has a preference and does not care what happens to the rest, whereas a political party wants its aims to prevail to the exclusion of others. If, for instance, some citizens want a constitutional reform and others oppose it, either the one or the other group must win its point, or if a compromise is made, one group loses what the other gains. But if one consumer wants to spend his income on better food and the other on better housing, there is no need for any agency to arbitrate this difference of opinion. Each can follow his preference without prejudice to the other, except to the extent that their needs require the use of the same scarce resources. In this event the conflict is decided by competitive bidding, regardless of whether the economic system is one of unplanned capitalism or a planned economy based on consumers' sovereignty.[2] Failure to notice this fact leads to gross overestimation of the number and magnitude of conflicts which a planning board will have to settle.

But there are conflicts which require a political decision. In matters of education, in the broadest sense of the word, the easy way by which other matters of consumption are settled is not practicable. The education of our children determines the character of the future community. My neighbor may be perfectly satisfied if his children grow up without education and may, therefore, refuse to let the community spend any of its resources on school buildings and the maintenance of teach-

---

[2] Even if industries were completely socialized, there would only be differences in the form, not in the essence of the procedure as long as the use of money is retained and consumers' sovereignty laid down as the basic rule. The reader who has any doubt on this point may consult, as one among many sources, H. D. Dickinson, *Economics of Socialism* (Oxford, 1939).

ers, but I shall be most dissatisfied with the idea that my children might be forced to live in the kind of community which
his children would make if they did not receive any schooling.
Besides, we generally feel that a parent's right over the fate of
his children is conditional, not absolute, and since the child is
not in a position to make decisions for himself, we limit the
power of the parent to make decisions for him, to deviate from
what we expect to be the child's wish when he has reached
adult age. We may therefore force the father—in a planned
economy, as we do today—to tolerate expenditure of community resources for the schooling of his children. To forestall
the evil effects of poor housing upon the community, we may
subsidize the construction of dwellings from public funds,
thereby causing a greater amount of resources to be spent upon
housing than the preferences of the individual families would
justify. We do not want people to consume opium or mari-
juana, and we will, of course, not provide for their production
except for medicinal use. We do not recognize the addict's
sovereignty as a consumer because we think that his habit will
disqualify him as a citizen and thereby damage the community, which should have the active support of all its members.
It is also because we feel that he is not now in a position to
make a choice that deserves to be respected and that after-
wards, when we have freed him from his vice, he will approve
of our course of action. There is a negative social need for the
prevention of the use of noxious drugs as there are positive
social needs for proper education and housing.

In all these instances, the political power of the majority has
to be used against the minority.[3] However, the majority has not

---

[3] These decisions must be made by a majority, because there are practically always
dissenters. It is difficult to see why Hayek believes that "common action is . . . limited
to the fields where people agree on common ends." (*Op. cit.,* p. 60.) As a description

merely to consider what influence upon the individuals it regards as desirable, but also how far it will go in limiting individual freedom. Probably none of us has any doubt concerning the opium addict, but many of us, even if we do not consume liquor ourselves, may question the wisdom or the right to withhold it from our fellow citizens. If a minority wants to enjoy a new type of art and is willing to pay for it, there is no reason why that minority should be denied facilities such as

of conditions in present-day capitalistic society, this statement is obviously invalid, as for example, the budget debates of legislative bodies show. Hayek's own ideal society could not possibly be bound by that rule, since he does not wish to eliminate, for example, defense and public education. Conscientious objectors will presumably always block complete agreement on defense as a common purpose; although people may agree that schooling is desirable, they will have very divergent ideas with respect to the ends which schools should strive to accomplish.

A few of Hayek's passages indicate that he does not always think of general agreement in this context but that at least sometimes he means to deny that even agreement within a majority is possible when economic issues are at stake. "Majorities will be found where it is a choice between limited alternatives; but it is a superstition to believe that there must be a majority view on everything. There is no reason why there should be a majority in favor of any one of the different possible courses if their number is legion. Every member of the legislative assembly might prefer some particular plan for the direction of economic activity to no plan, yet no one plan may appear preferable to a majority to no plan at all." (*Op. cit.*, p. 64.) This would clearly be a majority view and the resulting compromise would be very acceptable to Hayek: the majority would reject planning. But it is at least equally possible that the majority will successively eliminate by vote each of the less desirable plans and retain one which, although perhaps not the first choice of any one member, is considered preferable to no plan by a majority. If planning is regarded as a means to assure stable growth of the economy or other common advantages, the latter outcome is much more probable, for the same reason why—to modify an illustration used by Hayek—a group of people, wishing to take a hiking trip but having failed to agree on the goal in advance of their arrival at the starting point, are unlikely to return home because of inability to decide where to go, provided all of them find great pleasure in hiking. In any event, however, acceptance of one plan or rejection of all would be a legitimate action for the representatives of the people. "Dissatisfaction with democratic processes" or the belief that elected legislatures are "ineffective 'talking shops'" (*ibid.*, p. 62) will only originate if a sufficient number of voters become convinced that the advantages of planning are greater than the disadvantages of some plan and if at the same time a majority of representatives rejects all plans, regarding none of them preferable to an unplanned economy. In this event the remedy is at hand: the people should elect other representatives because the present representation does not express the will of the voters.

museums or theaters. The national plan must provide for the establishment of all churches in which people are enough interested to forego, *pro tanto,* their right to consume goods which would require an equal amount of resources. The majority, which perhaps thinks cubism, or whatever the new art is, a silly sort of painting in which nobody should indulge or may consider a particular cult superstitious and its doctrine misleading, may try to win the heretics over by persuasion, but must not resort to compulsion, economic or otherwise. The conflict between the educational aims of a majority and the right of a minority to its own convictions is by no means peculiar to a planned economy, but here it assumes increased importance. In a planned system, it may be necessary to implement the constitutional provisions protecting minority interests with special safeguards, but the best protection will not lie in laws. It will lie in the conviction of the majority that indoctrination by the community is only justifiable as long as it concerns the ethical standards without which no community can live, and that for the rest everybody must be free to follow his beliefs, follies, or hobbies; furthermore, that a wide range of intellectual experimentation is very useful, because the folly of today may blaze the trail for an important intellectual or artistic achievement a few years hence.

Another type of conflict requires political decision. The wishes of the consumers as individuals are not always identical with their desires as members of the community. The most important of these differences concerns time preference. We always attribute more significance to gains and losses in the present than to those in the future, but in private decisions the discount is much greater than if we are called upon to act as citizens. The strongest motive for time preference is the uncertainty and brevity of the human life. When we act as individuals, intense interest in losses or gains rarely extends further than the lifetime of our children. The community, on the other hand, appears to us an entity destined to last for a long time, if not forever. When we act as citizens, we wish to coerce ourselves to take the future more seriously than we would do as private individuals.

Those writers who maintain that consumers' sovereignty is incompatible with planning almost invariably fail to draw a clear dividing line between political and nonpolitical decisions. They believe that "the making of an economic plan involves the choice between conflicting or competing ends"[4] not only in the satisfaction of social needs but also with respect to individual consumption. They do not realize that government may in some fields function as a mere registration board and executive agency for consumers' preferences whereas in others it has to make "substantive" choices. Hayek commits this mistake even in historic analysis, where the character of government activities can be ascertained by direct observation of its effects.

Where, as was, for example, true in Germany as early as 1928, the central and local authorities directly control the use of more than half the national income (according to an official German estimate then, 53%), they control indirectly almost the whole economic life of the nation. There is, then, scarcely an individual end which is not dependent for its achievement on the action of the state, and the 'social scale of values,' which guides the state's action must embrace practically all individual ends.[5]

Yet in the Germany of 1928 the individual consumers rightly felt that they directed the bulk of production, and among the infringements upon consumers' sovereignty those

---
[4] Hayek, *op. cit.,* p. 65.   [5] *Ibid.,* p. 61.

by private monopolists were probably more important than
those of governmental origin. Of course, that would have been
impossible if the 53 per cent of the national income under
public control had all been in the same category with, for example, the military budget, in which the state really decides
how much should be spent on guns and how much on bar-
racks, and even what kind of uniform the soldier should wear
and what he should eat. But the 53 per cent included also the
budget of the German Federal Railroads, which did their business in precisely the same way as a private railroad corporation
would have done; the postal system (also operating the telephone and telegraph services), from which the citizen bought
communication service in the same way as he would have from
a private enterprise if one had operated in this field; the municipal, state, and federal electric plants and the municipal
gasworks which all offered their services for sale at the prices
they thought they could get, except that they sometimes re-
nounced monopoly gains which they might have been able to
make; they expanded their plants when they believed they
had a good market that would take more of their goods, and
stopped their investments in new machines and sometimes
their replacement of old ones when their sales did not permit
the use of existing capacity. They acted in every way in accordance with the laws of the market. By far the larger part of the
53 per cent was in this category.[6] Not merely did these govern-

---

[6] The part of the national income which was actually disposed of by political decision was certainly less than 25 per cent. This was the approximate share of the
budgets of the federal, state, and municipal governments without the budgets of
any government-owned enterprises. Although the budgets of the government enterprises may have contained some items which covered social needs in the sense in
which the term is used here, these expenditures could not compensate for expenditures for individual needs in the public budgets proper. The latter contained, for
instance, large sums for the construction of roads and canals, yet probably not more
than would have been spent if these projects had been privately operated and financed

ment-owned units actually operate in essentially the same fashion as private enterprises, but they could have done little else. They were bound by the rules of rational economic procedure, because the taxpayers would have been unwilling to make up any large deficit of the publicly owned enterprise.

In the drafting of a national plan the distinction between areas in which the state has purposes of its own and others in which it merely registers and satisfies consumers' desires is of the same fundamental importance as in the operation of government-owned plants. Since planning does not require society to judge all the preferences of individual consumers, a planned system does not need—as Hayek believes—"a complete ethical code" which represents "a comprehensive scale of values in which every need of every person is given its place."[7] Such a code would even be a logical impossibility because most consumers' purposes are ethically indifferent. It is no more virtuous to prefer beef to veal than veal to beef, or a washing machine to a radio set rather than vice versa.

It is possible, although by no means certain, that social needs and therefore political decisions on economic issues will occupy a larger space in a planned than in an unplanned economy. Very likely a planned system will register social needs more accurately and fully than does unplanned capitalism. On

---

by tolls. Also, a considerable part of the sum which the various government units spent on housing would have gone into the same channels from other sources without government interference.

Hayek's argument is open to other objections. If the telephone, the telegraph, the railroads, the gas and electricity supply, and so on, had been in private ownership, Hayek himself would certainly not have advocated complete freedom for these monopolistic enterprises to fix their rates, but would have insisted on public control. The effects which the state can exert upon the employment of national resources through the use of its price-fixing powers are much the same as the ones which government can cause via direct ownership. Hayek thus has failed to show how the problem which he considers incapable of a satisfactory solution can be avoided.

[7] Hayek, *op. cit.*, p. 57.

the other hand, some social needs require attention only so long as the standard of living is low, and the standard may be raised by planning. The housing problem is a point in question. To the extent that the plan fulfills its purpose of increasing the average annual income by eliminating waste caused by instability, individuals will spend enough on their dwellings to bring them up to socially desirable standards, and the need for subsidies will disappear.

Even if planning leads to increased community action in the service of social needs, that would, of course, be no reason for criticism. Human happiness requires that every need, be it individual or social, receive its proper weight in determining the course of production, and it is a strong rather than a weak point in an economic system if the communal purposes are fully recognized. The best way to prevent overemphasis on social needs is to leave their recognition to democratically elected bodies. Men are not easily induced to infringe as citizens upon their private wants. They will apply careful scrutiny to every public request for resources which might otherwise be used for the production of things the individual could enjoy in private consumption.

If an overexpansion of the political sphere is prevented by democratic control over the recognition of social needs, the bulk of resources will always, except in national emergencies, be used for the satisfaction of the private purposes of individuals. The reason is simply that in all types of society which do not attribute to the tribal or national community a mystic value, or which are not forced to defend themselves incessantly against common foes, the needs which by their very nature must be satisfied individually are quantitatively more important than the others. The principle of consumers' sovereignty can apply only to the sphere of private needs. Because this sphere is so large, the principle is of the greatest importance.[8]

Although a planned economy can be governed by the rule of consumers' sovereignty to the same extent as unplanned capitalism, will not the desire of the "planners" to regulate individual life lead to violation or abolition of that sovereignty? Hayek implies in several passages that probably planners would be seduced by power, even if they were not forced by the alleged inherent logic of their systems, to infringe upon the liberty of the individual. The principal guarantees against misuse of the planning power lie in the political constitution of the planned society; they have been mentioned before and will be extensively discussed later. Liberal convictions on the part of present advocates of planning cannot of themselves assure adequate respect for freedom by the future managers of a planned system; institutional guarantees are indispensable. The perusal of Hayek's book, however, shows that the attitude of present-day "planners" is an important item in the arsenal of the opponents of planning. When a writer who favors planning shows any skepticism about the value of liberty or the likelihood of its survival under a planned system, his utterances are used as evidence that the "planners" cannot be trusted to preserve freedom.

At the time of his writing, Hayek would have found it very difficult to discover any passage, suiting his purpose, in the substantial literature written by economists[9] who favored planning and had specialized in its problems. (He might have quoted some communist economists, but their rejection of consumers' sovereignty proves nothing except the truism that

---

[8] Some other aspects of the distinction between private and social needs are discussed in the chapter of "noneconomic" purposes of planning, see below, pp. 140 ff.

[9] On his quotations from Laski and Mannheim, see below, p. 236.

totalitarians have as little respect for economic as for other freedoms.) More recently, however, a book appeared which may lend a semblance of justification to Hayek's unwarranted indictment of the "planners": Barbara Wootton's *Freedom under Planning*.[10] The author, an excellent economist whose previous book on planning[11] was rightly regarded as one of the major contributions in the field, is very much concerned about human freedom, and she very well understands that freedom in the political and cultural sphere needs an economic complement, but she greatly underestimates the area of free decision that can be conceded to the individual without endangering the effectiveness of planning. She makes, for instance, the following statement:

Full consumers' sovereignty . . . is . . . definitely not compatible with economic planning. . . . It is not possible for the *same* questions to be settled *both* by the conscious and deliberate decisions of planners *and* as the unconscious, unforeseen, results of the behavior of millions of consumers acting independently of one another. The planners could, of course, carefully watch the market and take account of the fads and fancies of consumers there revealed: If they had sense in their heads, they would certainly include this evidence in the material upon which their decisions were based. But if they carried this attention to consumer behavior to such lengths that the final result of planning was just to copy as accurately as possible the picture that would result if no plan were made, the planners would in fact have ceased to plan. Planned decisions and unplanned market reactions are in fact *alternative* ways of determining economic priorities. Use can be made of both in different parts of the economic field (e.g., the output of saucepans can be planned and that of penny-whistles left to the market) but in the determination of any particular issue they are mutually exclusive. The case for planning is not that it is identical with, but that, in certain circumstances, it is superior to, the planless method of settling economic priorities.[12]

---

[10] (Chapel Hill: The University of North Carolina Press, 1945).

[11] *Plan or No Plan* (New York, Farrar and Rhinehart, 1935).

[12] (Reprinted from *Freedom under Planning* by Barbara Wootton, by permission of the University of North Carolina Press, copyright, 1945, by the University of North

Although planning would indeed lose its justification if the plan merely copied the prospective developments in an unplanned economy, the difference does not have to lie in the substitution of the planners' for the consumers' preferences. Under the kind of planning which will some day come into operation in the western countries, the "fads and fancies" of the consumers will determine economic priorities in all nonpolitical matters, as they would do in a perfect market, with fewer distortions than we find in the imperfect market of an unplanned economy. Planning will be a superior way not because it applies a better basic criterion in assigning these priorities, but because it represents the use of safer and less wasteful methods in their application, and therefore can satisfy the "fads and fancies" of the public to a higher degree with the same amount of resources.

It is hard to believe that Barbara Wootton should not, in principle, agree with this statement, for she fails to indicate any purpose which under planning should overrule consumers' sovereignty. She is far too democratic to recognize a purpose of the community that would not be a purpose of its members, and she decidedly does not wish to draw a "distinction between what people want to do and what they 'really' want to do"[13] and then to claim for the "planners" the ability to know the "true" desires of the consumers. What else is left except the rule that the citizens' desires, and that means in most instances

---

Carolina Press, p. 43.) Italics in original. Barbara Wootton speaks of "full consumers' sovereignty in this sense" and of "economic planning as we have defined it." The sense in which she uses these terms, however, is the same in which they are used in the present essay, so that the qualification is of no importance here.

[13] "Any such distinction is extremely dangerous and may be the cloak for some of the most wicked, because the most insidious, attacks upon freedom. For sooner or later what I 'really' want to do turns out to be a polite paraphrase of what you think I ought to want to do. But freedom means freedom to do what I want, and not what anybody else wants me to want—or else it has no meaning at all." *Op. cit.*, p. 5.

consumers' preferences as expressed on the market, should determine the actions of the "planners" and thereby direct production?

No answer to this question can be found in the specific objections which Barbara Wootton raises against the rule of consumers' sovereignty, but this discussion of the problem in concrete terms reveals some of the sources of her error. Her first argument starts from the unimpeachable and important premise that consumers' preferences can direct production only through a mechanism of correct pricing.

We can ... only draw conclusions about what pattern of production best pleases the consumers when we are sure that all the articles offered for sale are being produced in the most economical possible way and offered at the most economical possible price.[14]

In other words, price calculation is indispensable for consumers' sovereignty because consumers must know at what prices the different quantities can be offered, if they are to decide how much of each commodity they wish to see produced. Speaking in more technical terms, consumers' preferences cannot be expressed in a single demand price for each commodity, but only in a demand curve, and the point of intersection with the supply curve indicates the final price. If the consumers' desires are to be properly translated into directives for production, the planning board must sketch in advance physical changes as well as price changes—a point to be explained later; and to fulfill this task, the board must not only explore consumers' wishes and thus win the material for demand curves, but also determine costs and plot the supply curves.

The determination of the "minimum necessary cost of production" and consequently of the "minimum necessary price"

---

[14] *Ibid.*, p. 57.

is fraught with well-known difficulties. Barbara Wootton mentions specifically the failure of private cost calculations to express all social costs, but we might as well think of the better known (and often quantitatively more important) problems of the distribution of overhead costs, depreciation of capital equipment, and joint cost goods. Therefore, planning under consumers' sovereignty is a task for experts in price calculation, but it is not an impossible one. Certainly, even experts cannot solve, for instance, the imputation of joint costs to different products without some degree of arbitrariness, but the inevitability of allowing the "planners" a narrow range of discretion in setting prices is no reason to assume that the theory of pricing cannot be expressed "in any manageable compass without serious ambiguities in some of its most critical terms"[15] and still less "that the problem of determining the best possible use for resources of any community is scientifically insoluble."[16] If we have to give the planmakers the right to fill out, according to their own best judgment and in coöperation with the managers of plants, some small gaps which the rule of consumers' sovereignty has left open in the system of prices,[17] that is no good reason to discard the rule and fall back on "general judgments," which is only a euphemism for the planners' right

[15] *Ibid.*, pp. 60–61.

[16] *Ibid.*, p. 67.

[17] The gaps cannot be large as compared with the volume of the economy as a whole. The bulk of social costs, not expressed in private costs, can be estimated with a fair degree of accuracy and may be recovered by special taxes from the enterprises concerned, and indirectly from the consumers of their products, if such recovery seems expedient. Of the infinite number of proportions in which joint costs might conceivably be distributed between the products—for instance, to use a textbook example, between cotton seed and cotton fiber—only a very limited range is practically important. It may often be impossible to decide by an objective criterion whether a machine should be written off in eight or in ten years, but, as a rule, no expert would have any difficulty in stating that either six or twelve years (or both) are unreasonable.

to dictate to the consumers.[18] The problem of the best possible use of resources is soluble in the same sense as most of our practical problems, in economics as well as in technics and in every other field of human endeavor: We can approach the optimum although we cannot reach it.

In one of her other arguments against the rule of consumers' sovereignty, Barbara Wootton assumes "substantial agreement" among present-day economists with the statement that "the minimal cost of production can only be competitively determined." She adds that nothing "approaching this regime of perfect competition exists or ever has existed, or is likely to exist."[19] Her statement would have been completely correct if she had said, either that in an unplanned economy costs can be kept to their minimum amounts only through perfect competition, or that the calculation of minimum costs by a planning board requires certain procedures on paper which, if

[18] Barbara Wootton insists that these "general judgments" should be made "by the representatives of all on behalf of all"—in other words in a democratic fashion—and she seems to believe that this method offers enough protection to consumers' interests. But if the "representatives" are not instructed to satisfy needs according to demand, or if these instructions are not implemented by the creation of a mechanism for registering demand, what is there left for the "representatives" to do but to replace the preferences of the consumers by their own judgment as to what the consumers ought to have? In this way the consumers would still not receive what they want but what other people regard as the desirable ends of production.

It is really wrong to speak in this case of representatives at all. Unless the planmakers are obliged to direct production according to the desires of the individuals, they cannot represent the latter in decisions on the use of resources for consumption. If the planmakers are bound by the preferences of the individual citizens in the field of private consumption the planmakers need not be representatives chosen by election, but should rather be civil servants operating an economic mechanism to ascertain consumers' preferences and translate them into directives for production. Like all civil servants, the planmakers should, of course, be selected and supervised under the ultimate responsibility of the "representatives of all."

[19] Op. cit., p. 63. Her further contention that "we do not know, except perhaps in an extremely abstract sense, what a regime of perfect competition implies," is unjustified. The concept of perfect competition is unambiguous and no more abstract than any of the basic concepts of economics.

carried out in reality, would mean perfect competition. (The identity of the results of correct price planning with those of perfect competition will become clearer after the discussion in the next chapter.) But the planmakers can determine the minimum price through calculation by making appropriate assumptions without securing perfect competition on the real market. Therefore the practical difficulty of removing the obstacles to perfect competition need not prevent the planning board from knowing the minimum cost of production.

Barbara Wootton attributes much importance to the influence which producers exert upon consumers' buying habits. "Consumers (with insignificant exceptions)," she wrote in an earlier book,[20] "can only pick and choose between the things that are actually offered to them; but their behavior in so doing throws no light on the question whether they might not very likely have preferred to go without half the junk that they now buy, and be supplied instead with quite other goods that no producer has had the imagination to put on the market. Inevitably the whole trend and character of consumption are determined far more by producers than by those who actually use the goods that modern industry supplies. And in this respect there is probably not very much to choose between a planned and an unplanned system."

Nothing, of course, can be bought that has not been produced, and to this extent the consumer depends on the producer's ability to foresee the demand. Moreover, advertising and high-pressure salesmanship may sometimes induce us to buy another brand of cigarette or of beer than we would if the matter were left to our uninfluenced judgment. These practices may even cause us to buy some commodity for which we have

[20] *Plan or No Plan*, p. 174.

no use at all. The suggestion, however, that people might wish
to spend half their income differently if the market offered a
wider selection of goods, is not very plausible. The bulk of our
income is spent on food, clothing, shelter, transportation, and
on such recreation as going to the theater occasionally and
spending a few weeks annually in the mountains or at the sea-
shore. The limited insight of producers into our tastes may
deprive us of some delicacy which we would otherwise enjoy
now and then, or of some arrangement of our rooms which
would be particularly pleasing, or of a particularly efficient
type of car, or of some motion pictures which we would like
better than any of those which are really offered. Making the
most unfavorable assumptions, however, can we really believe
that in all this more than a small fraction of our total needs is
at stake? In any event, if the failure of the producers to realize
consumers' desires to their full extent curtails the latter's standard of living, there would be all the more reason to safeguard
consumers' rights carefully against deliberate infringement by
the planmakers—or by anybody else.

Nor is there much validity in another argument of Barbara
Wootton's; namely, "that people ... are generally unaware
whether they have got that freedom or not."

By and large, the pattern of production is a matter which the individual has to take as a datum under any system, planned or not. In the
Soviet Union the appearance of bicycles in the shops is the result, and
is known to be result, of the conscious decision of the planning authorities to give a priority to the manufacture of bicycles. In this country it
would be a mark, and would be known to be a mark, of some manu-
facturer's anticipation of profit. But for the vast majority of us either
the bicycles are there or they are not there, either they are priced at a
figure which we are prepared to pay or they are beyond our reach, and
that is the end of it.[21]

_____
[21] *Freedom under Planning*, p. 68.

It is not the end, not even under unplanned capitalism. If bicycles are rare in relation to effective demand, without being too high priced, bicycle producers will be swamped with orders and will thereby be induced to increase production; and if excessive prices are charged for a supply kept short, people will sooner or later ask why such high prices should be justified and will insist on the application of monopoly controls. In an unplanned private enterprise system it may take a long time before the consumer becomes aware of the overcharge and the antimonopoly measures may be unsuccessful. In a planned system, it will be a highly important task of the planmakers to render account to the public for the use of the national resources, to prove that all of them were used either for democratically approved social needs or for the best satisfaction of consumers' desires. It will be a task of the political representatives of the people and of the public press to search the reports for flaws and to tell the people whether they have, within the limits of possibility, received what they most wanted to obtain. The greater amount of reliable information will make it easier to determine where a monopoly exists and to apply means by which it can be broken.

Only one argument of Barbara Wootton's against consumers' sovereignty has at least limited validity. In all but wholly equalitarian societies "plural voting is permitted in the ballot box of the market."[22] The person with a high income can exert a greater "pull" on resources than the poor man, and the preferences of the well-to-do minority will therefore have a disproportionately great influence on production.

The fact that I am willing to pay 5 shillings for what you will only buy at half-a-crown is not necessarily proof that my want is twice as great as yours, or that it should (as under the rule of consumers' sovereignty it

[22] *Ibid.*, p. 64. Barbara Wootton speaks of "unjustifiable plural voting."

would) count twice as much in determining the pattern of production. The difference in the intensity of our respective money demands may merely be due to a difference in the amount of money which we have at our disposal.[23]

If plural voting seems undesirable, the obvious remedy is to abolish plural voting, rather than the ballot box. Dropping the metaphor, it seems better to modify the inequalities of money income than to prevent effective demand, partly determined by differences in money incomes, from directing production. Differences in income, it is true, cannot be entirely eliminated if production is to remain efficient. Some of us regret the necessity of a wage differential, but it would be illogical to maintain the margin between money incomes and frustrate its realization through the market mechanism, because the only sense in letting some people earn more dollars is our assumption that they should have more goods than others.

A case can be made, however, for interfering in selected instances with the effect of differences in income on the market and thereby on production. Some of these cases come under the category of social needs, which we have already discussed, but many of us also feel that certain individual needs are too vital to have their satisfaction depend on the ability to pay. Consequently, we may well decide to subsidize, for instance, medical treatment of poor patients, or the supply of scarce foodstuffs. This problem has no special reference to planning, except perhaps that a society which introduced planning to avoid the misery of unemployment may be generally more sensitive to human needs in personal emergencies.

Barbara Wootton's opposition to the rule of consumers' sovereignty is not typical of the general tendency of her recent

---

[23] *Ibid.*

book. She wishes to see planning established and freedom to be more fully realized than at present, and she only commits the mistake of not recognizing consumers' sovereignty as one of the indispensable and at the same time practicable methods of giving freedom meaning in economic life. Her splendidly written little treatise on the relationship of planning and liberty contains some important ideas which are representative of the school of thought often called "the planners." Precisely for this reason it was imperative to show in some detail why her position on the subject of consumers' sovereignty is neither a necessary consequence of the belief in planning nor compatible with the democratic principles which she herself regards as the only desirable basis of a planned system.

To the assumption that consumers' sovereignty, the use of money, and the institution of a market are retained in the planned economy, we shall for the purposes of the immediately following discussion add the further assumption that production is carried on by private enterprise. The concept of planning does not imply either the existence or the nonexistence of any of these institutions, and later on we shall glance at other types of institutional framework. But it is expedient to begin with a set of assumptions that would change as little as possible the familiar capitalistic environment.

The Two Schedules of the Plan

The making of a plan will always have to start with an inventory of resources. We must know how much arable land, how much pasture, how many workable mineral deposits of every kind, how much equipment of every description, and how much labor of every skill we have at our disposal before we can choose what we want to produce.

Since we want, as a rule, to give the consumers what they wish to have, we must find out their preferences. In this field, statistical methods have made great progress recently. We are not yet in a position to determine what a skilled auto mechanic in New Orleans or a farmer possessing a certain number of acres in a given part of Iowa will buy in a given year if his labor power is fully used, but some more effort will bring us to the point where we can answer these questions with sufficient accuracy.[24]

From its engineer advisers the planning board can obtain all the information it needs about the technical procedures in producing goods for the satisfaction of the consumers. It will also be advised about the required amounts of material, equipment, and labor. Yet all this will not suffice to work out a plan adequate for the guidance of an economy. If we want to decide which procedures are worth undertaking or are preferable to others, we cannot rely exclusively on a calculation in terms of physical quantities; we must supplement it by calculation in terms of economic value units.

The term "value" has so often been a matter of controversy among economists that it is necessary to explain the sense in which it is used here before presenting the arguments for value planning. Economic value is another expression for economic significance (utility), which implies that the degree of significance is expressible in numbers. The function of value is to make possible a comparison of input and output of any process of production, contemplated or completed. The value

---

[24] See the *Study of Consumers' Purchases,* a common undertaking of the WPA, the Bureau of Home Economics of the Department of Agriculture, the Bureau of Labor Statistics of the Department of Labor, the Central Statistical Board, and the National Resources Committee. The last-named used the data in its two volumes, *Consumer Incomes in the United States* and *Consumer Expenditures in the United States.*

figures for the output indicate utility gained and those for the input utility lost. The utility concept of value, therefore, implies that all cost is ultimately opportunity cost. The economic significance of material, equipment, or labor time, if considered in connection with a particular production process, is determined by the alternative of using the same resources for another purpose. If a production process shows more output than input, its net product must be more useful than that of the next best process. Value may exist in any type of social organization, but price is often understood to imply real bargaining.

The prices which, in a market economy, result from the bargaining of buyers and sellers express the value of commodities as it appears to the individuals concerned at the time of the bargain. The weighing of economic alternatives by bargaining individuals and by officials in a central agency can lead to different results only to the extent that the officials have more or less knowledge or calculating ability than the private individuals or that they have different purposes for which they use the goods. Since the latter possibility can be frequently neglected, the long-run market prices will often be identical with values calculated under the same conditions by some person or agency outside the market, or where no market exists. Therefore many economists avoid the term "value" altogether and speak only of "price," broadening the price concept so that it applies to situations where supply and demand are equilibrated by the decisions of a central agency instead of by bargains between sellers and buyers. There is no logical objection to this terminology, but in the opinion of this writer, we lose more by it than we gain. There is need for a term that covers only situations in which the economic significance of goods is expressed in demand for and offers of money by bargaining

individuals. There is also need for a general term for any numerical expression of the economic significance of goods. To
use the term "price" in the general as well as the specific sense
is not conducive to clarity.[25]

Under the institutional assumptions which we have made
in this discussion, the necessity of value planning can be easily
explained. Free choice for the consumers, together with the
use of money, makes it imperative to include a calculation of
incomes in the national plan. Obviously, before we know what
each group of the population is likely to buy, we must know
how much they have to spend. Income, however, is frequently
the difference between two sets of values: product values and
costs. Therefore, income cannot be calculated unless there is
an estimate of the values of goods produced and of the goods
absorbed in the production process. Furthermore, how much
of each commodity a group can buy depends on the amount
which it has to pay for other commodities. Consequently, if
the planning board devises a scheme for the satisfaction of
consumers' preferences three or four years from now, it must
estimate what the various goods will be worth at that time,
which means that it must include a value column in the plan.

Furthermore, with business in private hands and money used
as a general means of exchange, money will also be the standard of measurement by which the individual businessman
judges the success or failure of his undertakings. This means
that he will control the development of his business by a system of accounting in monetary terms. When the entrepreneur

---

[25] In this study the need for the term "value" is not so great as in other discussions.
Here we deal with value mostly in the form of price—present price or expected future
price. But there is no use in avoiding a term which has a legitimate place in the
vocabulary of economics, although in this particular instance it could be done without a great sacrifice of convenience or clarity.

studies the entries in his ledger, he draws conclusions as to advisable action. His accounting system instructs him what he ought to do to "keep out of the red." But at the same time, the entrepreneur in a planned economy receives instructions from the national plan. How can conflicts between these two sets of instructions be avoided? The planning board must make sure that the entrepreneur, to comply with the plan, is not forced to undertake any venture in which the value of the input would be greater than the value of the output. Every provision of the plan must be tested by value calculation, to examine whether it will not involve an industry or a single firm in any action that would make cost greater than product. This continuous examination is tantamount to the establishment of a value column beside the column of figures which describe the proposals of the plan in terms of physical quantities.

It will give the reader a broader view of the necessity for value planning if, for a moment, we deviate from our general institutional assumptions. A value column would be necessary even if private business were eliminated, production completely centralized in the hands of the government, and if consumers had no money income and no free choice of goods. Suppose the planning board, with full power to dispose of all the resources as it sees fit, acted in a despotic fashion, granting no autonomy at all to any production units and allocating goods to consumers through rationing cards without regard to their preferences, so that there would not be the same need as now for cost accounting in individual concerns and no need at all for ascertaining consumers' desires through a process of price formation. Still, the planning board could not hope to determine the desirability of production processes without calculation in value terms.

The engineers, let us assume, tell the board that one process, which is contemplated for use in a given branch of production, requires more coal, whereas another requires more complicated machinery, which can only be produced by a greater expenditure of labor. If this were an extreme example, in which the saving of coal was very great and the additional expenditure of labor not very considerable (or vice versa), it would be possible to arrive at a decision merely by taking a birds-eye view of the situation. On the other hand, if this were the only production process that has to be examined, the planning board might perhaps think out first the physical effects of one alternative, estimate the total satisfaction which consumers might draw from its realization, then do the same with the second alternative, and decide through a simple comparison.

But neither of these simplifying assumptions is justified. Differences in advantage of alternative technical procedures require such a combination of changes that their effects are revealed only by a thoroughgoing analysis. Nor can we afford to concentrate our attention on a few processes of production, for innumerable decisions of importance must be made daily in a modern economy. Therefore, beyond the primitive stages of technical development, a high degree of economic success is never obtainable except through calculation in units of economic importance. This rule is as valid for a collective agency guiding the economy under any kind of institutional arrangement as it is for the individual member of a society based on free exchange of commodities through money.

Perhaps this statement may seem to be contradicted by the experience that in most fields of human endeavor choices between alternatives are made without calculation in units of importance. Why should this device be necessary in economic life although it is not used, for instance, in warfare? A general does not decide by calculation in terms of "war-value figures" whether it is better to change one position for another or to wage a battle for a point of vantage although the price will be sacrifice in men and material. Even in preparing for war we do not undertake a numerical calculation to determine our choice between producing more machine guns or more tanks, more railroad cars or more cannon (although the priority and allocation systems, which during the last war were gradually worked out to direct the resources of the nation into the channels most useful for the war effort, might in a future emergency of even greater magnitude develop into a method of assigning "war value figures" to each unit of a production factor). Yet war, even modern war, is a simple matter compared with the organization of an industrial economy. For another reason, too, calculation in terms of units of importance is not applicable to war, at least not to the military operations in a proper sense. Such calculation takes time and therefore cannot be used in fields where the importance of objects changes too rapidly, because there the figures attributed to the objects would become incorrect before the results of the calculation were known. Such rapid change is very characteristic of war; in economics, on the contrary, although there is a perpetual change in conditions, yet there is much more continuity in that change.

The planning board will continually be faced with the question of how much it is ready to give up at present in order to achieve more in the future. In spite of all the controversies about the sufficiency of investment outlets—with some part of this debate we shall become acquainted in later sections of this book—most contemporary economists agree that at least for some decades there are great opportunities for an increase of the social product through electrification (unless atomic fission provides an abundance of cheap energy without costly distribution systems), improvement of road and airport systems, reclamation of soils which have deteriorated under the influence of wasteful methods, quite aside from the capital demand for the fructification of current and future inventions and for housing. If the planning board were to approve all the projects promising any increase in national income, resources for present consumption would be too severely curtailed. Therefore, the planning board will approve only the more profitable investments. Naturally, the board must work out a generally applicable yardstick. It must not in each instance decide anew how many units of future value justify the sacrifice of one unit of present value for any given length of waiting period, but this decision must be made once and then applied to all investments until underlying conditions change.

The minimum rate of productiveness, which the planning board will use as a standard, may well be called a calculation rate of interest. The market rate of interest indicates how many value units must be added to an amount available in the future to make it the market equivalent of a like amount immediately available. The rate of interest which an entrepreneur applies in his calculations when deciding whether or not to undertake a particular investment means the use of a standard of minimum profitability: he will not engage in the project if he expects no greater return than he can obtain by lending the money on the market. The planning board is in a very similar position when passing judgment on investment projects. To be sure, it is not interested in the money return which the capital would bring if lent to other borrowers instead of being spent on the project under review, but it is interested in the utility of the near-future consumers' goods which the resources would bring if used in consumer-goods industries instead of in long-range investment. The entrepreneur's calculation rate is identical with the market rate applicable to the kind of loan for which the money could be used if not self-invested. The calculation rate of the planning board, however, is different. The planning board acts for the community, and—for reasons previously explained—an organ of the community has to take the future more seriously or rather discount it less, than does the average private individual: the community, and therefore the planning board, has as a rule a lower time preference. The coexistence of a relatively low calculation interest rate of the planning board and a higher market rate of interest has a number of interesting implications, but space does not suffice for their discussion.

The low time preference of the planning board will induce it to favor investment at the expense of the present more than the average citizen, if acting as a private person, would be willing to do. The planning board, however, must also protect the present interests of the consumers. If it were to set the calculation rate of interest too low, it would be committed to the approval of too many investment projects, and too heavy inroads would be made by investment upon the means to satisfy present needs. If we assume that the planning board starts experimentally from a relatively high calculation rate and gradually reduces it, a point will be reached at which the marginal utility of the present goods which can be produced with one resource unit are just equal to the (present) marginal utility of the future goods which the same resource unit could produce and which will be available in larger quantity, because investment is physically productive. (The present marginal utility of future goods is of course to be calculated by estimating their future marginal utility—i.e., the marginal utility they will have when produced—and discounting it by applying collective time preference.) Assuming, for simplicity, that the present goods and the future goods would be of the same kind and different only in quantity, it may be found that, for instance, one resource unit, if used in a long-range improvement project, will make available within forty years twice the physical quantity of goods that can be produced by the same resource unit in a short-term process, delivering its product almost immediately. If it is also found that in this event the addition which the resource unit can cause to the stock of future goods has the same present value as the addition which it can make to the stock of present goods, any investment that would bring more than an increase of 100 per cent in forty years, or 2.5 per cent per year, would be worth undertaking. Consequently, the calculation rate should be just above 2.5 per cent.[26]

Very similar to the considerations concerning investments are those applying to the conservation of resources. The planning board will conserve irreplaceable resources even at greater sacrifice than private owners would make for that purpose.

---

[26] In this calculation it is assumed that the principle of compound interest does not apply. The principle applies whenever the yield of a future year, if not immediately consumed, can be made the source of further yields in the more remote future. Since we are speaking here of physical yields, the direct applicability of the principle depends on the character of the product. Steel can be used to make more steel, shoes cannot be used to produce more shoes. The principle may be indirectly applicable, however, if the increased production of shoes in, say, the fifth year will release resources for the increased production of capital goods which will lead to a greater shoe production later. In this whole matter, however, only the figures and not the essentials of the time preference problem are at stake, and therefore in the text above no assumptions were made which would make it necessary to take compound interest into account.

But unconditional conservation would mean nonutilization and would entirely subordinate the interests of present consumption to those of an indefinite future. Here again a balance of marginal utilities must be sought: the current marginal utility of the future, discounted by the application of the collective time preference (which, of course, involves a lesser discount than the one resulting from the application of private time preference) must be kept equal to the marginal utility of the present. If intense present exploitation of the resource makes the product more abundant now and consequently scarcer in the future, the marginal utility of the future will rise above that of the present, indicating that the degree of exploitation must be reduced.

This view of the problem is probably shared by the majority of economists who have dealt with the theory of conservation.[27] Eduard Heimann, however, has recently denied that economic equilibrium concepts are applicable to the problem of irreplaceable resources. He argues that there can be no "equilibrium price, in the proper sense of the word, of minerals.[28] To be sure, there is a momentary price, whose relationship to the cost of production will determine the degree of utilization of the equipment in the short run and the possible expansion of the equipment in the long run. But . . . these concepts, in their original application to products, imply what is explicit in the classical concept of a balanced circular flow, that of Quesnay: namely, that the thus determined output can be reproduced indefinitely." He concludes "that the foundation on which all our industry rests is inaccessible to equilibrium eco-

---

[27] See esp. S. von Ciriacy-Wantrup, "Private Enterprise and Conservation," *Journal of Farm Economy*, February, 1942.

[28] If, for this reason, an equilibrium price were impossible, the argument would also apply to an equilbrium of marginal utilities.

nomics. The strictest application of such economics is ... compatible with the physical destruction of that foundation."[29] He quotes a statement by Harcourt A. Morgan: "For permanent industrial development we therefore first need permanent sources of raw materials, which are furnished by nature," and adds: "This, however, is not a question of value equilibrium; it is one of physical planning."[30]

If there is to be a value plan, it must translate all physical provisions into value terms, and it must provide for an equilibrium between marginal cost and marginal utility of the product in every industry and production unit. There can be no sector of economic life, and certainly not such an important one as the exploitation of mineral resources that would remain outside the calculation of a value equilibrium. If Heimann were entirely right, value planning would be impossible, and consequently, full planning would be impossible, at least in a private-enterprise economy.

Actually, Heimann applies an inadmissible test to the usefulness of the valuation process. This usefulness is not disproved by the statement that, in obeying the signs resulting from this process, we may be led to the "physical destruction" of the "foundation on which all our industry rests." Any policy which merely limits but does not preclude the use of irreplaceable resources is open to this criticism. Our present form of industrial civilization cannot be continued indefinitely unless new sources of materials are opened up every time that the old sources are threatened with exhaustion— and, of course, we cannot be sure that these discoveries will always occur in time.

[29] Eduard Heimann, "Developmental Schemes, Planning and Full Employment (Economic Theory of TVA)," *in* Abba P. Lerner and Frank D. Graham, eds., *Planning and Paying for Full Employment* (New Jersey, Princeton University Press, 1946), pp. 103–104.
[30] *Ibid.*, p. 105.

Planning can do much to reduce the danger, by applying a lower time preference in all calculations, but it cannot devise a scheme for putting the economy on a perpetuating basis, because this would mean dropping all time preference. Probably we could not live if we took the remote future quite as seriously as the immediate present, but in any event this is not the attitude of human beings, neither as private individuals nor as citizens. If we are considering the very remote future, none of us would pay more than an infinitesimal price, in terms of present goods, for the prevention even of very substantial losses. The economic plan cannot ignore this basic psychological fact, nor its obvious consequences for the less distant future, which consists of milestones on the road to the remote one. The plan must determine the volume of production in each field by calculating the equilibrium between the value of the prospective return, estimated with a discount according to the time preference of the community, and the value of the cost goods.

It would be a comparatively easy task for the planning board to determine the calculation rate of interest if all elements of instability were banned from the planned system. But no planning can achieve so much. Among the elements that cannot be expected to operate in a calculable way are not only natural forces outside human life, but also the inventive spirit of man. Suppose there is a period in which this spirit is particularly fertile, and consequently many new possibilities of improving production are discovered. If the board simply applied its current rate of interest, formed by experience of past periods, it would arrive at obviously wrong decisions, for too many investment projects would seem to be justified by this yardstick, and resources available for present consumption would be de-

pleted. The planning board will have to recalculate its rate
of interest on the basis of a new—and higher—time preference,
following from the more abundant prospective satisfaction in
the future and the greater scarcity of resources at present. But
it will not be sufficient for the planning board to take into
account merely the strain on resources at the time when the
change appears. Investment usually requires a far greater expenditure in material, machine capacity, and labor in the later
phases of the expansion process than in the beginning. This
can be observed in the progress of the individual project and
also in the interdependence of expansion processes in different
fields. After an individual factory has been completed, the
necessity for supplementary investment will very frequently
appear—not only need for new supplier or customer plants,
but also for homes, schools, stores, roads, and recreation facilities for the workers. The planning board, therefore, must calculate the full strain which will be imposed on resources when
requirements are at their peak, and from this anticipated scarcity must derive the rate of interest that will equate the value
of marginal quantities of present and future goods. (Since
resources will be less scarce in the first period of heavy investment, a lower short-term interest rate may well be established
for that space of time.)

Psychological Arguments against the Possibility of Value Calculation

Before we take any further steps in our analysis, we should
once more make sure that we understand completely the meaning of calculation, as the term is applied here. In a market
economy, the individual businessman inquires from supply
firms about their prices, watches his own sales and those of his

competitors, draws conclusions on the probable demand, and decides what prices he can charge for his products and, therefore, what he can afford to pay for his supplies. In all these deliberations the businessman tries to be one step ahead of the market, but as a rule he cannot raise his sights higher. Since he cannot hope to anticipate the more distant future, it is not unreasonable for him to take his information from present market conditions. It is true that long-range tendencies, of which he cannot become aware through the observation of current events on the market, may suddenly spoil all his calculations, but as long as no such catastrophe occurs, that method serves him well in the conduct of his business.

The planning board is in an entirely different position, having to guide the market and to correct its tendencies so far as they do not conform to long-range requirements. Therefore, the board cannot take its own guidance from current developments on the market. For an anticipation of the prices which will exist two or three or five years from now, present prices are of little use. Thus the planning board must calculate values independently of the market, at least of the market in an institutional sense, where real buyers and sellers meet. It will estimate future supply and demand conditions, thus constructing a "paper" market, and calculate the prices that will equilibrate the two.

The question whether values can be calculated without a market in the institutional sense has been intensively discussed in the recent literature on socialism. The socialist writers, who presented the argument for the affirmative, were guided by aims which are not necessarily implied in the function of planning, and they were not primarily interested in planning as it has been defined in this essay. Their problem was not how values expressing future supply and demand conditions could be calculated, but how substitutes could be found for the role of private entrepreneurs in the formation of present prices. For this purpose they suggested the establishment of what we may call a semi-institutional or artificial market, at least for capital goods. Prices should be tentatively fixed by the collective agency, and the managers of individual plants should be instructed to determine output and purchases of factors on the basis of these prices as if they were entrepreneurs acting under perfect competition. The collective agency would observe the results and change prices accordingly. Whatever the merits of this solution, it cannot be applied to our problem, because the planning board, which has to anticipate future prices, has no opportunity to correct its tentative calculations through observation of buyers' and sellers' attitudes. The artificial market suggested by socialist writers is different from the "paper" market required for value planning.

Yet these socialist authors, primarily Oscar Lange[31] and H. D. Dickinson, have done an excellent job in refuting some of the arguments by which the possibility of value calculation without the institution of a market had been denied. They showed clearly that the "real" process through which the market arrives at an equilibrium price and the calculating process which a central agency must apply for the same purpose have traits in common which make it impossible to question the practicability of advance calculation of values by a planning board. The line of reasoning in the following paragraphs is, to a great extent, a mere adaptation of the arguments found in the writings of the Lange-Dickinson school.

---

[31] Oscar Lange and F. M. Taylor, *On the Economic Theory of Socialism,* Benjamin Lippincott, ed. (Minnesota, 1938); Dickinson, *op. cit.*

Among the opponents of the possibility of value planning, Ludwig von Mises[32] occupies the first place. His position is based upon an argument which he took from a school of psychologists. Since the substance of value is utility, that is, the capacity of goods to satisfy human needs, the quantity of value attributable to each good must be determined by the urgency of the need which it satisfies. But, according to the psychologists on whose opinion Mises relied, the urgency of human needs and the intensity of their satisfaction cannot be measured, although it is possible to establish a scale of needs or satisfactions. There are no units of satisfaction that can be counted. I cannot reasonably say, so the argument runs, that I want good A twice as much as good B,[33] I can only state I want A more than B, and I can make a table of commodity units showing their sequence in a series of increasing or decreasing utility for a particular consumer.[34] For a time, this position was upheld not only by Mises and many other writers of the Austrian school, but by the majority of economists everywhere. Perhaps it is still the majority opinion.

Yet if the argument were correct, the formation of prices on a market in the institutional sense could not be explained. The economists who deny that satisfactions are measurable have never adequately explained how prices, representing measurable quantities, could be formed out of expected satisfactions, if these were not also magnitudes consisting of units and, therefore, capable of measurement. They have often argued as if

---

[32] *Die Gemeinwirtschaft* (Jena, 1922), translated under the title *Socialism* (New York, 1937).

[33] To say that I want a certain good twice as much as another is obviously tantamount to saying that I expect twice as great a satisfaction from the one as from the other.

[34] Sometimes this has been expressed by the proposition that ordinal but not cardinal numbers can be assigned to different intensities of satisfaction.

there were some magic power in the market mechanism able to transform magnitudes which could only be ordered in a scale, into magnitudes which could be determined by counting units, as prices certainly can.

All price theory must start from the assumption that buyers have tentatively made up their minds about the prices which they are willing to pay, if necessary, before they get to the market, just as sellers have made a preliminary estimate of the minimum amount for which they will give away their goods. In the absence of specific conditions which would justify a different interpretation, the willingness of a buyer to pay, if necessary, twice as much for good A as for good B means that he expects twice as great a satisfaction from good A as from good B. To be sure, the exceptions may be very important. The purchase may involve such a large portion of the buyer's income that the change in the marginal utility of money—increasing marginal utility as income is depleted through purchases—must be taken into account.[35] In such transactions, the willingness to pay twice as much for one commodity as for the other indicates that somewhat more than twice the satisfaction is expected. But even in these instances of deviation, the ratio of prices is derived from the ratio of desires and thus proves the existence of the latter. A ratio, however, can exist only between measurable quantities. Nor can any valid objection be derived from our inability to measure accurately the change in the marginal utility of money. The issue is not whether a technique for a perfectly accurate measurement of

---

[35] There are, of course, also many times when the buyer knows that he need not pay under any conditions as much for the good as his maximum estimate would warrant, and when therefore he does not stop to think how much he would pay if necessary. Therefore, evidence for the measurability of satisfaction can often be found only in the attitude of the marginal buyers or of those who hold a near-to-marginal position. This does not affect the essential character of the problem.

satisfactions is available or whether there is any technique to measure satisfactions under all circumstances, but whether or not such measurement is possible on grounds of principle. Even if we found a single instance in which we could say that one satisfaction is approximately, by a wide margin of error, n times as great as another satisfaction, that would refute the idea that there is a fundamental obstacle to measuring satisfactions and, consequently, utility of goods.[36]

There have been recent attempts to show that the market process can be explained without assuming the existence of utility as a measurable magnitude, by using the concept of the marginal rate of substitution. This rate is defined as indicating how much of commodity A would just compensate an individual for the loss of the marginal unit of commodity B.[37] At first sight, it seems to describe the formation of prices only by referring to the preferences of individuals—that is, to their judgment that some combinations of goods are more useful than others—and not to imply that they can judge how many times good A is preferable to good B. Yet, as the authors of the concept themselves have stated, a marginal rate of substitution can be established not only between two goods but also between one good and all the others, or more accurately, between one good and the best combination of other goods. The latter rate is identical with the marginal rate of substitution between that good and money. Suppose we ascertain the marginal rate of substitution between either of two goods, A and B, and the best combination of other goods, and find that the rate for commodity B is twice as high as that for commodity A. Could

---

[36] For discussions of this question, the reader is referred to the surveys of Lippincott-Taylor-Lange, op. cit., and Dickinson, op. cit., and also to Heimann's excellent study of socialist literature in Social Research, February, 1939.

[37] J. R. Hicks, Value and Capital (Oxford, Oxford University Press, 1939), p. 20.

we then not say, just as well, that the marginal unit of *B* is twice as useful as the marginal unit of *A*? The difference between the two statements is merely a verbal one, for we have really measured the utility of *A* and *B* in terms of the utility of the best combination of other goods or in dollars.[38] The concept of the rate of substitution between goods can only be formed on the silent assumption that utility can be measured.[39]

It is not an economist's job to determine how these facts can be reconciled with the theorems of psychology. Of course, no statement in the field of economics must violate a valid rule of psychology, but no rule can be upheld in any branch of science if it does not permit an explanation of all parts of reality. The phenomenon of price formation cannot be explained except on the assumption that satisfactions are measurable. This

[38] The same slight inaccuracy that we have observed earlier is also contained in the assumption that the following two statements are equivalent: "Of the best combination of other goods, twice as much must be substituted for the marginal unit of commodity *B* as for the marginal unit of commodity *A*," and "Good *B* has twice the marginal utility of good *A*." Twice the quantity of the best combination of other goods is not quite twice as useful as one times that quantity, because of the decreasing marginal utility of the combination; therefore, the marginal unit of *B* is not quite twice as useful as the marginal unit of *A*. However, for obvious reasons, the marginal utility of the best combination declines more slowly than the marginal utility of any single commodity, and the decline may therefore be neglected as a "small quantity of the second order of smallness"—since we are dealing with marginal units and thus with small quantities in the first place.

It seems to this writer that the mere concept of a combination of goods being the equivalent in desirability of one particular good implies that desirability is measurable. Evidently, we can speak of the total desirability of a commodity group only if the desirability of the component parts can be added up. But if addition is possible, all other mathematical operations must be possible too. Adding means counting, and there is no counting except by units; if there are units, their aggregates can be subjected to division and multiplication as well.

[39] A more direct but also more abstract method of proving this proposition can be derived from an argument of Oscar Lange. The concept of a rate of substitution implies that an individual is able to judge not only whether a stock of commodities is preferable to another stock of commodities, but also whether a given change in one stock is preferable to a given change in the other. As Lange has shown in his study on "The Determinateness of the Utility Function" (*Review of Economic Studies,* Vol. I, No. 3, June, 1934, p. 222), this is the same as saying that utility is measurable.

will have to be taken into account when the issue is settled among psychologists.[40]

Now, since value planning is necessary and fundamentally possible, how is it to be carried out? Even if the market mechanism is entirely preserved, as we have assumed, the planning board will not be able to use this mechanism for its own task of price determination. It has to determine not the prices which reflect present market conditions, but those which will result in the future when supply and demand conditions are changed. Yet the planning board, although unable to ascertain through the market the prices which should be inserted in the plan, will have to use for its purpose the same principle on which the market mechanism operates. Price formation on the market is a search for an equilibrium through trial and error. Sellers and buyers change their charges and biddings until a price is established which just equilibrates supply and demand. The planning board can carry this process out on paper with infinitely less cost and loss of time than it can be carried out by

---

[40] Another version of the psychological argument is used by some economists. They object that the concept of social utility, and therefore that of value in a social economy, implies not only the possibility of arithmetical operations with units of individual satisfaction, but also that individual satisfactions can be added up to social satisfaction. This is regarded as impossible because of the lack of a common standard of reference for satisfactions or desires of different individuals. Even granted, it is said, that it makes sense for A to maintain that he wants one good n times more than another, yet the statement is inadmissible that A's desire for a good is m times greater than B's desire for the same good. We may well leave this question open and still assume that A's as well as B's desire contributes to the social utility and therefore to the value of the commodity. The common standard of reference is not of a psychological but of an institutional character; it is a product of either force or social philosophy. If we are orthodox equalitarians, we shall assume that each person's total needs count as much as any other person's. If we are not equalitarians in the strict sense, or even not at all, we shall deviate from this rule, to a given extent, for reasons of ethics or expediency. Even if we knew A's total desires to be twice as strong as B's—whatever this might mean—it is not at all certain that this knowledge would influence our judgment as to the proportion in which their respective desires should be satisfied.

sellers and buyers in reality. The board need not take all imaginable variations of supply and demand into account, but only those which are within the limits of practical possibility, and this brings its task down to manageable proportions.

However, this is an object of controversy. In his *Collectivist Economic Planning*[41] and in a later article in *Economica*[42] Friedrich Hayek, relinquishing the old Mises position, conceded the formal possibility of planning, but maintained that the planning board would never finish solving the innumerable equations through which the value of individual commodities would have to be calculated.[43] Hayek refers to the type of equations used by Walras, Pareto, Wieser, and Cassel for the description of price equilibrium. All commodities, consumers' as well as capital goods, are useful only in combinations, and it is only their combined effect which we can directly observe. For each purpose a different combination is used, yet if an optimum condition is to be attained, each commodity must have the same unit value in all combinations. Therefore,

---

[41] Friedrich A. Hayek, *Collectivist Economic Planning* (London: Routledge, 1935).

[42] "Socialist Calculation: The Competitive Solution," *Economica,* May, 1940.

[43] Professor Hayek, in his article in *Economica,* seems to question that the formal possibility of value planning (or, to use the terminology of previous debates, of "pricing in a society without a market") has ever been denied. He opposes the contention of Lange "that the demonstration that the formal principles of economic theory apply to a socialist economy provides an answer" to Mises and other critics: ". . . the question raised by Professor Mises and others was not whether they ought to apply but whether they could *in practice* be applied in the absence of a market" (p. 127, italics mine). But Mises considers value calculation in a socialist society not merely a practical but a formal impossibility. On this point his reference to psychological theory (citation of the psychologist Cuhel in *Socialism,* p. 114) leaves no doubt. Consequently, Lange's demonstration that there was no formal obstacle to socialist calculation in value units did provide an answer to Mises. It is true that formal possibility does not prove practicability, which neither Lange nor Dickinson ignored, but Hayek's concession that an affirmative answer to the first question was possible meant certainly, as Lange stated, a "retreat to a second line of defense." Whether it meant the granting of the "essential point" is a matter of opinion, but there is no justification at all for Hayek to accuse Lange and his school of "covering up their own retreat by creating confusion about the issue" (*op. cit.,* p. 127).

it is possible to establish a system of simultaneous equations, in which the combined effects, in terms of utility produced, and the physical quantities of each element in each combination appear as the knowns and the unit values of the elements as the unknowns.

Starting from consumers' goods, we may consider that people like to ride to a motion picture after having eaten a good meal. They would not enjoy the picture, or at least would enjoy it far less, if they had either to see it while they were hungry or after the exertion of a long walk from their homes. Thus we cannot directly establish the utility of a motion-picture ticket alone, but only in combination with the meal and with gasoline for transportation. When the planning board, or any one else, tries to find out the utility of a motion-picture ticket, the object of inquiry is not the negligible utility which the show ticket would have among men deprived of all other enjoyments, but its utility in a social environment where a given standard of living is customary. Therefore, the situation can be illustrated by an equation of this kind:

$$x+y+3z=10u$$

where x means the utility of a motion-picture ticket, y that of a meal of given quality, z that of a gallon of gasoline, and u a counting unit of utility, for instance the utility of a dollar.

There is no difficulty at all in finding as many equations as we wish, since there are almost innumerable combinations of goods and we have always enough to calculate the unknowns. The results obtained for consumers' goods can then be used to calculate the value of producers' goods. For instance, having calculated the value of the motion-picture ticket, we may establish a similar equation expressing the utility of the various capital goods that are required for a performance, and add the necessary number of other equations—taken from the production of other consumers' goods—so that each element can be calculated. The kind of value planning which forms an indispensable complement of physical planning may well be described as a continuous effort to solve that type of equation. The equational system of the Walras-Pareto school was originally developed only to illustrate the interdependence of prices, not to prove that the calculations could actually be undertaken by a collective agency for society as a whole. Of the writers who proposed the equations, Pareto at least, whom Hayek quotes to this effect, was definitely opposed to the idea that calculation would be practicable. He argues that the multitude of equations which would have to be solved would defy any effort undertaken with mathematical means and that "the only means to solve them which is available to human powers is to observe the practical solution given by the market."

Once more the opponents of planning have offered an argument which, if correct, would prove that even the capitalistic market could not function. There are two ways of solving equations, the one which we have all learned in school (and which was referred to above), and the other which we may call the method of experimental variation, or the trial-and-error process. Instead of following the rules of the mathematical textbook, we may systematically change all the unknowns of the equations until we arrive at magnitudes which will satisfy the conditions. If we try out changes chosen entirely at random, the procedure will take an impossibly long time. Frequently, however, we may be able to eliminate certain types of assumptions because they are unrealistic, and thus limit the range of variation. It is this method, limited experimental variation, that prevails in the practice of a market economy.

The form in which experimental variation is practiced there is exceedingly wasteful, for it does not consist merely of changing figures on paper. We can change our purchases as consumers as well as our combinations of factors as producers, until we feel that we have made the best use of every dollar, that we are producing the most profitable product in the cheapest way, and, generally, that we have nothing to gain from further change. We do it on paper as far as we can, that is, we try to calculate in advance how we can economize in production by using substitutes for individual cost goods or by choosing entirely different combinations, and if we are very careful, we even draw up a consumer's budget to see how we can secure, for instance, our supply of vitamins and other necessary elements of our diet in the most satisfactory way and one that is still not too expensive. But in an unplanned economy we cannot get very far by paper calculation, because we know too little about the reactions of others to the same problems. Soon we reach the point where we have to change the relevant magnitudes in reality and watch the reactions of our customers, suppliers, partners, and competitors. These reactions will, for the most part, make changes in our own dispositions necessary, and then again we have to find out how these affect the attitude of others.

The planning board, on the other hand, applies the trial-and-error process on paper to those processes of production in which the optimal course for one firm or individual is determined by the actions of others. This form of experimental variation is an immense economy in time, effort, and material as compared with the experiments in steel and timber, copper and labor, selection of occupation and expenditure of consumer dollars, which is the prevalent form of approaching an

equilibrium under the *status quo*. The apparent advantage of
an unplanned market economy lies merely in the fact that it
employs every person, producer or consumer, in the solving
of the equations, and that the sacrifices involved in their trials
and errors do not, for the most part, become visible in the
public budget.[44] But this does not make the sacrifices any less
real. Planning does not require the solving of any equation or
any other determination of magnitudes that would not be
necessary in an unregulated market economy.

Since the market actually solves all the equations that must
be solved, we have a right to suspect that the problem is not
quite so formidable as it looked to Pareto and Hayek, but at

[44] Hayek, in his criticism of Lange and Dickinson, seems to be oblivious of the
trial-and-error character of all actions on the market. "Professor Lange as well as
Dr. Dickinson assert that even if the initial system of prices were chosen entirely at
random, it would be possible by such a process of trial and error gradually to approach to the appropriate system. This seems to be much the same thing as if it
were suggested that a system of equations which was too complex to be solved by
calculation within reasonable time and whose values were constantly changing could
be effectively tackled by arbitrarily inserting tentative values and then trying about
till the proper solution was found." ("Socialist Calculation," pp. 130–131.) But the
latter method is the way in which prices are formed today, except that the tentative
assumptions are not chosen entirely at random, but within reasonable limits, which
could just as well be done in a planned system.

A little later Hayek discusses the question of whether central direction or an
unregulated market will reach "anything approaching the desirable equilibrium"
with greater speed. "How great the difference in this respect would be between a
method where prices are currently agreed upon by the parties of the market and a
method where these prices are decreed from above is of course a matter of practical
judgment. But I find it difficult to believe that anybody should doubt that in this
respect the inferiority of the second method would be very great indeed" (*ibid.*,
p. 132). It is perfectly true that the reaction of the buyer to the offers of the seller
come forth more quickly if he is independent of a central agency, but the seller's offer
itself is only one tentative step toward the equilibrium price, and the buyer's reaction
is another. The question how speedily a reasonable approach to the equilibrium price
is achieved depends not merely on the quickness with which one step follows upon
the other, but on how many steps prove to be erroneous. A man running in a zigzag
fashion toward a goal may reach it much later than a person approaching it in a
slow walk, but on a straight, direct path. The most important question is, therefore,
whether the planning agency can cut out unnecessarily roundabout ways by calculating reactions of buyers and sellers to one another on paper before having them carried
out in reality.

what point did they overestimate the difficulties? Pareto, in the passage quoted by Hayek, argues that to calculate the utility of each of seven hundred commodities for each of one hundred consumers, even under simplifying assumptions, the solution of 70,699 equations would be required. He assumes that this "exceeds practically the power of algebraic analysis," and speaks of the "fabulous number of equations which one obtains for a population of forty million and several thousand commodities." No businessman tries to anticipate the utility of each of his products for each of his customers. Very appropriately, he is satisfied with estimating the demand of consumer groups, and there is no reason at all why the planning board should not do the same. Thus the equations will not reach a fabulous number, but it is quite possible that a few hundred thousand combinations have to be taken into account. Why this should exceed the power of algebraic analysis is difficult to see. It probably does not exceed the amount of calculation work which a hundred middle-sized engineering firms have to perform in a week.[45]

The real weakness of value planning, at the present level of knowledge, is not at all the necessity of using too much mathematics; it is rather the inability to use mathematical techniques on a sufficiently large scale. It is a crude method to search for an equilibrium by experimentally varying all the determinants until they fit together, and, although it is infinitely more eco-

---

[45] The human ability to perform a large number of mathematical operations in a limited period of time has been very much increased by the perfection of calculating machines, which, of course, were not yet very efficient at the time when Pareto first proposed his argument. Nowadays, however, even an otherwise impregnable argument, based on the limitations of the human mind in solving equations, would not seem very strong. Further improvement in calculating apparatus, perhaps even the wider use of machines and procedures already available to some experts, may well remove any conceivable difficulty of that kind in the very near future.

nomical to carry out these variations on paper than in reality, a further great economy of effort might be achieved through the development of mathematical short cuts. A future generation may look upon the trial-and-error process very much as a second-year schoolboy, knowing the use of multiplying and dividing techniques, looks at the abacus. But in the meantime, the abacus method serves the purpose of demonstrating that the problem is soluble, practically as well as theoretically.[46]

The Coördination of the Two Columns

The extensive discussion of the role which value planning must play if the planned system is to work has diverted the attention of economists from the function of physical planning.

---

[46] There exists a school of mathematical economists who try to find out the actual demand curves for individual goods. The standard work in the field is the book by the late Professor Henry Schultz, *The Theory and Measurement of Demand* (University of Chicago Press, 1938).

The efforts of Schultz and his predecessors were concentrated on an analysis of prices in past periods. Their demand curves are intended to show how, at given moments, the statistically ascertainable prices were formed under the influence of factors which determined the slope of the demand curve and its location in a system of coördinates. Schultz undoubtedly thought of future prices too, but only in the sense that the analysis of past developments should enable interested individuals, groups, or agencies to make relatively accurate forecasts of marketing conditions in the very near future and to estimate general trends over a longer period of time, in an unregulated market economy. He did not consider the possibility that his techniques could be used for an effort to calculate future prices several years in advance as part of a plan of all production and consumption. He even listed the increased interest in economic planning as one of the factors which might distract the attention of students from the field which he was trying to develop (*op. cit.,* p. 660).

In reviewing the work of Henry L. Moore, A. C. Pigou, Wassily Leontieff, Ragnar Frisch, Jacob Marschak, and René Roy, Schultz found that the problem of statistical demand curves had been attacked from two different angles. Some authors had used time series of prices and had tried to derive demand functions from price movements under various historical conditions. Others had tried to construct demand curves from family-budget data on different income levels. Schultz himself, in his attempt to establish the demand curves for various agricultural commodities, uses the time-series method, although he recognizes that the family-budget method also has advantages and extensively discusses its mathematical problems.

The time-series method, however appropriate for the purpose which Schultz had

This function is easy to state. Future supply and demand conditions can only be determined if we calculate the physical effects of our present undertakings. Evidently, we can achieve nothing in the line of price anticipation unless we know what physical changes in production we have to expect. The prices resulting from an unplanned market are misleading as a guide for action because they tell us nothing about the physical situation which will exist when our actions have worked out.[47]

Thus physical planning is basic to value planning. But it would be an oversimplification to say that the establishment of the physical-quantities scheme must precede the establishment of the value scheme. Value calculation is necessary to test the worth of the contemplated physical arrangements, just as the physical data (including needs) determine the values. Thus neither can be finally established before the other is worked out, and we have to approach the correct results by a process of adjustments on both sides. The planning board must not draw up two separate plans, but two interdependent columns of the same plan.

---

in mind, is not usable for the determination of future prices if a substantial change of conditions must be assumed. This method tries to deduce one cause, the structure of demand, from the observed effect, the price. If we have found the structure of past demand through an analysis of past or present prices, we still do not know what changes in the demand structure will occur between now and the time for which we attempt our prediction. A comparative analysis of family budgets reveals the determinants of the demand for individual commodities and makes it possible to separate the relatively constant factors (psychological data) from those subject or even destined to change (incomes and prices of competing or complementary commodities). The promise of the work of Schultz and his school for the progress of planning technique rests on the possibility of developing the family-budget method to a higher degree of perfection.

[47] Note Heimann's remark that "the nature of price, expressive as it is of an only momentary situation, appears to be inadequate to the regulation of long range processes" ("Literature on the Theory of a Socialist Economy," *Social Research*, February, 1939). The point has also been discussed rather extensively in an earlier article by Heimann: "Planning and the Market System," *Social Research*, November, 1934, pp. 488 ff.

The problem of how to coördinate the value and physical-quantities columns must arise in every effort at national economic planning in one form or another, and it will become urgent as the plan becomes comprehensive and provides for far-reaching changes in production and consumption. Judged by these criteria, the problem must play a very great role in the Russian Five Year Plans, and yet we are almost without information about the techniques which the Soviet agencies are using for its solution. It seems strange and regrettable that the theory of national economic planning should have to be developed entirely from a priori considerations, when there is already a country where the economy has been guided by all-inclusive plans for almost twenty years. On no other phase of the planning effort are we so much in need of empirical information as on the relationship of physical planning and value planning. Yet the official Soviet publications in English, full as they are of details about the engineering aspects of planning, leave us unenlightened on the fundamental economic aspects, and even the few books which deal with pricing, finance, and credit in the Soviet Union contain very little about the process of mutual adjustment between the physical and value plans or even about the methods by which the value figures are established. We know hardly more than that the problem, in its general outline, is known to Soviet economists.

The Financial Plan has its counterpoint in a Material Plan, which determines the production and consumption of raw material and manufactured goods, the progress of new construction, the reconstruction of existing factories, works, plants, etc. Obviously, the two plans must agree; they are, in effect, two versions of the same plan and each serves as a check on the other.[48]

---

[48] L. E. Hubbard, *Soviet Money and Finance* (London: Macmillan, 1936), p. 46.

Thus one of the best informed writers on the economics of the Soviet system describes the coexistence of the two plans. The Financial Plan is not exactly a value column, but an estimate of the revenues and expenditures of the various industrial units. Yet it is built upon the estimates of values of raw material, labor, and products, so that it represents a derivative from value calculation, and its relationship to the physical plan must, broadly speaking, be the same as that of a value column.

Although Soviet economists have not overlooked the necessity of anticipating changes in values which correspond to the planned physical changes, their ideas on this problem are very vague. By their Marxian tradition, they were committed to the labor value theory, which is entirely inadequate in making clear the function of value in a planned system. Their theoretical ideas clashed with practical necessities, and since it was extremely difficult for them to abandon or greatly modify their theory, they must have refrained as far as possible from working the problems out clearly even in their own minds.[49] This is evident from the reluctant and almost haphazard

---

[49] An effort to revise the value theory so as to make it more applicable to the practical task of planning was undertaken by a group of Soviet economists in 1943. This group worked out proposals for the revision of the content of courses on economics in Soviet universities. The text of the proposals was published in English translation by Raya Dunayevskaya in the September, 1944, issue of the *American Economic Review*. Naturally, proposals to change the treatment of economic questions in the classroom involved a criticism of opinions held by the teachers, and therefore the suggested reform of instruction amounted to a reinterpretation of the Marxian doctrine, or rather to an abandonment of some Marxian principles in the form of a reinterpretation. While retaining the terminology of the labor theory of value, the group made a definite move in the direction of a utility value theory as the basis of plan calculation, especially for the valuation of different types of labor. See my note "From Marx to Menger," in the *American Economic Review*, June, 1944. Although the note was based on the abbreviated version of the Russian statement, as published in *Science and Society*, Spring, 1944, and therefore contains a few inaccurate references and arguments, the main line of reasoning is not thereby affected.

The text of the proposals mentions that instruction in economics on the college level had been suspended in the Soviet Union "for several years," previous to the

fashion in which value planning was developed. If there had been a clear realization of what value would mean for planning, the Soviet economists would have seen that it was of decisive importance to keep the monetary unit as stable as possible in terms of commodities, because fluctuations or rapid depreciation of money was bound to make all value calculation very difficult and largely inaccurate. But there was a great amount of indifference toward the inflation of currency in the period of the first Five Year Plan, before practical experience forced a change of mind, leading to the bank reform of 1930–1931.[50] The idea was widespread that fixing of prices by the government would remove all dangers from the increase in currency,[51] although price fixing means the freezing of a barometer which the planners have to watch.[52]

---

academic year 1942–1943. This interruption can hardly be explained except as an effect of the "purges" of the 1930's. If this interpretation is correct, the desire of the authors of the proposals to preserve at least the language of traditional Marxism can be easily understood.

The contention by Brooks Otis (*American Economic Review*, March, 1945, pp. 134–137), that the statement of the group did not involve a fundamental revision of doctrine because the marginal-utility theory in its pure form "is in no way inconsistent with Marxism" seems to me untenable in view of many passages in Marx's own writings.

[50] Hubbard, *op. cit.*, p. 50.

[51] See Arthur Z. Arnold, *Banks, Credit and Money in Soviet Russia* (New York: Columbia University Press, 1937), p. 429.

[52] According to information furnished by Charles Bettelheim in his excellent book *La Planification Soviétique* (Paris: Librairie des Sciences Politiques et Sociales, 1939), some Soviet economists distinguish between the "material" and the "synthetic" balance sheets, which seems essentially the same distinction as between physical and value planning. "Synthetic balance sheets make it possible to examine very different objects from a single point of view (that of exchange of value, money expenditure, etc." (*ibid.*, p. 111). Among those who stress the necessity of supplementing the "material balance sheets" by "synthetic balance sheets," Bettelheim mentions Margolin, the author of a much-discussed article on "The Balance Sheet of Money Revenues and Money Expenditure in the Population" in one of the official Soviet periodicals. It seems that the school of economists to which he belongs is writing studies on the elements of the synthetic balance sheet, but that its compilation is not yet a part of the work of the official plan-making agencies. Bettelheim makes

Nor did Soviet economists see the difficulties which the "multiple price system" was bound to create for value planning—as far as we can judge from what was done. Up to the "derationing" legislation of 1935, the Soviets kept different sets of prices for rationed and unrationed goods. This would not have made value calculation impossible, if a system of accounting prices had been built up, independent of the prices that were actually charged on the market. No thoroughgoing attempt of that kind was made, although wholesale prices, which mainly guide production, were less arbitrarily determined than retail prices.

Thus it is not the fault of the investigators that they found little to discover about the coördination of physical and value planning in Soviet Russia. Since Soviet planners have no clear conception of the task, we would have to analyze their practice to see how they have developed the indispensable minimum of value calculation and are fitting it into their physical plan. But no outsider has ever been admitted to the consultations of the *Gosplan* or been permitted to study the records on planning in the Soviet archives.

Since we can learn so little about the coördination of the two columns in the actual procedures of the Soviet government, nothing is left but to return to our attempts to solve the problem by deduction. In this way, however, we cannot hope to find out the best method, any more than the inventors of the gasoline motor were able to suggest all the details of a 1947 automobile. We shall again have to be satisfied with showing how the problems could be solved, if no better way were found.

---

the statement: "While the elaboration of the material balance sheets for fuel, metals, construction materials, tools, etc., has been promoted in the USSR by a relatively strong impulse, the question of the synthetic balance sheets has made very little progress" (*ibid.*).

Planning is certainly one of the activities which cannot be fully learned except "on the job."

Suppose the planning board has made an inventory of resources and with the advice of engineers has assembled enough facts to draw all the important supply curves. Furthermore, it has sufficient information to show how consumers react to changes in their income, and for each level of income to make reasonable estimates concerning the demand curves for the important commodities. Now it is attempting to draw up the plan in its two columns for a period of years.

Let us assume that planning begins at a moment when there is unemployment of men and machines. Whatever else may be unknown, there is one fact from which to start. The planning board certainly intends to provide for the employment of all available man power, at least as far as the workers are willing to work at present wages. By considering the composition of the available man power with respect to skills, which determine income groups, and the amounts of interest and profit which correspond to a given level of wage income, it will arrive at a tentative figure indicating the total income of each of the major social groups after the process of reëmployment is completed.

On the basis of this tentative set of figures, the planning board can undertake a preliminary calculation of the demand for various commodities. Suppose that it is found that the demand for automobiles will be m, that for radio sets n, that for dresses and suits o, and that for shoes and boots p, and so on for all the important industries. Now the board has to examine all these industries to find out whether their working staffs add up to total employment of industrial labor, and if the division of their staffs into skilled and unskilled, manual and white-collar labor is in accordance with the original assumptions. If the corrected scheme shows a deficiency in employment, there must be some fault in the assumptions, for instance, too low a figure for the total national income or wrong proportions of consumer expenditure on various commodities. The possibility of a deflationary process which would drain purchasing power need not be considered if there is general confidence that the plan will work, since by providing a market the plan gives every entrepreneur a foreseeable chance to earn profits, and nothing but the fear of unprofitableness can cause saved money to be withheld from investment in production and the creation of incomes.[53] If, however, there are reasons to believe that some funds may still be kept back because of lack of confidence in the period of transition, the deflationary effect must be estimated and either checked or compensated by the issuance of new money. More will be said about this point later.

The result of the preliminary calculation which we have so far explained is a scheme showing how all available man power could be employed and products exchanged, if prices were the same as before the expansion and incomes conformed to our

---

[53] The theorem that total employment will be achieved if everyone spends his income or saves only as much as will find an outlet in real investment, is related to but not the same as Say's law. The latter implies an automatic expansion of demand as a consequence of any expansion of supply, and thereby denies the possibility of an equilibrium with underemployment, because it considers money a neutral element. But even one who believes in the possibility of an underemployment equilibrium— for instance, on the basis of the Keynesian theory—will grant that this is not the only imaginable state of equilibrium and that the monetary factors which tend to keep production on a comparatively low level can be put out of effect by deliberate action of community organs. In other words, here we have to rely on that part of Say's reasoning which nobody who believes in the possibility of theoretical explanation of economic phenomena can reject: namely, that there is no useful good which cannot become the object of exchange for other useful goods, or that the money earned in one type of employment (if it is not hoarded) will be spent on the products of other branches of production and thus sustain the employment of a corresponding number of workers there.

tentative assumptions. But prices and price relations will certainly have changed. Some industries, under the influence of decreasing cost, will be able to offer their products more cheaply; others, governed by increasing cost, will have to secure a higher unit price. Frequently "bottlenecks" will make it impossible for supply to follow demand, and a price considerably above production cost will be required to equate the two. The calculation of national income with which the planning board started would have been inaccurate anyhow, but the price changes make the difference from reality even greater.

Changes in the assumed prices and incomes make changes in the physical plan necessary. Suppose the automobile output and sale was q before the plan was made, and the tentative draft of the plan assumed that it would be q plus r. But closer calculation shows that there are still advantages to be gained by increasing the output of the individual automobile factory, and on the basis of the saving of labor and energy per unit of product a price drop is held possible that would permit demand for automobiles to grow to q plus r plus s. However, any increase in automobile production requires more steel. If the steel mills are operating under conditions of increasing cost, the saving of labor and energy in manufacturing automobiles will be partly outweighed, the price can be reduced only to a lesser extent, and the demand will not be q plus r plus s, but only q plus r plus s minus e.

These developments in automobile production and the automobile market will affect other sectors of the economy. If people buy more automobiles, some of them will buy fewer refrigerators or even suits and dresses. This is the group which, before the price change, had not yet reached the decision to buy an automobile, but was close to it and now finds that with some saving in other fields it can afford a car—or a new car—and that in this way it will get more satisfaction out of its money. But there is another group which was ready to buy automobiles before the price drop and now finds that it has to pay less and, therefore, can afford to buy more of other commodities. Income structure and demand schedules will supply the elements from which the net effect of these conflicting tendencies can be calculated.

There are still other developments that must be taken into consideration. A rise in the price of steel will force an increase in the price of a great many goods, affecting demand. The increased use of automobiles will add to the demand for complementary goods, such as tires and gasoline. This again will require changes in supply and will produce changes in incomes.

To find the state of equilibrium among all these interdependent magnitudes, the planning board will have to apply the method of experimental variation—which we described before in discussing the determination of interrelated values— to the relationship between elements of the value column and those of the physical column. This task is facilitated by the fact that most of the innumerable effects which any change in values or incomes must produce are negligible in comparison with the whole volume of the economy. A change in the value of steel affects practically all branches of industry, agriculture, and commerce, but it affects the railroads and the automobile industry far more than the textile industry or cattle ranching. Some marked changes in demand will not make much of a change in factor requirements and producer incomes, since approximately the same materials—although in different proportions—are required for, say, the automobile and refrigerator industries, and the wages of a skilled worker or a clerk in either of these two industries will be almost the same. For these reasons, it is possible to make a rough estimate of the effects that we may expect from a given change without entering into calculation of all details, and later to approach accuracy by taking minor consequences into account.

How helpful this kind of procedure is can best be explained in terms of the administrative problems of planning. The planning board will need a large staff, organized in departments, so that each department concentrates on the conditions of a particular industry. The results of departmental investigation must all be reported to a central committee or bureau which integrates them into a plan. But the flow of information is not all in one direction. The central bureau will have to keep every department informed of the results obtained by the other departments, as far as these affect each department's own work. Now, if the central bureau had to wait for the details to be worked out in the field of each single department, probably no plan could ever be completed. But since the most important effects of any change can be estimated with comparative quickness, the central bureau can send the departments preliminary instructions which will greatly simplify their tasks. If, for instance, a decrease in the manufacturing cost of automobiles coincides with increasing cost conditions in the production of steel, the central bureau will be able almost immediately to notify the departments in whose field steel is most important to expect a rise in the value of steel, with an indication of an upper and a lower limit of that rise. In this way, departments for railroads, for the machine-building industry, for construction, and so forth, know that a great many technical possibilities are ruled out as proposals for the plan. They will know that they must not take any expansion projects or even replacements into consideration unless they are necessary enough to justify the use of more valuable steel. They will have to send back to the central office estimates of the changes which these restrictions will produce in their physical requirements, in the prices of their products, and in the incomes originating in their respective spheres. In the meantime, the details of the steel price will be worked out, which will then show the need for lesser adjustments.

The essence of the whole method is the gradual narrowing down of discrepancies within the plan.[54] Neither in the mutual adjustment of different prices nor in that of the value and physical-quantities columns is it necessary to obtain accuracy from the beginning. It is only important that in each successive phase of the planmaking process more apparent possibilities are ruled out as inconsistent with other magnitudes already

---

[54] The study by S. Morris Livingston, *Markets after the War* (Department of Commerce, Bureau of Foreign and Domestic Commerce, March, 1943), uses a simpler method of planmaking. Livingston analyzes the way in which the American people, as a whole, spent its income at various times in the recent past. This analysis enables him to establish a ratio between national income and effective demand for each type of producer and consumer good. He then estimates the postwar national income on the assumption of full employment, taking into account the productivity of the American labor force, as shown in war production, and the prospective equipment of American industry. Finally, he tries to answer the question of what the demand for each commodity would be on the basis of the estimated postwar income of the nation, if the prewar spending habits and other determinants of the distribution of effective demand among various consumer goods were to remain unchanged.

It is one of the virtues of this excellent study that the explanation is immediately followed by a list of reasons why the results must not be accepted at their face value but must only be regarded as a first approximation. The study achieves its purpose of giving the businessman an idea of the magnitude of postwar markets. The method, however, is too crude for the elaboration of a plan by which the economy can actually be guided. An estimate of the size of individual income groups and an analysis of their prospective spending patterns through family budgets will be necessary if sufficiently reliable demand curves are to be established. Such a detailed analysis will also offer more opportunity to take account of probable changes in postwar as compared with prewar conditions.

established as parts of the plan. Let it be repeated that this is the principle on which the market operates, and the most important advantage of planning lies in the possibility of performing these operations on paper before they have to be performed in reality, thereby cutting out the costly fluctuations through which the market has to seek its equilibrium.

III. The Execution of the Plan

CONTROL FIGURES

VEN THE WISEST planning board cannot be expected to draw up a faultless plan. Developments beyond the control of the planning board—for instance, changes in the types or quantities of goods which foreign countries are able to export or import—may occur during the planning period. Furthermore, the means that are applied to carry out the plan are not likely to be equally effective at all times and places. It is essential to discover as early as possible any circumstance that may require corrections in the plan or the use of supplementary means for its execution. Developments must be subjected to careful current observation for any tendency to deviate from the original estimates. The execution of the plan must be continually checked by control figures, picturing the actual production and consumption and the progress of expansion projects.[1]

---

[1] In Soviet Russia, the term "control figures" is used in a somewhat different sense. There the Five Year Plans for every industry and finally for every factory are broken down into goals for each of the five years and even for shorter periods, and these goals are called control figures. Therefore, they do not describe achievements, but rather magnitudes that ought to be achieved—like the original plan figures, only for a more limited period. They enable the planning board to judge whether or not adequate progress is being made toward the fulfillment of the Five Year Plan, which would be impossible or at least very difficult if the achievements for the individual

All enterprises must currently report their outputs, sales, employment figures, pay rolls, and purchases of material and machinery. Banks must report their loans and deposits; statistical agencies, the data of foreign trade and population movements. In many of these fields, of course, this is the type of statistical information which is available even today, and no change, except perhaps a speeding up of publication, will be required; but in other fields the reports will have to compile business data which are now the secret of trade associations or are not assembled by anyone. The categories of this control-figure system will have to be the same as the categories of the plan, and in their entirety they must give a full description of all the relevant physical processes, prices, and monetary operations, and of the formation of income. The planning board will have to devise an administrative machinery which will call the attention of the responsible men to any point in the body economic where actual developments differ from preëstimated developments and corrective measures of some sort or another will therefore be necessary.

The Inducement of Individuals to Compliance

The planning board and the producer.—A plan need not change all the activities of all the citizens, but it can be carried into effect only by causing many individuals to act differently, on many occasions, from the way in which they would have acted if left entirely to their own counsels. The choice of the

---

month or year had to be compared with the goals for the whole five-year period. The same purpose is served by control figures in the sense in which the term is used in the text. It is clear that, in any event, goal figures and achievement figures must exist for every year, month, and even week, to make an adequate control possible, but since the short-run goal figures are essentially of the same character as the elements of the plan, it seemed more appropriate to reserve the term "control figures" for the short-run achievements.

methods by which compliance can be secured depends largely on the character of the legal, political, and economic institutions. In the foregoing section, we found it expedient to assume an institutional setting for the planned economy as much like the existing economic order as possible without defying the purpose of planning. In particular, it was assumed that enterprise would, as a rule, be in private hands. We shall continue with this assumption.

The existence of private enterprise does not in itself imply the absence of compulsion. To be sure, private enterprise can only be justified on the presumption that there are at least some things in the conduct of the individual business which the owner understands better than any central agency. This leads to the recognition of a sphere in which the owner of a business can act as he sees fit, but outside this sphere he may be compelled to act according to directions. In contemporary society the entrepreneur is already subject to compulsion in various forms and has to accept it as a condition for the conduct of enterprise.

However, to impose the plan on entrepreneurs wholly or mainly by compulsion would be not only undesirable but hardly practicable. It is logically possible to imagine a sphere in which the entrepreneur is his own master and another in which he has to obey the orders of the planning board without any right of remonstrance, but it would be difficult to keep the boundary between these two spheres clear and thus avoid constant friction. Therefore, it is preferable that the entrepreneur be induced to accept voluntarily the instructions of the planning board.

The way to achieve such voluntary acceptance is to make it visibly profitable to the individual entrepreneur. The gain which the whole economy has to expect from a well-calculated plan is not in itself a guarantee that each individual entrepreneur will automatically profit from compliance, and still less that the profitableness of compliance will be obvious to him. But there must be ways to secure, for every entrepreneur who coöperates with the planning board, an adequate share in the gain which will accrue to society as a whole and to disperse any doubts about its certainty and magnitude.

In his book, *Jobs for All*[2]—preceded by an earlier book containing similar suggestions[3]—Mordecai Ezekiel, of the United States Department of Agriculture, has proposed a method for such an arrangement. A central government agency, with the assistance of business organizations, is to work out a plan providing for an expansion of all economic activities from a depression level to full employment. If the plan is well balanced, a magnified volume of production will sustain itself, because the workers of one industry will buy the products of all others. For the individual entrepreneur, the only risk in complying with the plan lies in the possibility that the others might not do so and thus might fail to provide a market for his own products. As a protection against this risk, Ezekiel suggests that the government enter into simultaneous contracts with all large concerns, obligating them to carry out their part in the plan and promising in return to compensate them for all damage that might result from such compliance. The entrepreneur would have to commit himself not only to a fixed volume of output but also to a maximum price for his products, since the government could of course not guarantee a sales volume if the entrepreneur were free to set the price. At first sight it

---

[2] *Jobs for All Through Industrial Expansion* (New York: Knopf, 1939).

[3] *$2500 a Year* (New York: Harcourt, Brace, 1936).

might appear that several other commitments would have to be inserted in the contracts between the government and the individual firms, for instance, a minimum price. It is unnecessary, however, to guard in the contracts against all deviations from the plan figures. Where deviations are not likely to assume dimensions that would seriously disturb the functioning of the plan, the individual entrepreneur may remain free in his decisions. Price reductions below the assumed figures will in all probability not be frequent enough to be a disturbing element of importance, and from a long-range point of view it would be undesirable to discourage the entrepreneurs from reducing their prices. The sales guarantee would, of course, not protect the entrepreneur from the consequences of his own errors of judgment or incompetence which may lead to his inability to sell with profit at the guaranteed price.[4]

The system would be the "Triple A" reversed. Producers would contract not for restriction but for expansion of output,

---

[4] This summary of the sales-guarantee proposal does not entirely coincide with Ezekiel's own version but includes some modifications which this writer considers desirable. Ezekiel wishes to construct the sales guarantee in such a form as to give it the effect of a minimum price. To this end it is combined with a contractual ceiling on the output. Ezekiel proposes, by way of example, that the entrepreneur should commit himself not to exceed the guaranteed "quota" by more than 20 per cent, and his normal sales price would be 10 per cent above the price at which the government guarantees the sale of the "quota." Under these circumstances, the maximum advantage which any entrepreneur can obtain through any price reduction is an increase of sales by 20 per cent. In reducing the price by 10 per cent below "normal," he may secure for himself a part, if not the whole, of this increase, and only in a negligible number of cases will the balance of the possible gain in sales volume offer an inducement to reduce the price still further below the guarantee level. If the increase in output is left without a ceiling, the situation may be different. In Ezekiel's scheme, the undesirable effects of the minimum price are kept within narrow limits through the provision that the contracts are to run for one year only, a period which would afford an early opportunity for reducing the minimum but which seems too short in all instances in which the entrepreneurs have to increase their equipment in order to comply with the output figures of the plan. On the latter point, see below; also, *Jobs for All*, p. 17. The general arguments for and against a ceiling on the output of the individual firm are also discussed later.

and the government would underwrite their plans. Just because the plan assumes that the expansion of one industry provides the market for the expanded operations of the other, the government's risk would never even approximate the fiscal burden which inevitably results from any serious depression.

Since the recent form of the Ezekiel proposal has been submitted only briefly, some questions had to remain open. Among other points, it is doubtful exactly how the risk of expansion is to be divided between the government and the firms. Whenever the entrepreneur needs new capital equipment to comply with the plan, the period must be determined for which he will receive a sales guarantee for his products. Should this period include the whole lifetime of the equipment? Ezekiel's idea, on the contrary, seems to be that, as a rule, the government should commit itself for one year only, which may suffice when the expansion can be carried out with equipment already available; although the plan must comprise a number of years, there is no reason why the government guarantee should cover a longer period than that for which the individual firm must make its decisions. But when large investment is necessary, the entrepreneur must stake his capital for many years, or even—as for a power dam, a new mine, and so on—for several decades, and he must certainly receive a guarantee for at least a considerable part of this time. Since the plan can hardly be drawn for more than, say, five years, this will sometimes mean that the government will have to accept a commitment for more than one planning period. The risk is naturally far greater when the guarantee extends beyond that space of time for which a plan of balanced production can be worked out, and it is probably justified and desirable to have the entrepreneur share the possible loss. This can be achieved either by limiting the guarantee to a period not covering the full amortization of the equipment or by providing only for partial compensation if its usefulness is prematurely lost. The entrepreneurs themselves might well find it good policy to insist upon such a sharing of risks, since the chances of survival of private enterprise will be greatly improved if the entrepreneur's position does not become too similar to that of a mere receiver of rent.

Ezekiel does not entirely rely on voluntary coöperation. Much as he prefers to avoid compulsion, he finds it necessary to suggest the imposition of a penal tax on individual entrepreneurs or whole industries who refuse to assist in the elaboration of the program or to accept contracts, and he speaks also of other sanctions that might be applied against recalcitrant individuals or groups. It is important to examine the need for these compulsory provisions.

Expanded production for an assured market is likely to be good business. There is little reason to suspect that during the Great Depression any considerable number of firms would have refused to enter into contracts of the type which Ezekiel proposes. Because of their mistrust of government action in economic life they might have been convinced that the whole program would ultimately be a failure, but they would certainly have tried to get the most out of the experiment as long as it was going on.

Only in the later phases of expansion, or if the program does not start from the depth of a depression, a number of firms may wish to exclude themselves from further increase in production. Once the very low point in the utilization of existing capacity has been passed, a firm or group of firms may see greater prospects of gain in raising prices than increasing out put. This would by no means imply that they want to wreck the program; on the contrary, their chances to secure higher prices would depend on the increase in purchasing power which expanded operations of other industries could not fail to produce. But from a desire of some entrepreneurs to remain behind the others in the expansion process, a general slowing down of the movement might easily result, with unemployment as a consequence.

This danger is not peculiar to a planned economy. Attempts of producers to keep production at a low level in order that prices may remain high are known from century-old experience. The existence of a plan reduces rather than strengthens the incentive to a monopolistic attitude. In an unplanned economy, it is not merely greed for greater gain that causes entrepreneurs to restrict competition; it is just as much fear of loss. Expansion is risky, and in the mind of an entrepreneur who weighs the chances that restricted production with higher price may bring him greater profit than expanded production with lower price the fear of the risk is added to the lure of higher unit revenue. In many industries the advantages of production on a large scale would outweigh the profit from higher prices but could not outweigh the double advantage of greater receipts per unit plus diminution of risk. Economic planning makes expansion very much safer for the entrepreneur who keeps within the plan and will often induce him to expand his operations when otherwise he would decide for the opposite policy. Yet even in a planned system the monopoly problem exists and must be attacked.

How much harm the noncoöperation of an entrepreneur in an expansion scheme will do to the plan depends on the type of industry in which it occurs. If, for instance, the manufacturers of suits refuse to expand their operations according to the plan, the damage may well be relatively small. Consumers will not be able to buy as many suits as they could have bought if the suggestions of the planning board had been carried out, and some adjustments may be necessary in the production of commodities that are either closely competitive or complementary to clothing. But these adjustments will be distributed over a number of industries and therefore will not affect any one industry very seriously. The deficiencies in satisfaction and employment in the field of clothing itself will remain the greatest effect of the manufacturers' failure to comply with the plan.

Much greater disturbance may result from the refusal of entrepreneurs in one of the important producers' goods industries to accept the planning board's proposal for expansion. If there is not enough steel or electric power, a number of manufacturing industries may be seriously affected, and in these the loss of consumers' satisfaction and workers' employment may be many times greater than in the production of the particular commodity which is the primary object of dissension.

In branches of production which are not vital for the success of the plan, either because they are quantitatively unimportant or because effects on other industries are negligible, a controversy between the planning board and the firms may well be put to trial. There is no reason to assume that the planning board will always be right and the firms always wrong. Although in an unplanned economy the entrepreneur's judgment on how demand and production cost will develop is necessarily unreliable, since his scope is, in the main, limited to his own business, in a planned economy he can obtain the relevant data from the planning board, and he may be better able than the board itself to draw conclusions for his firm. Therefore, a limited freedom for the entrepreneur to reject the suggested expansion (on the basis of the proposed product price) would work as a useful check on the plan, besides making the whole proposal politically more acceptable. An entrepreneur who rejects the suggestions of the planning board would, of course, act entirely at his own risk, and thus would not receive any guarantee of sales at a given price. This will in itself operate as a strong deterrent to rejection of the plan.

Since compulsion is to remain a rare exception and is by no means to take place even in all disagreements between individual entrepreneurs and the planning board, the compulsory powers must be so constructed as to be elastic. There should be no automatic sanctions. In each instance the planning board must decide if the dangers to the success of the plan are great enough to justify compulsory measures. On the other hand, whenever the planning board finds that voluntary compliance is not forthcoming and deviations are intolerable, compulsion must be quick and unquestionably effective. The penal tax which Ezekiel proposes may not meet these requirements in the best possible way. There may be difficulties in so constructing a tax that it becomes applicable only at the discretion of the planning board, and in an ultimate showdown an industry group may prefer to pay even a very high tax for a while, thus forcing a delay (perhaps a disastrous one) in the application of the plan. It is at least equally doubtful if much can be achieved by antimonopoly laws such as the Clayton Act. Aside from other reasons, the effectiveness of such legislation declines as industry becomes more concentrated, and there is no likelihood that the concentration process will be slowed down in a planned economy.

What better weapons can the government apply to combat monopolies? Whenever one or more firms refuse to expand production as much as the planning board thinks desirable, the government can see to it that new enterprises are created. The planning board will know what production resources, including entrepreneurial skill, are available, and if the government has sufficient control of credit facilities, as it certainly should have (this point will be discussed later), it can set up capable businessmen, equipped with the necessary capital, as competitors to existing firms that refuse to expand.

The calling in of new enterprises will sometimes involve waste, since the cost of constructing new plants may well be higher than that of expanding facilities already in existence. As long as the sums involved are not too large, the waste can be accepted as part of the cost of executing a plan. But it would not be justifiable to spend any considerable part of the community's resources upon the construction of new factories merely because the owners of existing equipment refuse to put it to full use. Therefore, a stronger weapon should be provided for the government. If, after careful consideration, the conclusion is reached that a firm is obstructing the national plan, either in the expectation of monopolistic gains or from motives of political resentment or just out of unwillingness to do the work which economic progress requires, the government should have power to expropriate that enterprise, after due compensation, and either run it under public management or transfer it to coöperating entrepreneurs. The granting of such powers would be within the logic of principles already recognized in our society. If rights of private ownership are not permitted to obstruct the building of railroad or power lines which the public interest demands, there would be little consistency in shrinking from interference with such rights when a whole stabilization plan is at stake. Of course, this does not mean that property rights are at the mercy of the government,[5] but that they can be interfered with under specified conditions and in ways prescribed by law and subject to review by the courts.[6]

The fight against monopoly has far better chances of success in a planned than in an unplanned economy. One of the reasons is the opportunity to apply stronger measures of enforcement when a plan is in operation, but perhaps even more important is the greater ability to judge when monopoly exists. Suppose the planning board has worked out proposals showing that production in a particular industry can and should

---

[5] Certainly no expropriation should be admissible for the sole reason that an entrepreneur refuses to accept a partial risk of expansion, when he is offered a sales guarantee for a period shorter than the amortization period of the equipment that he would have to purchase or construct. (See above, p. 82.) Ways can be found to protect the public interest as well as the rights of the firm; for instance, the latter may be given the choice of greater chances of profit with participation in the risk or protection from risk (except for consequences of incompetency or poor judgment) with very limited profits. Ultimately, of course, the planning board may always carry out a necessary expansion as a public enterprise.

[6] Very likely Mordecai Ezekiel did not choose his proposal of the penal tax primarily on grounds of economic expediency; he was probably motivated by the fear of legal difficulties which might stand in the way of a more direct enforcement. Unless one is a constitutional lawyer, it is impossible to venture an opinion on the possibility of overcoming or circumventing these obstacles, but the attitude of the judiciary will certainly be influenced by the whole character of the relationship which the plan establishes between the individual and the community, and more particularly by the advantages which the plan offers to the individual entrepreneur. If further concessions to the individual operator's interests—for instance, an extension of the period for which the sales guarantee is granted—improve the chances of judiciary approval of enforcement measures, the price may not be too high.

For tactical reasons, it may be more expedient not to grant powers of expropriation to the government before an open refusal to comply with the plan has been actually encountered. It is certainly easier to overcome political and legal difficulties if the danger of obstruction has been demonstrated by facts than if it appears merely as a theoretical possibility. On the other hand, the presence on the statute books of the power to transfer plants from private to public administration, or from a non-coöperating to a coöperating entrepreneur, may so strengthen the hands of the government in its negotiations with firms that the danger may be entirely averted.

be expanded. The entrepreneurs who oppose these proposals will probably argue that their production cost is higher than the planning board has assumed. If this argument is either a pretense or a mistake, the profits of the industry must turn out to be higher than those of others. There are certainly possibilities of hiding profits for a time, but they are not very great in a planned economy in which the comparison of conditions in one industry with those in others is so much easier than under "pure capitalism." There is a considerable likelihood that any extraordinary profits, earned by a firm or group of firms which defied the planning board on the issue of expansion, would eventually be discovered and would lead to coercive measures.[7]

---

[7] A. P. Lerner has suggested that monopoly should be prevented by fixing the prices of commodities produced under noncompetitive conditions through counterspeculation. "The government through a special board estimates what would be the price of the good that would make demand equal to supply if there were no restriction of the kind which we wish to abolish. It then guarantees this price to all the sellers in the case of a sellers' restriction or to all buyers in the case of a buyers' restriction. The buyers (or sellers) then know that the price will not move against them if they buy or sell more and that they will not get a better price if they restrict their dealings. The Board of Counterspeculation then buys in the free market what it has promised to sell to buyers at the guaranteed price or sells in the free market what it has undertaken to buy from the sellers at the guaranteed price." (Abba P. Lerner, *The Economics of Control* [New York: Macmillan, 1944], p. 55.) If the sellers were to refuse to supply the government with their product, they would presumably be prosecuted for restraint of trade, or the government would open competing plants.

In a more recent article Lerner has significantly modified his proposal. ("An Integrated Full Employment Policy," in *Planning and Paying for Full Employment*, p. 176). "Counterspeculation does not mean that the government must actually buy and sell all these goods itself. All the government need do is to guarantee the price to the producers who have been able to influence the price by their own restriction of sales. The government will tell them that they can sell as much as they want to at the guaranteed price. The producers sell at the market price, whatever this may happen to be, but the government reimburses them if they have to sell at less than the guaranteed price *while in the opposite case they must pay the difference to the government*." (Italics mine.) Whereas in the original form the proposal would mean that the government frustrates the expectations of the monopolists by its own market policy, the second form would presuppose a contractual relationship, which closely

So far we have discussed merely the possibility that entrepreneurs may not want to expand their operations as much as the national plan suggests, but it is also possible that they may wish to expand them more. Even without specific powers of compulsion, the planning board, if supported by other government agencies, will probably not find it difficult to check these attempts, if it so desires. The position of an entrepreneur who embarks on a system of expansion is always vulnerable. He has no guaranteed market. Often he will need credit, and when the banking system is under the control of the government, it will frequently be impossible to finance an undertaking which the government considers harmful. If these indirect means do not suffice to restrain an entrepreneur whose expansion projects threaten to interfere with the execution of the plan, the board must be able to impose direct restrictions. How-

resembles the arrangement proposed by Mordecai Ezekiel and suggested in preceding passages of this book. The principal difference—and at first sight this appears to be an advantage of the Lerner plan—would be the absence, in the latter, of any production quotas: The government would let the producers "sell as much as they want to at the guaranteed price," in the expectation that the producers will expand their output only "up to the point where the extra cost to them of adding another unit (their marginal cost) is as high as the guaranteed price" (*ibid.*, pp. 174–175).

This expectation presupposes rising marginal costs. Modern industry, however, knows many instances in which production remains within the area of declining marginal costs, either because too much capacity was originally established and therefore no plant can reach the optimal value of operations, or because the absorptive capacity of the market is not large enough even for the full output of a single plant of optimal size. In these instances the flooding of the market can only be prevented by the decline in price which the producer has to expect if he expanded his operations too much, and this limitation would be removed by the price guarantee. It is precisely under conditions of declining costs that monopolies are most easily established, because these conditions on the cost side favor concentration of enterprise.

Moreover, a guaranteed price without production quotas might easily involve the government in heavy losses, in the event of important technological improvements, of which the government, in an unplanned economy, would not necessarily have any advance knowledge. Suppose the firms introduce cost-reducing machinery during the guarantee period. The guaranteed price will then operate as a premium—and perhaps a very high one—on overexpansion of output, and the government has to pay the premium.

ever, the planning board may take an attitude of benevolent neutrality toward expansionist deviations from the plan. Even more than in connection with restrictive deviations, it may wish to let the entrepreneur find out if his opinion is correct as long as the plan as a whole is not upset, and sometimes a compromise solution may be found. The planning board may refrain from issuing a guarantee for the excess production but may provide the necessary supplies, or it may issue a restricted or conditional guarantee.

On these, as on other matters, the planning board will have to negotiate and bargain with individual firms. It is important to remember that the initiative for expansion may not always come from the planning board but sometimes, and perhaps frequently, from the firms. We can envisage firms or industries competing for inclusion of their expansion projects in the plan. In passing on their proposals the planning board will have to be guided by the estimates of consumers' reactions, and a project will be acceptable in the inverse proportion of the price which the firm will charge for the products of its expanded operations. In trying to convince the planning board that their respective projects are worthy of being carried out, the firms will have to lower their price expectations, and it will be up to the planning board to use this competition for the benefit of the consumer.

Sometimes a firm may propose to charge a price below production cost, in the hope that the latter may be lowered when experience has been gained in the period of introduction. As a rule, the planning board will have no objection if the firm wishes to subsidize the production of an article, but there may be exceptions. The supplies necessary for that particular production cannot perhaps be produced in existing plants. If the

planning board is to guarantee the profitableness of an expansion in, say, the steel or aluminum industry, which is to provide a firm with the necessary raw materal for the production
of a new article, the board may require assurance that the
demand will have some degree of permanence; but the firm,
producing the article on an experimental basis at a loss, may
or may not be able to give such assurance. Or the firm may not
even contemplate a permanent production but may wish to
start the production of an article in order to kill a competitor
who would introduce a rival product and it may intend to
discontinue its own production when this goal is reached.
The planning board will hardly wish to support such tactics.
On the other hand, the planning board may sometimes consider the introduction of an article so desirable that it will
recommend a public subsidy. If society becomes more equalitarian, the necessity for such subsidies will increase because of
the decreasing importance of the market for luxuries.[8] Many
of the innovations in consumers' goods, from the bicycle to the
radio, were originally introduced at a price prohibitive for the
masses and were accessible only to the privileged few. Even in
a society with complete equality of income there would be
purposes of special urgency for which expensive innovations
could be used. But it is doubtful if these would be frequent
and important enough to offer a full substitute for the initiat-

[8] At the present time, we are undoubtedly moving in the direction of an equaliza-
tion of incomes, but to this writer, at least, it seems uncertain how far the equalitarian
trend will lead. There are two counteracting tendencies. On the one hand, the underprivileged, in the world as a whole, are gaining in political power and in skill to
use it. They are naturally trying to increase their share in the national income and
thus to reduce the amount of inequality. On the other hand, their interest has been
partly diverted from equality to security. It is imaginable that the point may be
reached when the workers would accept the existence of profits without further
attempts to reduce them for the benefit of wages, if they are protected against fluctuations in employment and assured an undiminishing share in the increase in the productivity of labor.

ing function of luxury consumption, and therefore public subsidies may be necessary.[9]

Although the planning board may tolerate many deviations
from its original proposals, there is one requirement on which
it must always insist. Every large producer must make his intentions known to the planning board in advance and, as a
rule, must carry them out as announced. The planning board
must know the approximate quantities of material and labor
which an individual producer will buy in the coming period,
the payments of various kinds which he will disburse, and the
portion of purchasers' income that will be absorbed by the
marketing of his goods. There must be a law to make such
advance reports compulsory. In itself, this is no hardship on
any entrepreneur, and the data which the entrepreneur will
be given by the planning board will greatly facilitate reliable
estimates. But there remains a possibility that an entrepreneur
would like to change his output or his mode of operation during the period for which he has committed himself, either
because there has been some change in conditions or because
he wishes to correct his own calculations. If conditions, impossible to foresee, have arisen—for instance, if a crop has turned
out to be smaller or larger than had been expected—the planning board will have to admit adjustment without penalty.
Again, safeguards must be established to make deviations exceptional, although it may not be desirable to "freeze" the entrepreneur's plans entirely. A penal tax, graduated according
to the degree of deviation, would probably be the best method
to confine these subsequent changes to real emergencies.

---

[9] There is, of course, no doubt that subsidies will be necessary for scientific experiment. Even today such subsidies amount to considerable sums in the public budgets
of all civilized nations. The transition to subsidies for the introduction of new commodities on the market would often mean the crossing of a hardly discernible
borderline.

As an important link in his organization, Ezekiel proposes the establishment of Industry Authorities, consisting of representatives of labor and management, plus representatives of the consumers and the government. These committees, each for its industry, are to work out the production plan and subdivide the guarantee of output among the individual firms. Ezekiel is not unmindful of the warning example of the NIRA, which demonstrated how easily institutions of business self-government—the Code Authorities—can be made to serve monopolistic purposes. Yet what he says to show that his own organization would be free from this danger is not entirely convincing. It is true that the functions of the Industry Authorities in his project are more specifically defined and that every industry has before its eyes the definite prospect of increased marketing opportunities as an incentive to refrain from restriction. Yet the lure of monopolistic profits may sometimes be great enough to outweigh these advantages. Then all safeguards may prove ineffective; the Industry Authorities, if they are dominated by monopolistic tendencies, need not counteract the plan—they can influence it in the formative phase.

The presence of labor and consumer representatives in the Industry Authorities does not greatly diminish this danger. Consumers' representatives are, as a rule, not nearly so well informed about the conditions of a particular industry as the managers, and therefore cannot conduct an argument with them on equal terms. Labor representatives may be offered a share in the spoils of monopoly, and European experience indicates that in this way a formidable alliance can be formed against the consumer.[10]

---

[10] The reference is primarily to German experience with self-governing bodies in the coal and potassium industries during the Republican period.

It is easy to see, however, why, in spite of these dangers, Ezekiel considered Industry Authorities necessary, and why many previous advocates of planning have been led to similar proposals. It would be easier for the planning board to negotiate agreements with industry organizations instead of individual firms, and at first it may even seem an overwhelming task to allocate to individual firms their proper quotas in the expansion scheme. It might indeed be insoluble if a bargain had to be made with each firm, however small. But small business can be sufficiently relied upon to follow in big business' steps. Barbershops and grocery stores, even without a guarantee of customers, will emerge in towns where great corporations build new factories with government guarantee of sales. Little business' requirements of merchandise, material, equipment, and labor can be estimated by the planning board without their entering into commitments, once the board knows the pay rolls of the large factories. The question may be raised whether, for reasons of fairness, small business should not also receive guarantees, but this decision can wait until the plan is well established. Even if the small businessman does not receive a formal guarantee, he possesses much greater economic security in a planned than in an unplanned economy.

In any event, the stage of concentration which industry has reached will make it possible for the government to negotiate the sales-insurance contracts with the individual large concerns instead of with Industry Authorities. For obvious reasons, this will not remove all monopolistic influences, but the government will be able to play one concern against the other and, with some energy and skill, to ensure that the plan will be far less distorted by monopolistic forces than it would be if it were the product of negotiations with entrepreneurs' associations. The difference between monopoly and oligopoly may not always be great in a market economy, but it will be very important in an economic order where the oligopolists have to deal not with unorganized consumers, but with one central agency representing the public.

The exact legal relationships between the planning board and the producing firms could only be discussed in a separate essay. The producers would certainly be protected by the general provisions of the federal Constitution against arbitrary acts by the planning board, but what specific legal guarantees, if any, should be added cannot in all likelihood be finally determined before there has been a chance to observe how the relationships develop in practice.[11]

[11] Morris A. Copeland, in his article "Business Stabilization by Agreement," (*American Economic Review*, June, 1944, pp. 328–339), has proposed a system of contracts on a somewhat different basis. The contracts are to be concluded by the government with individual firms, each of which "undertakes to place an order for an article to be delivered or job to be done during a definite future period" and in return receives a bonus either in cash or in tax credit. These "definite period agreements" are to be supplemented by two other types of agreement, namely, "stable inventory agreements," in which the firms obligate themselves not to liquidate their inventories during a business recession and, in turn, receive a government guarantee against inventory losses and compensation for carrying charges, and "slack period reserve agreements," by which "the subscriber undertakes, in return for a bonus, to have a construction or other project ready for prompt activation on, say, three months notice" from the government. The government would offer enough agreements to produce full employment but no boom which would be bound to collapse; if firms place excessive orders, not covered by agreements, their overoptimism is to be curbed by special taxes and other "mild restraints." If, on the other hand, the stimulus provided by the bonus proves to be insufficient to reach the desirable level of production, the bonus might be increased or the gap filled by public works.

In the Ezekiel proposal, the community relieves the entrepreneur from a risk which, by the very fact that it is eliminated from private calculation, ceases to be serious. The government insures the individual firm against losses from large production, and since nobody will then be restrained by such fears, general full production will be attained and losses minimized. No such element is contained in the Copeland plan. The sacrifice which the government will have to make by paying the bonus will fall with its full weight on the Treasury. There is no assurance that an average rate of 4 to 5 per cent of the value of the orders, as suggested by Copeland, will suffice to overcome the entrepreneur's fear of being left with a large stock of

One kind of business demands maximum protection as soon as the plan is inaugurated. This is the production of goods and services which affect the formation of public opinion: newspapers and broadcasting corporations. Although the present conduct of these firms as private enterprises striving for profit is by no means ideal if we consider their function in a democracy, there is no doubt that the situation would be a good deal worse if their policies were determined by the government with the deliberate intention of influencing public opinion in favor of the party or group in office. Evidently, the effects of the most severe kind of censorship can easily be reached if a governmental agency is free to decide what physical facilities, from newsprint to electric power, are to be put at the disposal of any newspaper or radio station. The planning board, therefore, must be put under an obligation to provide the material, machinery, labor, and energy for these plants upon the demand of the producers, and the latter, of course, will have to forego the advantages of a public guarantee of their sales. The disturbing effect upon the plan of miscalculations on the part of newspaper enterprises or radio corporations is very limited and certainly would be a cheap price to pay for so important a safeguard against a manufactured public opinion. Even if it were found necessary to add the film industry to the list of especially protected industries, the situation would not be fundamentally altered. Of course, the firms could and should be obligated to submit their physical requirements to the planning board sufficiently in advance to minimize the adverse

unsalable goods. Thus the Ezekiel model of contracts will probably prove more effective and economical than the Copeland model and will be preferable as a basic arrangement. The two techniques, however, are not mutually exclusive. "Stable inventory agreements" and "slack period reserve agreements" may well be fitted into a system of sales guarantees and may prove very valuable.

effects upon the plan, but not so long ahead that their own operations, which need flexibility, would become unduly rigid.

The planning board and the consumer.—The principle of guaranteed sales offers a method by which an economic plan can be put into effect with compulsion of the producer only in exceptional circumstances. Will it be necessary to subject the consumer to compulsion? This question may arise even if the planning board reorganizes consumers' sovereignty in planmaking. Suppose the planning board has compiled a plan which, except for some educational objectives, gives the consumers the goods that they want, to the best knowledge and belief of the board. Will it not then be necessary to ensure by compulsory measures that the consumers will really buy these goods in the quantities in which they are provided? If the planning board was in error, it may seem better to make the consumers honor the commitments into which it has entered rather than to have the plan upset; and if the consumers have changed their minds, it may seem best not to permit an immediate change in their selection of goods but to make them wait for the next planning period.

If the planning board has provided for a larger production of refrigerators and a smaller production of bicycles than the consuming public would like to buy, and if prices are calculated on the wrong assumption that the plan coincides with consumers' preferences, queues will be formed before the bicycle stores and the refrigerator stores will lack patronage. Those consumers who have enough time and physical strength to stand in a queue for many hours will be the only ones to obtain bicycles, which is clearly a very unsatisfactory method of selection. A remedy may be found in changing the prices, so that more would be charged for bicycles and less for refrigerators, but in an economy where production is carried on by private enterprise this leads to other difficulties. The producers of bicycles would make an extra profit, for no better reason than that the planning board made a mistake in its original scheme and must now remedy it, and the producers of refrigerators would, for the same reason, suffer a loss, which they could not be expected to bear themselves. Presumably a tax would have to be levied from the entrepreneurs who are permitted to charge more than was originally provided in their contracts with the government, and from the proceeds a subsidy paid to those who must sell below the precalculated price. This arrangement may seem to offer a tolerably good solution. One of its advantages would be that it would involve only a very mild and indirect form of compulsion, since it would still leave the individual a chance to obtain a preferred good, if his interest is sufficiently strong to stand the higher price. But it will be very difficult to carry out the price adjustment without delay and in such a fashion that the compensation for one group is entirely covered by tax collections from the other.

Price adjustments are not the only way by which demand can be diverted from commodities which are not available in sufficient quantities and directed to those which are relatively abundant. Another method, containing a far stronger element of compulsion, is rationing, which may be wholly or partly substituted for buyers' competitive bidding in the market economy. In its extreme form, a rationing system would entirely supersede the market machinery and the use of money. Instead of a universal means of exchange, by which all sorts of goods can be bought, the consumer would have in his pockets a set of ration cards, each of which would constitute a claim for a specific commodity. Since bread cards and clothing cards are not interchangeable, the consumers would have no means of expressing their preference for clothing, if they felt that this need was undersupplied, and to prevent queues the government could simply reduce the rations to the quantities available. The details of this technique have been worked out in the First and in the Second World War. It has, so far, been applied only to the necessities of life, and if it were extended to "luxury" goods, considerable modifications would in all likelihood be necessary.

However, quite aside from the inconvenience for the consumer, there is another very serious argument against distribution by rationing in any but emergency situations. With the disappearance of money from use by consumers, the ultimate test of all value calculation would become impossible. In a system of planning in which money is used the planning board has to estimate prices in advance, but ultimately it is up to the consumers whether or not they will "ratify" the product prices by spending their money on the products in the estimated amounts. The willingness of the consumers to pay the estimated prices proves directly that the anticipations of the planning board concerning the utility of the finished goods were correct, and indirectly, since producers' goods values were derived from the anticipated figures for consumers' goods, it confirms the cost calculations of both the planning board and the entrepreneurs. Thus consumers' sovereignty provides the final possibility of control for the whole process of accounting, by which production in all its phases is guided.

If rationing cards take the place of money in the consumers' pockets, an attempt may still be made to maintain bookkeeping in production with the value of factors and products expressed merely in book money, but this would have to be entirely based on the planning board's estimates of the utility of final products. The planning board would never be able, except through very indirect and inaccurate methods,[12] to find out if it had read the minds of the consuming public correctly. It is unlikely that on this basis an accounting system could ever be operated in a satisfactory fashion.[13]

If the bookkeeping idea is dropped and value calculation is entirely abandoned, then the system must suffer from all the inadequacies of purely physical planning. Not only would private enterprise become impossible, since money profits would naturally disappear with money, but the choice between ways of production could no longer be made with any claim for accuracy in determining the most desirable. Thus it is not enough to say that rationing will restrict the consumers' freedom, it will also reduce very greatly the efficiency of production.

Since change in previously established prices is fraught with difficulties and rationing is inacceptable as a regular procedure, what means of correction are available to the planning board in the normal course of events, when it discovers mistakes in its anticipation of consumers' preferences?[14] No economy can

[12] The planning board may, for instance, inquire from the stores whether or not consumers were more anxious to obtain their quota of socks or of neckties. It may also expect to receive complaints or be criticized in the legislative body, if there is a relative undersupply of some goods. But since the critic has little opportunity to distinguish between undersupply due to mistakes and undersupply due to irremediable bottlenecks of production, the planning board will probably not be able to learn much from this criticism, even with the best intentions on the part of the planners.

[13] If the use of money by consumers is retained in a rationing system, the choices which consumers make in spending their money no longer express the utility of the goods, since the public would like to spend more money on some commodities, if it were permitted to do so. Consequently, the value figures which are based on the behavior of consumers in their expenditure do not offer reliable evidence for action which is intended to maximize the utility of output.

[14] It has sometimes been maintained that mistakes in estimating demand will be of greater importance in a planned economy because there they will be all in one direction, whereas in an unplanned economy each individual entrepreneur makes his esti-

operate without storage facilities and stocks of reserves to close a possible gap between supply and demand for a specific commodity. In a planned economy, in which many developments can be foreseen which are unforeseeable without a plan, these gaps will be less frequent. But since price changes are more difficult under planning, more emphasis must be laid upon the possibility of supplementing from reserve stocks the supply of a commodity for which demand is greater than anticipated and of putting in storage part of the supply if the demand is less.

Frequently, reserve capacity will have to take the place of reserve stocks. From an engineering point of view, it would seem ideal to have capacity always just equal to average demand, but economically this would not be the best solution. Factories cannot be quickly enlarged when additional demand shifts to their particular products, and therefore serious losses in satisfaction are unavoidable unless plants are large enough to satisfy some supernormal demand. Even for physical reasons there is need for reserve capacity. For instance, if milling space and transportation facilities were only just able to handle an average crop, a part of a rich harvest would have to go to waste. It is far better to carry the additional cost of some excess capacity in normal times rather than to be helpless in the face

---

mate, and mistakes are likely to cancel out. This last statement has never been true in a general way, for, in the absence of reliable data for calculation, the estimates of the individual entrepreneur are very often governed by the sentiment of the "business community," and if they are incorrect, the majority of mistakes will be of the same kind. With increasing concentration of business, which means concentration of decisions in a few hands, the chances for the canceling out of mistakes have been further reduced. Whatever chances of that kind remain must be weighed against the possibility which the plan offers of substituting calculation for guesswork. Moreover, decisions of the planning board are, of course, not one man's decisions. Many minds will have to coöperate in an estimate of any importance, and the errors of one individual are not likely to have any great influence upon the result.

of unforeseen developments. In a planned economy, the danger of underestimating the unforeseeable and committing the mistake of "irrational rationalization" is perhaps greater than in an unplanned economy, where the limitations of foresight are more obvious.

With the aid of reserve stocks and storage and with some possibility of price manipulation, the need for outright compulsion in the form of rationing or in any other form can be confined to exceptional conditions, and powers for such measures should be granted to the government only when an emergency arises. Yet it is worth while to consider some of the exceptional situations which would justify a system of planning in which rationing would be substituted—partly or wholly—for money as a means to distribute the goods.

Since planning without the use of money (or with money in a subordinate role only) means the abolition of consumers' free choice and a fortiori of consumers' sovereignty, and since without consumers' freedom a plan is essentially reduced to a physical scheme, such planning will be suitable only for situations where physical possibilities and necessities alone must be considered in order to arrive at the right decison of what ought to be produced. This will be true, first, when the satisfaction of consumers is not an end in itself but a means to an end. In an army, for instance, the purpose is not to give the soldiers the food and lodging and clothing that they would like best, but to satisfy their physical needs so that they will be able to beat the enemy. Therefore, the soldiers' "ration" can be determined largely, although not entirely,[15] by the judgment of army dieti-

---

[15] Although consumers' freedom is actually abolished in the army or restricted to such peripheral fields as recreation, it would be wrong to believe that the existence of that freedom in our economy has no influence on the soldiers' way of living. In determining the kind of food and shelter which soldiers should get army authorities

tians about the necessary vitamins and elements of nutrition, without regard to subjective preferences. Second, physical needs prevail in a state of poverty. In parts of the world reduced to semistarvation, there will be little use in maintaining a machinery for choice between radios and refrigerators. The merely physical considerations of what is necessary to sustain life and of the means by which the primary necessities of life can be produced and transported to the places where they are needed will then supply all the data required for decisions. A supplementary system of rationing, superimposed upon a monetary economy, becomes necessary in times of war to the extent that a nation's condition resembles either that of fighting soldiers or comparative poverty.

There may be instances when the planning board has temporarily lost its bearings and is unable to make reasonable estimates about consumer behavior in the coming period, so that rationing may be necessary as a stopgap. This contingency, although hardly important in itself, illustrates a significant fact. The necessity of compulsion in executing a plan arises mostly, if not entirely, from lack of foresight in drafting the plan. The more thoroughly and comprehensively the planning board collects and analyzes the data, the more clearly it can foresee the effects of the individual measures which it proposes; it will therefore be less likely to make mistakes and it will be better able to avoid measures which would forcibly prevent either consumers or producers from following their natural reactions to the provisions of the plan. Thus comprehensiveness in planning is not only, as has been stated previ-

have always realized that they have to take the consuming habits of the men into account, and these habits were formed in an environment where the men were free to spend money income according to their preferences.

ously, compatible with the use of merely persuasive means in plan execution, it is the condition of such a noncompulsory policy.

It is certainly simpler to foresee how consumers will behave if one has the power to prescribe their behavior. That is the reason why, on the surface, the right of compulsion toward the consumer seems to simplify the task of the planning board. To those who believe that the consumer, by ever-changing, incalculable whims, is likely to spoil the schemes which the planning board has worked out, it seems natural to suggest that freedom of choice should be taken away from the individual. In fact, however, men are conservative in their consuming habits, and such things as rapidly changing styles in clothing are surface phenomena, which do not affect the economic system deeply—and which are, moreover, to a large extent created by producers to stimulate interest in particular types of consumption. Changes in consumers' taste are no important source of economic insecurity or instability, and the planning board can calculate them in advance with sufficient accuracy. For the planning board, it would be a poor bargain to be freed from the necessity of anticipating the consumers' wishes and to lose the ultimate test of utility by which it can recognize the imperfections of the plan and the opportunities of improvement.

THE FUTURE OF PRIVATE ENTERPRISE

We can now form a more complete idea of the position of private enterprise and of the chances of its preservation in a planned economy. The conception of private enterprise in a planned economy is contradictory to the thesis that planning is possible only on the basis of full socialization of industries. This thesis would be less widely accepted if it were not for the coexistence of socialism and economic planning in the only country where either exists in completeness: Soviet Russia. Yet certainly this coincidence cannot be taken for sufficient evidence that an economy has to be socialistic if it is to be planned. Are there better arguments to support the thesis?

In the preceding analysis of plan execution it has been suggested that the plan should be carried into effect through negotiations between the government and private firms. This is unavoidable if private enterprise is to exist in more than a formal sense in an economy under government guidance. Yet these negotiations will take time and effort which an abolition of private enterprise would save. It is therefore possible to make a case for full socialization as a step to increase efficiency.

Another argument for the desirability of socialization is the disadvantage of divided responsibility for the success of the plan. Costs, for instance, may be higher than the planning board estimated. Perhaps the planning board has committed an error; on the other hand, it may be that the producer firms, or some of them, have been negligent or incompetent in organizing the production process. The representatives of the people may not be able to distinguish between these possibilities clearly enough, and fruitless controversies and wrong decisions may be the consequence.

Finally, not all the private entrepreneurs may wish the plan to succeed, and some may deliberately act as wreckers. It is very difficult to judge the likelihood of a serious attempt of that sort, since much depends on the political atmosphere in which the plan is started. Certainly the government needs resolution and a firm hand, and any plan will collapse unless a majority of voters stand determinedly behind it. But given these conditions, there is every reason to assume that an attempt at sabo-

tage can be defeated. The position of the owner in modern
society is not an impregnable fortress from which a successful
attack can be made to frustrate actions of the community. On
the contrary, in a society of equal suffrage, where the majority
of the voters own little, those whose economic position is based
on property are safe only as long as their fellow citizens remain
convinced that the exercise of property rights is in the interest
of society as a whole. It is true that the owners of small property very often attach an importance to their holdings out of
all proportion to what the latter contribute to their standard
of living, and this has often worked out as protection for the
large owners. Yet if big business were ever to make a concerted
effort to wreck a stabilization plan, the chances are that its
property rights would not be preserved.

The right to invest money in an undertaking and employ
others in its operation cannot be counted among those democratic rights which must be protected for their own sake; nor
must the superficial analogy between the free competition of
ideas for majority support, which is a true characteristic of
democracy, and the competition of enterprises for the market,
which is characteristic of capitalism, mislead us to the assumption that the former cannot live without the latter. From a
democratic point of view, the justification of private enterprise
must not be sought in what it means for the owners or managers of large enterprises but in what it does for the masses,
particularly for the consumers.

What we may have to fear, if private business is retained in
a system of planning, are some inconveniences and delays and
greater inequality of income than might otherwise exist; what
we may hope for is an easier acceptance, an effective check
upon the plan, a greater diversity of the sources of economic

progress, and, so far as small business is concerned, greater consciousness of freedom for a considerable number of people. Even if the small shopkeeper does not, in general, lead a much more independent life than the wage earner, he feels freer, and this subjective factor is an important social asset. On the whole, the advantages of preserving private enterprise in this period of history seem far greater than the price that must be paid in terms of difficulties, at least in the United States.

It is impossible to foresee the fate of independent private entrepreneurs in the more distant future. Although a planned system offers greater possibilities of rationalizing even small-scale enterprise, technical progress may be of such character and speed that in any economic order the small concern has to give way. The future of large-scale private business is even more a matter of historical speculation.

The existence of the economic plan greatly diminishes the guesswork which the entrepreneur has to undertake. It makes his function less adventurous and thus it becomes less a matter of intuition and more strictly a matter of calculation. The plan detracts from the role of the large entrepreneur as a pioneer of economic progress, because the initiative in experimentation with new commodities or new methods of production, and for economic expansion in general, will be largely transferred to agencies of the community. But the entrepreneurs will have an important part in the formation of the plan itself, and still more in the system of checks by which the execution of the plan must be controlled. In negotiating guarantee contracts with the government, the owners of large enterprises have ample opportunity to compare the provisions of the plan with their knowledge of business and to call attention to mistakes. The entrepreneur is the first to notice any discrepancy between the demand for his products as estimated in the plan and the real demand on the market, or any deviation of costs from the preëstimated amounts. No one can tell now if the advantages will prove to be so great in the long run that the people will consider large-scale business worth preserving. But there is neither need nor good reason for any decision on this problem before history has furnished more facts. For our own age, planning is a great enough task without change in the system of ownership.[16]

The establishment of a national plan will not revolutionize, but it will modify, the technical aspects of business. Relations between supplier and customer firms will still be governed by contracts, but their transactions will be of a different character. Since all large firms will have bound themselves with respect to the maximum price for their products, price bargaining will

---

[16] Some economists may perhaps object to the term "preservation of private enterprise" as indeterminate because of the vagueness of the property concepts on which it is based. There is no doubt that the concept of private property has undergone a great many changes in the course of history, and for the last decades most of them have been in the direction of increasing restrictions imposed upon the freedom of the owner in the interest of the community. As far as planning involves a shift of decisions from the individual property owner to communal organs, it is in line with this trend.

One of the recent developments of great importance for the concept of property—an importance which has hardly been realized to its full extent—has been the regulation of foreign exchange since 1931, which affected not only bank accounts and securities but all sorts of revenue-bearing property. In some totalitarian countries emigrants were not permitted to retain even their personal property. When Sudetenland was separated from Czechoslovakia, the removal of factory equipment—"installations"—was explicitly forbidden, and this prohibition was sanctioned by the British government. Thus a sort of superproperty of the state over all private property within its boundaries has been established. Perhaps more remarkable than the restrictions themselves was the relative complacency with which they were accepted outside the countries of their origin. Of course, during and after the war the spoliation of individuals became even far more frequent.

The weakening of the belief in an absolute right of property, the growth of the idea that property rights must not stand in the way of what is (rightly or wrongly) believed to be the interest of the community, has been closely connected with the experience that property is again, as it was in periods preceding the epoch of laissez

form only a minor part of the negotiations between suppliers of capital goods and their customers. Competition, in the main, will no longer find its place in the negotiations between firm and firm but in the bids which the firm will submit to the planning board.

LABOR ARBITRATION

The price of labor, like other prices, must be estimated in advance by the planning board. Yet this price is not merely dependent on statistically ascertainable conditions governing supply and demand, but—at least in the short run—is also a product of social power, resulting from conditions outside the market. This is also, to some extent, true of other prices, but factors such as public opinion or the tactical advantage of one political party over the other or the psychological atmosphere in the ranks of the sellers or of the buyers have a greater influence on wages than on the prices of machines or of steel. Unless a means is found either to control or to calculate these influences in advance, the provisions of the plan may easily be upset by the unexpected strength or weakness of labor in its dealings with management, and the community may be faced with the choice of abolishing either private wage contracts or planning.

---

faire, greatly dependent on community action for its utilization and the maintenance of its value. This is evidently true of real estate; not only the degree of police and fire protection offered by the local community, but also its road-building policy, the parks and recreational facilities which it provides, the schools which it maintains influence the value of the lots within its limits. Similarly, the value of industrial plants becomes more and more dependent on governmental monetary and credit policies, governmental arbitration of wage conflicts, and so on.

The need for a plan is another expression of the dependence of individual effort on communal effort. A plan which is not carried out with legal compulsion does not take away any property right—the owner's right to do with the objects of ownership as he pleases. But the right means something different when the ways in which it can be profitably used are no longer determined by the anonymous forces of competition but by a social agency.

Even in our present economy, which is almost entirely based on private contracts, experience has led to the elimination of many uncertainties in wage movements. In an ever-increasing number of industries collective agreements between trade unions and employers or employers' organizations determine in advance the wage rates or the way in which they are to be adjusted. If the planning board can convince both sides that it is to their interest to embody in their agreements that wage which the board has found to conform to the expected development of conditions, the way would be open to an optimal solution. But so much wisdom can hardly be expected. The stronger group is unlikely to forego its advantage, voluntarily. There is no assurance nor strong probability that contracts will fix wages right at the objectively desirable level.

Fortunately, it is not necessary for the effective operation of a planned system that wages be exactly on the level which the economic theoretician would designate as correct. It will be possible for the planning board to adjust the other elements of the plan to wages which are either somewhat too high or somewhat too low. If wages are too high, there will be a tendency toward unemployment, and the planning board will have to withdraw some of the labor supply from the market. The labor day may be cut down more than the individual worker might desire, or compulsory schooling may be provided for young people at an age at which they would otherwise seek employment, or the retirement age may be advanced, or vacations increased, or military or public labor service introduced or extended. If, on the other hand, the wage fixed is too low, a great competition of employers for labor must be expected. If this competition is permitted to raise the wages of workers above the level established by the collective agreement, the problem will disappear.[17] But if the employers, through an agreement among themselves, prevent competitive bidding for labor, luck will determine which employer can obtain the services of needed workers. This will detract from the average efficiency of labor and will create some disturbance in the execution of the plan, but partial adjustment may be sought by lengthening the working day in those enterprises for which enough labor cannot be obtained.

Yet these expedients will not save private wage agreements under planning unless three conditions are satisfied. First, the parties to an agreement must permit themselves to be dissuaded from insisting on wages that are either excessively high or excessively low. Second, the planning board must be advised of the agreed wage for a sufficient time in advance so that the necessary adaptations can be made. Third, there would have to be effective safeguards against labor disputes at the expiration of agreements. A major strike or lockout, quite aside from its outcome and merely through its effects on production, might well upset any plan. For this purpose at least, a machinery of government control is necessary, which can be used when the parties fail to agree and which, moreover, will by its existence prevent excessive use of power by one group.

A planned economy needs agencies by which labor conflicts can be arbitrated. The arbitration boards need not have unconditional powers of compulsion, but they must be able to impose an award whenever conflicts threaten to become too destructive, either through their magnitude or their frequency,

---

[17] It must be remembered that collective wage agreements, as we know them, only prevent the employer from paying less than the agreed wage, but do not prohibit him from paying more. Therefore, it is legitimate for an employer to add to his working staff in times of labor scarcity by offering higher wages to workers in the service of other employers, unless there are special regulations to the contrary.

to permit the orderly execution of the plan. That such boards are no innovation is known to every student of social history. Arbitration agencies with powers of compulsion existed not only in fascist countries but also in pre-Hitler Germany with its extremely democratic constitution; they also exist in democratic Australia and New Zealand. In the United States and in many other countries the right to strike is restricted in fact if not in law, even where no capitalistic bias dominates the government, simply because the public cannot look dispassionately upon any labor conflict of major importance. If there is no resort to more drastic measures, at least public opinion is mobilized against the group which refuses arbitration, and this pressure is often irresistible. The present American system of a legal right to strike, which can be restricted by extra-legal means at the discretion of the national administration, of a governor, and sometimes of a chief of police or a city council, offers less guarantee of fair treatment to labor than a system of semicompulsory arbitration such as would be required for the execution of a national plan.

Whenever arbitration boards settle labor conflicts, they will have to impose a wage level that is as close as possible to the economically correct one. The economically correct wage is not necessarily, or even frequently, on the same level with the marginal productivity of labor. It is desirable to keep the wage moderately above that level to provide an extra stimulus for saving wages by technical improvement. Unemployment, which would otherwise result from a wage exceeding the marginal productivity of labor, must be counteracted by indirect "job-rationing" through a short work week, and so on.

Even aside from the desirability of making wages approximate their economically correct level, there are very great technical difficulties which stand in the way of any other policy. Like every court, the arbitration board, which is by the very nature of its function a judicial or semijudicial body, must know the law on which its decisions are to be based. The conditions which economic theory establishes for optimal output are sufficiently definite to form the content of such a law, and there is no other workable concept of which this would be true. In unplanned economies, where the need for social arbitration has also been keenly felt and the optimal wage is so difficult to ascertain, arbitration boards have experimented with the concept of the "living wage," but this is not a satisfactory solution. There is no point in trying to keep the general wage level of a country at a height which we think is decent, if by that attempt we force a great many people into unemployment with a standard of living still much further from decency than that of ill-paid workers.[18] On the other hand, if economic conditions permit a wage level which exceeds what we, under the influence of tradition, consider the minimum level of decency, why should not the workers receive the higher wage? Thus arbitration boards should be instructed to set the wage as high as the industry can bear without discharging more workers than can be absorbed in another industry, without an excessive degree of "job rationing." In either an unplanned or planned economy, this is the only workable rule, but without a plan, the board can only guess the rate which industry is able to pay, and consequently its decisions are not only subject to error but also lack authority. It is for this reason that arbitration boards so often fall back upon the expedient of simply splitting the difference between

---

[18] The concept of a living wage may very usefully be applied if it is not a question of changing the general level of wages, but only the wage of one industry that was working under sweatshop conditions.

what workers demand and employers are willing to give. Obviously, this bad procedure must in the long run ruin every arbitration system under which it is practiced. The necessity of arbitrating labor disputes, which is becoming more urgent every day, is one of the forces driving us toward a system of full planning, since only in such a system are the commands of economic reason sufficiently unequivocal to afford a basis for the settlement of social conflicts.[19]

CHOICE OF OCCUPATION

Our discussion of the possible conflicts between the requirements of planning and the economic liberties of the individual is still incomplete. We have spoken of freedom to own, freedom to consume, freedom to strike, but this still leaves out freedom to choose an occupation and freedom to save.

Free choice of occupation can be maintained in a planned system at the price of admitting wage differentials, just as in an unplanned economy. It is not to be expected that the natural inclinations of individuals will furnish aspirants for different vocations in exactly the proportions in which they are socially needed, but through the premium of greater earnings people can be attracted to a trade or profession which otherwise would not have been their first choice, and through the deterrent of low reward they can be kept away from activities which they would have preferred if the earning opportunities had been equal. However, there will probably always be some occupations which are so attractive that overcrowding must be

---

[19] In the words of Barbara Wootton (*Freedom under Planning,* p. 119), planning substitutes "arbitration by rational principle" for "arbitration in a void." ". . . whereas a Trade Union which is asked to negotiate, not in order to get the best possible terms for its members, but so as to keep wages in harmony with some predetermined pattern, finds the sense knocked out of its position, an arbitrator might well find that such guidance would for the first time put sense into his" (p. 114).

prevented by other means than low compensation, since there is a minimum under which the latter should not be permitted to fall.[20] In these fields restricted admission to schooling and severe examinations will have to be used, as they are used today.

As far as occupational plans are concerned, it is again extremely important for the planning board to be informed of the intentions of individuals at an early date. If the planning board receives this information sufficiently in advance to influence the individual's final decisions by changing the scale of earnings or to adjust the plan to the use of abundant labor in one type of production and to labor shortage in another, restriction of choice can be kept to a minimum; again, coercion is only needed to correct situations which lack of foresight has permitted to arise. Fortunately, the necessity of choosing an occupation fairly well in advance is evident to everyone, and thus the planning board will have no great difficulty in ascertaining the number of aspirants for all types of work. Although some persons may wish to change their plans later, these changes will rarely, if ever, be so frequent and so one-sided as to create serious difficulties for the execution of the plan.

FREEDOM TO SAVE AND THE RATE OF INTEREST

The value plan, as has been pointed out, must contain a calculation of incomes. But it is not enough to know how much people earn and how, as consumers, they will distribute their purchasing power among the various commodities. It is also

[20] The compensation for medical services, for instance, cannot always be kept as low as would be necessary to deter enough aspirants from becoming doctors, for a badly underpaid physician might be driven into malpractice and might therefore be a public danger. Thus the present policy, in the United States and some other countries, of restricting the admission to medical schools is defensible and may have to be continued, although it has the great disadvantage of working in a mechanical (and sometimes in an undemocratic) way.

essential to know how much they will withhold from consumption and whether this amount will be equal to the value of the capital goods which are to be produced if the plan is followed. Approximate equality between money saved and money invested[21] is one of the presuppositions of a smoothly working plan, and it may well be asked whether this condition can be satisfied if people are free to spend or to save as they please.

In a planned system, oversaving, as well as undersaving, may be understood in either a short-term or long-term sense. In the former it means that more or less is being saved during the current planning period than was anticipated when the plan was made; in the latter sense the term refers to an expected excess or deficiency of savings which is contrary to the intentions of the planning board for future planning periods.

Short-term oversaving presents two problems. First, it creates a deficiency in opportunities to invest funds. Ordinarily, savings would have to be used for the purchase of real assets, and, with the sums saved exceeding the estimate, the production of such assets as provided in the plan is not sufficient to absorb the sums which savers wish to invest. Therefore, some of the funds will have to rest idle for the remainder of the planning period, and the interest will have to be paid from general reserves, or some flexible interest rates will have to be

---

[21] For reasons of space it is impossible to discuss in any detail the famous proposition of Keynes that the two amounts are necessarily equal. This proposition rests on a set of definitions and assumptions which this writer, like some others, does not believe to be useful. (For a critical survey of the controversy see Howard S. Ellis, "Notes on Recent Business Cycle Literature," *Review of Economic Statistics*, 1938, pp. 111 ff.) In choosing these definitions and assumptions—in particular, by assuming the economy to be "lagless" (*ibid.*).—Keynes obliterates his own arguments against the fallacy "that any individual act of abstaining from consumption necessarily leads to, and amounts to the same thing, as causing the labour and commodities thus released from supplying consumption to be invested in the production of capital wealth" (*General Theory of Employment, Interest, and Money*, p. 19).

lowered so that the return from the invested portion of savings will suffice to pay interest on the whole. (However, the remedy is not applicable on a large scale, since variability of interest must be strictly limited if the whole system is not to become unstable.) Second, short-term oversaving creates a surplus of consumable goods, which the public has failed to take out of the market and which the government will have to take over under the sales guarantee, unless it prefers to compensate the entrepreneurs by money payments for their loss. If the surplus consists of ordinary necessities of life, the government will not find it difficult to use the goods with some advantage—a human if not a fiscal advantage—since it has to provide for the subsistence of a considerable number of people—such as soldiers, inmates of institutions, the poor—and it may add to their dietary and clothing. The articles of more refined consumption are largely of a durable or semidurable character, and they can be stored and their disposal spread over a longer period of time. Any such surplus disposal, of course, involves financial loss, but hardly of a magnitude that would lie heavy on a modern economy which makes full use of its resources.

The effectiveness of the remedial measures may be increased by the methods of financing. The government can provide the money by taking the excess savings out of the market through public loans, but it may well prefer to increase the taxes on the most saving-minded part of the population, namely, the upper classes, and thereby depress the current rate of saving. Tax measures would also provide a possible method of correcting short-term undersaving; they would then have to alleviate the burden on the upper classes and lay taxes on mass consumption. But aside from social objections to such a policy, it may be doubtful if the effect would come quickly enough, and therefore, it will, as a rule, be preferable to take the physical resources which are needed for the scheduled amount of capital production from reserve stocks, to be paid for from reserve funds, so that changes in taxes to correct the deficiency in saving become unnecessary. In extremity, the government may have to resort to temporary rationing in order to free resources for the amount of expansion provided by the plan.

Long-term oversaving or undersaving means a conflict of intentions between the planning board and the individual. If the planning board is not backed by the political representatives of the public, there is no reason why its intentions should prevail in a democratic state. If the board finds such backing, and still individuals do not save as much as necessary for the execution of the plan, the cause must be a conflict between social and individual time preference. In these circumstances the effects of undersaving can be corrected by taxing the public, with the proceeds to be loaned to public or private entrepreneurs who wish to expand, and the measure will be most effective if the tax burden is laid on those in the population with the least propensity to save, although this again may be unacceptable for social reasons. As an alternative, the government may induce its citizens to save more by offering a higher rate of interest (on its own or on private borrowings) and covering the difference between this rate and the return from the investments by the proceeds of taxation. This method, however, is not generally applicable because the public does not always respond to higher interest rates with an increase in savings.[22]

---

[22] See Gustav Cassel, *Theory of Social Economy,* trans. by S. L. Barron (New York: Harcourt, Brace, 1936), pp. 238–239. His arguments are presented in many textbooks. Robert Mossé, in his very interesting article "Planned Monetary Economy" in *Annals of Collective Economy* (Geneva, 1941), considers the financing of invest-

Long-term oversaving will certainly not be an important problem in planning. Whatever individuals wish to save will, under all but exceptional conditions, be less than what the planning board will wish to use for improvements of production techniques—a clear consequence of the excess of individual over social time preference. This would be different, of course, if a point could be reached at which possibilities for increasing the future national income by producing more or better equipment in the present had become scarce, so that stagnation would be an inescapable fate. Then, even a planned system would be exposed to the danger of oversaving and might have to resort to appropriate taxation as a remedy. Heavy death duties would in any event offer a final solution, since they would transfer the accumulated savings into funds for public consumption, and the resulting problems of public ownership—for rigorous limitation of private inheritance leads inevitably to the acquisition of business interests by the community—would be more easily soluble in a planned system, in which private initiative does not have the same significance as in an economy without a plan. In the period of transition before the death duties became fully effective, an adequate supply of money could be maintained by credit creation for public spending, and the plan would give the data needed to determine the magnitude of these operations. The lack of demand for loans would probably reduce the rate of interest to zero, which would further ease the problem because it would reduce

---

ment by borrowing preferable to financing by taxation, because the former method has the advantage of reducing "to the minimum the people's sacrifices by allowing them to choose the moment to spend their incomes. He who accepts to delay his satisfaction would receive a monetary payment for this particular type of effort" (p. 28). Mossé does not, at this point, take into account the complication arising from the difference in time preference between the community and the individual.

that type of income from which the largest portion is saved. Adjustments in the plan would, of course, be necessary. The planning board would have to take into account the high spending power which, under the circumstances, people in advanced years would possess as a consequence of previous savings and would use liberally because they could not transfer much of the money to their children. The board would have to provide an adequate supply of goods fit for the consumption of older people, and also for public consumption.

Yet these are merely hypothetical considerations, for—in the opinion of the writer at least—mankind is unlikely to exhaust, within the next centuries, its technical opportunities for the advantageous investment of all it can save—barring a development of atomic-fission technique that would lead us into a true economy of abundance. Although no absolute proof is possible, existing and prospective uses for capital will probably suffice even if the rate of saving should increase as a consequence of a greater per-capita income, which we may well expect of successful national planning.[23] The rise in the rate of saving, moreover, is by no means a certainty; the calculations of William J. Fellner show that in the past the secular upward

---

[23] Protesting the idea of Mordecai Ezekiel and myself, that "the markets would be forthcoming if a sufficiently large part of the economy were induced to expand output . . . because the firms are each other's markets," Abba P. Lerner raises the objection: "Here again there is the complication that as output and national income increase, saving also increases, so that demand increases less than supply. If there is an increase in investment sufficient to make up for the increase in saving all will be well, but such an increase in investment is not guaranteed." ("An Integrated Full Employment Policy," p. 190.) Dr. Lerner does not, of course, believe that planning is caught in an inescapable vise between underemployment and oversaving, but he does contend that special measures of fiscal policy to maintain a sufficient rate of spending will always be of prime importance. Stating that Dr. Ezekiel and I, although we have not rejected such measures, refuse to regard them as the most important tools of economic stabilization, Professor Lerner protests "the relegation of this matter to a kind of footnote." The text above will make it clear why I find it impossible to change the "footnote" character of my approval of deficit spending and similar means.

trend in national income has not brought about a reduction of the propensity to consume, which is the reciprocal of the propensity to save.[24] As Professor Fellner points out, his results do not disprove the thesis, well established from household budgets, that people with higher incomes save more than people with lower incomes do *in the same society and at the same time*. "The reaction of income recipients," he writes, "to an increase in their incomes may well depend on whether the notions of the community on the 'standard of living' are given or whether they are changing.... For this reason, the marginal propensity to consume is likely to exhibit an entirely different behavior for a simultaneous comparison of various income groups on the one hand, and for an historical comparison of various periods on the other."[25] For the effects of a transition from an unplanned market economy to a planned system, or of an improvement in planning once it has been established, the historical comparison would offer far better guidance than the analysis of contemporaneous conditions.

The assumption that objective opportunities for investment will be available does not settle the oversavings problem entirely. It might still be argued that people will fail to take full advantage of these possibilities and that therefore government spending will always, or very frequently, be required to secure an adequate amount of total expenditures. The Keynesian denial that interest can equilibrate investments and savings can be made the basis of such a theory. Following this line of thought, Dr. Lerner criticizes Dr. Frank D. Graham[26] and this

---

[24] William J. Fellner, *Monetary Policies and Full Employment* (Berkeley: University of California Press, 1946), pp. 55 ff.

[25] *Ibid.*, pp. 61–62.

[26] See his article "Full Employment without Public Works, without Taxation, without Public Debt, and without Inflation," in *Planning and Paying for Full Employment*.

writer for putting "so little emphasis on the possibility of too low a total rate of spending" and he finds the reason in the fact that we "revert to some remnants of a classical theory of interest. According to this classical theory an excess of saving over investment lowers the rate of interest and in this way restores full employment equilibrium by discouraging saving and encouraging investment. Modern theory has shown that this does not happen except as a result of a long process of depression, which would almost certainly destroy our form of society long before it reduced the rate of interest."[27] According to the Keynesians, liquidity preference will hold the rate high until incomes have shrunk, and then discouragement resulting from the reduced absorptive capacity of the markets will for a long time offset whatever favorable effects the eventual drop in the rate might have upon investment. It is unnecessary to discuss here the strong and weak points of this theory in an economy of unplanned capitalism. A Keynesian, if asked what causes the fluctuations in investment, considering that they are not supposed to reflect changes in the rate of interest, would certainly answer: changes in the marginal efficiency of capital, that is, in the expected chances of selling future products profitably to consumers. The existence of a plan of economic development will give the entrepreneur a much higher degree of certainty in judging the profitability of contemplated investments, and even more so if sales guarantee contracts were sufficiently extended into the future to cover the markets of the goods the production of which will eventually result from the investment.[28] Even from the theoretical position of Dr. Lerner and of the Keynesian school the problem of oversaving must

[27] Lerner, "An Integrated Full Employment Policy," p. 190.
[28] See above, pp. 81–82.

lose much of its formidableness in a planned economy. Whatever may be true of the present-day market rate of interest, the calculation rate of a planning board will certainly not be determined by liquidity preference in the Keynesian sense. The effect of changes in the calculation rate upon investment cannot be doubted, for this rate indicates the degree in which the board is willing to provide for material and man power needed for expansion and improvement of the production apparatus and to take other steps to assure the profitability of the projects concerned.

Even if it is recognized that a planned economy would not know a general tendency of investment to lag behind saving, there may still be misgivings about the effects of "rigidities." Today monopolistic restrictions often make socially useful investment unprofitable for the individual entrepreneur. Might not the same be true in a planned economy, and might not this factor create an excess of savings over investments?

In the previous discussion of monopoly dangers it has been explained how a planning board would have to deal with "rigidities." These methods may not succeed in eliminating all monopolistic features from the economy, but they can be trusted to prevent obstruction of investment outlets on so large a scale that savings would be forced into idleness. Any monopolistic restriction of output in capital-goods industries reduces the rate of return that can be expected from additional money capital, but this will not lead to the accumulation of idle savings as long as the rate of return can be kept above the minimum rate of interest at which the banks or the public are willing to part with cash. The rate of return for additional funds depends on the relative importance of the investment outlets that are still free from monopolistic restriction, for if all additional savings must be invested in a few fields, their yield is bound to fall very rapidly. If, on the other hand, control of monopoly can keep a large part of industry under conditions approximating free competition, additional savings can be invested without much depressing the rate of return, and the chances that this rate can be prevented from falling below the minimum rate of interest are far better.

The minimum rate of interest that prevents hoarding is determined by two factors: the cost of loan management and liquidity preference. (The question of hoarding arises only where funds are withheld from consumption and investment. Therefore time preference, which is preference for present as against investment, has no influence at all on the antihoarding minimum rate.) It is certain that banks cannot afford to lend funds to investing entrepreneurs unless the interest compensates them for administrative expenses and risk. The long-term influence of liquidity preference is controversial, and since it is impossible here to enter into a discussion of that controversy, the author can only state his opinion that liquidity preference is not a determinant of the rate of interest in the long run. To prevent long-term hoarding it will suffice if control of monopoly keeps the rate of return on increments of invested capital above the cost of loan management, in the improbable event that profits from new investments should show a tendency to fall below that modest level. Short-term hoarding is a product of economic uncertainty, of the danger of misfortunes against which cash reserves are held, and of the possible emergence of unexpected investment opportunities for which ready cash can be used with a high return. Since planning minimizes uncertainties, short-term hoarding by savers is bound to become insignificant.

Since the community has effective means at hand to correct
the consequences of oversaving or undersaving if they become
dangerous to economic stability, it will not be necessary for
the success of a plan to prescribe the amount which an individual must save. The corrective measures, it is true, may sometimes mean that certain persons are induced to change their
intentions or may see their intentions frustrated—those, for instance, whose desires as consumers clash with the intentions
of the planning board for expansion and those who are taxed
to finance investment. But this is not fundamentally different
in an unplanned economy. Here, too, it is a frequent experience that an individual cannot carry out his original intentions
because the effects of his course of action change the presuppositions from which he started. Or by changing the conditions of other people he may destroy his own chances of success.
A man may, for instance, try to gain more economic security
by hoarding money and, because his example is followed by
many others with disastrous effects on the volume of employment, he may unwittingly produce greater insecurity for himself.[29] Freedom of action never means the freedom to achieve

---

[29] This statement resembles a well-known Keynesian proposition, but is by no
means the same. There is general agreement that hoarding may produce a shrinkage
of the national income and thereby unemployment and instability. Nor can any
economist quarrel with the thesis that, under specific conditions which cause entrepreneurs to refrain from the investment of loanable funds regardless of the rate of
interest, saving can have the effect of hoarding, and that the decrease in income,
which under such conditions will follow from saving, may even frustrate the effects
which the saving individual hopes to obtain for himself. The object of controversy
between Keynesians and anti-Keynesians is the frequency of these conditions. The
liquidity-preference theory of interest and other elements of the Keynes theory, if
accepted, justify the assumption that investment of loanable funds is not even assured
in prosperity, and that oversaving can, therefore, be partly or wholly responsible for
the eventual termination of the prosperity period. Most anti-Keynesians, on the other
hand, maintain that during prosperity, or at any rate at the peak of prosperity, all
available funds are invested, thereby eliminating oversaving as a cause of depression,
since the germs of economic paralysis must be found in the period of the boom.

all the results we want without interference by others. It never means protection from the social effects and reactions of our own deeds, but merely the liberty to decide which steps should be taken, at the risk of all the physical and social consequences that may follow for the author of the action. It is in this sense that freedom to save is compatible with economic planning.

Saving, of course, is not the only source of money available for investment. The amount of such money is also influenced by the inclination of businessmen to entrust funds, which they are temporarily unable to use in their own concerns, to the banking system under conditions which facilitate their partial use for middle- or long-term loans. The amount of money for investment is also influenced by the degree to which banks are willing to use the funds provided by consumers' savings and producers' temporary cash surpluses as a basis for a superstructure of additional credit. These two factors, however, can be kept under control even more easily than saving and will, therefore, create no difficulty for the drafting and execution of the national plan.

Even today, the policy of the banks is very largely under the control of the government, and with the coöperation of other government agencies the planning board would have little difficulty in determining the ratio between deposits and loans.[30] The propensity of entrepreneurs to keep large liquid reserves cannot be directly regulated, but if the degree of propensity is known in advance, no damage will result from its being either high or low, for undesirable effects can be offset by changes in the supply of money. Today it would be difficult to estimate in advance the extent to which the entrepreneurs will insist on keeping liquid cash reserves, for the uncertainty of

[30] See below, p. 203.

conditions leaves a wide range for the influence of optimism and pessimism, and nothing is less calculable than the "bullishness" or "bearishness" of the business world. But in a planned economy the attitude of entrepreneurs will depend on objective conditions, which the plan reveals before they actually occur. The existence of the plan will also remove the main obstacle to government regulation of money supply. Aside from deficit spending, which is not always a commendable method, the way to increase money in circulation is through the loan of additional funds to private borrowers by the government or the Central Bank. But will these agencies find borrowers? In an unplanned economy entrepreneurs are often reluctant to incur debts, because they do not feel sufficiently sure that they can carry out their transactions successfully and thus meet their obligations. In a planned economy the entrepreneur produces for a guaranteed market and has therefore no reasonable motive for such hesitations.

There is no reason why in a planned economy firms or individuals should not be free to borrow from one another and to agree on a premium for lending as they see fit and as supply and demand relations warrant. But both supply and demand will be more influenced by public policy than they are in an unplanned economy. This influence will be stronger on the long-term than on the short-term rate, because of the greater significance of the former for the execution of the plan.

In an unplanned economy, the rate of interest is determined by the time preference of individuals, and in a planned economy, the calculation rate of interest will express the time preference of collective bodies representing the nation. For reasons which are by now undoubtedly familiar to the reader, the latter rate must, therefore, in the long run be lower than the former. But in periods of rapidly growing investment the situation will as a rule be different. There, an unplanned economy would apply the lower current rate, whereas a planned economy will be guided by the higher rate that the planning board must anticipate as a product of the process of expansion.

Whenever the calculation rate of the planning board is lower than the time preference of private individuals, the planning board will encourage investment that private individuals would not consider sufficiently rewarding if left to their own decision. Yet if the investment is not to be carried out as a public enterprise, which can only be done in a limited number of industries unless the ownership system is changed, it must be made profitable for the private firms. There is a simple means to this end. The government must lend the necessary funds to entrepreneurs at a rate that is at least not higher than its own time preference. There is no reason why a private entrepreneur should refuse to invest funds with the prospect of moderate gain if he has only to pay a proportionately moderate rate of interest. The way of providing the funds for these loans will be taxation, tax-subsidized loans, or credit creation through the banking system. Through the public loans, the calculation rate of interest of the planning board will become the actual market rate.

The planning board will, as a rule, prevent substantial fluctuations of the long-term interest rate within one planning period, as a part of its policy of reducing adjustments in the current plan to a minimum. For this and other reasons, the board will frequently discourage entrepreneurs from introducing technical innovations before the end of the planning period. It will be impossible, however, to keep the long-term rate completely stable even within the same period. Some new technical methods may be so advantageous that postponement of their use would be unjustifiable. Moreover, the board may not wish to change the rate abruptly from one planning period to the other and may prefer, if a rise or decline seems necessary, to inaugurate it in the old period in order to make the change more gradual.

We have tried to explain the difference between the determination of interest in a planned and an unplanned system. But interest theory has still another significance for the theory of planning. If some opinions on the general nature of interest were correct, the need for a production plan might not exist because then it might be possible to achieve economic stabilization through credit policy alone. This point will be discussed later, and it will then be possible to clear up some questions which have not yet been fully answered. Further analysis will also confirm a conclusion, which this section has probably suggested to the reader, namely, that monetary and credit policy loses much of its difficulty if it is associated with a plan of production. As long as nobody knows what will or should occur in the realm of production, the management of credit is necessarily based on a series of unsafe guesses. Once a production scheme has been established, it is comparatively easy to provide for the arrangements in the field of credit which will fit the contemplated production processes. As long as credit governs production (as it does for the most part in an unplanned economy) it is difficult to control; as an instrument which should help perform production tasks set by the plan its performance can be regulated with a high degree of accuracy.

The same is true of monetary phenomena in general. The money required for transactions depends on the physical volume of production, the desired price level, and the velocity of circulation. The first two items are part of the plan, and in an economy in which everything else is stable (in the sense of not being subject to unexpected change) the velocity of circulation is nearly a constant over periods of short and medium length. Consequently, it is not difficult for the planning board to calculate the required amount of money, and since there is continuous expansion and therefore demand for loans, it is easy for the banking system to put the additional money in circulation.

Excursus on Planning and "Economic Maturity"

Since theories of economic stagnation are very prominent in the controversies of contemporary economists, it seems desirable to say more about the significance of the stagnation problem for planning than was possible in the preceding chapter, where an extensive discussion would have interrupted the trend of thought. Even in this excursus, however, space does not permit more than to take cognizance of some of the most important arguments of the stagnationists and their opponents.

The reader is already familiar with the principal relationship of the problems of planning and of economic maturity: If we were faced with a cessation of growth of our economic organism for unalterable reasons, a lack of opportunity for the profitable investment of savings would very probably exist in a planned system as well as under unplanned capitalism.

Most, if not all, stagnation theorists refer to the fact that there are no longer great land reserves which can be settled and thus turned into markets for industrial goods, and that population growth in the western countries has slowed down and will soon come to a standstill. "Extensive growth" of the industrial economy is therefore no longer possible on anything like the nineteenth-century scale. If more goods are to be sold, the same number of people living in areas already settled have to buy more commodities. "Intensive growth" must be substituted for "extensive growth." The stagnation theorists believe that the substitute cannot be adequate.

Whatever we may think of the proposition that investment opportunities, in an objective sense, are more limited than they were in previous periods, the stagnation theorists are very probably right in assuming that those opportunities were more obvious in the decades of territorial expansion and rapid population growth. Although there may still be enough chances of profiting by investment, capitalists may not see them so easily or may feel more hesitant about relying on them than their predecessors did in judging the prospects of investment in the nineteenth century.[31] These difficulties, however, need not affect a planned economic system. A plan would make the opportunities for investment more clearly visible and may thereby give sufficient encouragement to the capitalists. Governmental sales guarantees, granted on the basis of the plan, will intensify this effect. If the capitalist were still too reluctant, public investment would have to take the place of private ventures and could be far more safely undertaken than in a system in which the course of economic development is uncharted.

---

[31] "Efforts to disprove the 'stagnation thesis' by showing that the American economy still has room for expansion are ... futile. ... The argument is not that gross national product at full employment can increase no further; it is only that full employment is increasingly difficult to attain and maintain as a country becomes more industrialized, more fully populated, more fully developed, and richer." (Benjamin Higgins, "The Doctrine of Economic Maturity," *American Economic Review*, vol. 26, no. 1, March, 1946, p. 134.) In Professor Higgins' argument, the term "full use of savings" could be substituted for "full employment," since full employment is possible only if all saved funds find their way into real investment. The Higgins article is a defense of the stagnation theory against the attack by George Terborgh in his book *The Bogey of Economic Maturity* (Chicago: Machinery and Allied Products Institute, 1945).

Disregarding crude varieties of the stagnation thesis, which assert or imply an impeding saturation of human needs and which sporadically infiltrate into scholarly writings, only one form of the argument touches the oversavings problem in a planned economy. Some stagnation theorists are inclined to assume that inventions now have a tendency to result not only in the saving of labor but also in the saving of capital. If that were true on a sufficiently large scale, the outlets for savings might become wholly inadequate, since current savings might have to compete for the remaining investment opportunities with capital released from its previous use by capital-saving inventions.

In its early stages, economic progress was achieved through the use of more capital per unit of product value—by "deepening" capital. The transition from the use of no capital goods at all to the use of tools, and from the use of simple tools to that of machines, were such "deepening" processes. In the later phases of technical progress, capital-saving inventions share the field with labor-saving innovations. Present controversies concern the numerical ratio between the type of technological change that means "increase in depth" and the one that means "loss in depth."

Efforts have been made to find an answer to that question in an empirical way, by comparing the amount of invested capital with the value of goods produced, or by calculating the share of capital goods in the total commodity production. When these calculations are extended over a sufficiently long period, it seems possible to find a trend. But what is a sufficiently long period? It is generally agreed that "deepening" innovations prevailed over "flattening" ones before the turn of the century. If the forty-seven years of the twentieth century had not been so largely filled with economic upheavals it would be easier to find out by statistical investigation whether inventions tend to become more capital consuming or more capital releasing. But war, inflations, and the Great Depression have distorted the picture, so that it is hardly possible to isolate the technological trend from the effects of other changes. For instance, the figures given by Simon Kuznets in his *Commodity Flow and Capital Formation 1932–1938*[32] show that "capital formation for business use exclusive of inventories," that is, investments in machinery and business construction, increased very rapidly during the period 1932–1937.[33] It might be tempting to interpret this fact as a "deepening" of capital for technological reasons. Further investigation, however, reveals that the total volume of these investments in 1937 did not reach the 1929 figures.[34] The drop during 1929–1932, when real investment came almost to a standstill, had been so great that even the rapid rise during the recovery period of the middle 'thirties was not sufficient to bring back the former volume. Can we then draw the opposite conclusion, namely that a "loss in depth" of capital use occurred in the 1930's? Obviously, we would be rash in so doing, for how do we know that we are really dealing with two "natural" peaks of business activity when we compare 1937 with 1929? Perhaps the prosperity of

[32] (National Bureau of Economic Research, Bulletin 74, June 25, 1939.)

[33] Kuznets calculated several pairs of indices of growth, by which to compare the increase of "capital formation for business exclusive of inventories" during the 1932–1937 and the 1921–1929 periods. The calculation whose basis appears most meaningful in terms of the present discussion led to an index of 2.62 for 1932–1937, as compared with 1.77 for 1921–1929. For all particulars about the calculation, see Kuznets, *op. cit.*, pp. 7–9.

[34] "Capital formation for business use exclusive of inventories" was lower by 1.76 billion dollars in 1937 than in 1929. The main "deficit" was in construction, whereas the production of machinery slightly exceeded the 1929 total, although a small deficiency appears here too if the calculation is made on a per-capita basis.

the middle 'thirties, and therefore the rise of investment would have continued far beyond 1937 and would have reached a much higher peak, if deficit financing had not been abruptly curtailed. The smaller capital consumption may therefore reflect the policy of Congress rather than any technological phenomenon. Or to choose another and equally significant example: the growth of capital invested in manufactures slowed down in the early 'twenties.[35] The explanation seems to be that in the preceding period the production of equipment and construction of plants had been enormously stimulated by the war, and these plants were used to produce the record amounts of consumers' goods which the markets absorbed during the 1924–1929 prosperity. Capital formation had been accelerated for "noneconomic" reasons and, as a consequence, leveled off for a time. It would be a misinterpretation to use the slow growth of invested capital during these years as evidence of any indigenous changes in the economic structure.[36]

Although the empirical material does not enable us to prove conclusively the existence of either a "deepening" or a "flattening" trend in the use of capital during recent periods, it does at first sight seem to show that the former trend toward a deepening use has ceased to be very marked at a relatively early stage of capitalist development. Carl Snyder has made a comparison between the growth of product value and capital invested in American industry as a whole and also in various individual industries. Each capital investment curve runs al-

---

[35] See the curve showing the fluctuations in "capital invested" in the chart "National Wealth and Income of U.S.," drawn by Carl Snyder in his article "Capital Supply and National Well-Being," *American Economic Review*, vol. 26, no. 2, June, 1936, p. 203.

[36] For other reasons why available statistical data are inconclusive, see William J. Fellner, "The Technological Argument of the Stagnation Thesis," *Quarterly Journal of Economics*, August, 1941, pp. 642 ff.

most parallel to the corresponding product value curve for the greater part of their length; only for the first decade, 1880–1890, do the capital curves rise in a decidedly steeper slope. It becomes clear from these graphs that capital did not appreciably increase its share as a cost element relative to that of labor during the period in question. Does this mean that the replacement of labor by capital, the essence of the mechanization process, did not continue after 1890? Obviously, that conclusion would force us to change fundamentally our view of the industrial development in the age of advanced capitalism.

No such revision of our basic concepts, however, is needed because the growth of product values has been accelerated by an extraneous factor: the increase in real wages. According to Paul Douglas, the rise of real wages in all manufacturing industries between 1899 and 1925 was 30 per cent.[37] If this change were statistically eliminated—for instance, if the value product were calculated in Keynesian "wage-units"[38] instead of in dollars—the curve of invested capital would rise far more steeply—at least as far as manufactures are concerned—than the curve of the value product; since even with the 30 per cent real wage increase the curves are approximately parallel. In other words, if wages had been stable in terms of living costs, capital costs would have attained an ever larger share in aggregate value of produced goods. A considerable "deepening" must have taken place much later than 1890.

Another part of the Douglas material also supports this conclusion. Professor Douglas has worked out a comparison of the growth of earnings with that of physical productivity. He

[37] Paul H. Douglas, *Real Wages in the United States.* Publications of the Pollak Foundation for Economic Research, no. 9 (Boston and New York: Houghton Mifflin, 1930), p. 510.

[38] John Maynard Keynes, *The General Theory of Employment, Interest and Money,* p. 41.

found that in the average of manufacturing industry in the United States real earnings had by 1925 reached 130 per cent of the 1899 figure, whereas the physical product was 154 per cent of its amount in 1899. Has the difference been absorbed by entrepreneurs' profits? Both 1899 and 1925 were prosperous years and there is no evidence of a spectacular rise of the rate of profit from the one to the other. Certainly, the difference between the rise of workers' earnings and the rise of the physical productivity of labor has not benefited the consumer, since the cost of living index stood much higher in 1925 than in 1899.[39] Consequently, we have to conclude that the bulk of the difference was of no benefit to anyone: it represented higher capital cost.

We have every reason to believe that in some fields of economic activity other than manufacturing the deepening process has been even more marked during recent decades. In power production, the great dams and networks which now supply our homes, farms, and factories with current simply did not exist in 1890. In farming, the use of complicated machinery is a relatively recent development and has assumed proportions which, in the United States, are commemorative of the Industrial Revolution.[40] Barring an "atomic revolution,"

---

[39] It might be argued that the rise in the cost of living index alone would not sufficiently warrant the conclusion and that consumers' incomes must also be taken into account. But a substantial part of total consumers' incomes, that is, wages, has already been taken into account in calculating the difference between growth of physical productivity and that of workers' earnings. The farmers certainly did not do conspicuously better in 1925 than in 1899. These two groups form such a large part of the consuming public that no more detailed calculations of real incomes seem necessary to substantiate the proposition.

[40] To support his opinion that for "the economy as a whole, including fields other than manufacturing, there is no good evidence that the advance of technique has resulted in recent decades, certainly not in any significant measure, in any deepening of capital," Alvin Hansen refers to the service industries and to housing. In the former, he states, "the capital stock has not increased significantly even in relation

it seems probable that in these fields the deepening trend will continue at least for a considerable time to come. The backward sections of our country, especially the South, are lagging behind in the mechanization of farming and, with the exception of the TVA area, in electrification, and much capital will be needed if they are to attain the standards of the more advanced regions.

Even in the very improbable event that a "flattening" trend were ascertained in the American economy at its present stage, there would be little danger that a planning board, if put in charge of the direction of economic development in the United States, would have to face any problem of oversaving within the next decades. In the first place, as Hansen himself has pointed out, loss in "depth" of capital use may be compensated by gain in "width." In other words, even if most of the new inventions were capital saving, they might enable us to produce commodities so much cheaper, that the resultant expansion of production leads to an absorption of both the released capital and of the current savings. Moreover, the difference in the state of economic development between the North and the South of the United States is almost dwarfed by the difference between the more advanced and the more backward parts of the world at large. An enormous amount of savings will have to be invested in equipping China, India, Malaysia, the Near and Middle East, and Latin America if these countries are to be brought up to the level of western Europe, not to speak of the North American level. Enormous sections of the globe are

---

to population." In the latter, "real capital has little more than kept pace with population growth." (Reprinted from *Fiscal Policy and Business Cycles* by Alvin H. Hansen, by permission of W. W. Norton & Company, Inc., copyright 1941, p. 356.) Taking these statements at face value, it would still be necessary to weigh this loss in depth against the gain in manufacturing, agriculture, and power supply before the conclusion for the whole economy could be upheld.

still living under conditions similar to those which preceded the Industrial Revolution in Europe, and therefore there is ample room for a repetition of the story of the nineteenth century on a global scale. In one respect such a repetition is already on its way. The population of many colonial areas is growing by leaps and bounds, for the same reason which was responsible for the increasing numbers of the white race in the preceding epoch of history: decline of the death rate. Because of this population increase, industrialization is an imperative necessity for these countries. Even if no problem of oversaving is found to exist in the western world, there will be excellent reasons for facilitating development loans to the overpopulated regions of Asia, for only by supplementing agriculture with industry can the Malthusian mechanism in its most sinister form be prevented from operating among that large part of mankind.

Certainly, serious obstacles of a technical as well as a political nature stand in the way of large-scale investment of "western" savings in the development of colonial and semicolonial areas. The channels for the flow of loan capital from one country to the other would have to be broadened. However heartily we may welcome the striving of the peoples of the underdeveloped areas for political independence, it is a tragic coincidence that these aspirations are reaching a climax at a historical moment when a huge influx of capital from the "old" industrial nations has become a life and death question for the colonial world. Undoubtedly, India would find it much easier to obtain capital for her economic development if she remained within the British Commonwealth of Nations, and the Dutch East Indies will jeopardize their capital supply of which they stand in great need, if they cut themselves off from Holland politically.

There is still hope, however, that obsolete and untenable systems of colonial domination may be replaced not by a splitting up of empires but by their transformation into partnership systems between natives and Europeans. Generally, it is too early to despair of reforms which might render capital transfer possible on an even much larger scale than in the nineteenth century.[41] If these efforts succeed, the western nations may have reason to fear, not an excess of savings over investment but an excessive competition for the available savings with resulting high interest rates and difficulties in providing the capital for exploiting new inventions.

[41] For an example of such pessimism, see Hansen, *op. cit.*, pp. 360–361. Professor Hansen, however, has not been deterred from attempts to reduce the obstacles in the way of international capital transfer. He was one of the most vigorous and probably one of the most effective advocates of the Bretton Woods' agreements. Perhaps the conclusion of these agreements should be regarded as a reason to take a more favorable view of the possibilities of international investment than Hansen did in his book. Although the International Stabilization Fund and the Bank for Economic Development, which were created by these treaties, may not represent the final form in which the goals pursued at Bretton Woods will be realized, and in no event can mean more than a good start on the right road, it seems at least clear that leading statesmen and experts in the economically advanced nations are willing to overcome some old prejudices in order to facilitate the flow of capital across the frontiers, and that some effective means have been found to reduce the risks.

IV. "Noneconomic" Functions and Purposes in Economic Planning

War and Postwar Planning

THIS DISCUSSION has so far been based on the assumption that the planning board wishes to provide consumers with as many material means as possible for the satisfaction of their individual needs, except as this purpose is modified by the educational aims of the community. The difference in social weight between the needs of the different consumers, following from the different income levels, has been accepted as a datum—of course, without any implied approval and with the realization that there are possibilities of reweighting or even abolishing differences altogether.

But from the start we have been aware that planning, being a method of organizing production of goods, may be used for all kinds of human purposes, because these all depend wholly or in part on availability of goods. We must distinguish planning for consumers' satisfaction from planning for other aims. The name of "economic" purpose applied to consumers' satisfaction and that of "noneconomic" purpose applied to other possible objectives of planning cannot be defended on any ground except that it probably conveys the right meaning to the reader. The terms, therefore, will be used between quotation marks.

A very important example of a "noneconomic" purpose of economic planning, and one to which we have referred before, is the successful conduct of a war. Modern war is as much an economic as it is a military undertaking, and the economic requirements of warfare cannot be satisfied without planning.

The basic reason why an unplanned economy is ill-adjusted to war requirements is the time necessary for its trial-and-error processes. In war, far more than in peace, time is of the essence. An economic plan means that undertakings are tried out on paper and therefore need not be tried out in reality. Thus the necessary amount of coördination, which is as important in the economics of war as in those of peace, can be achieved far more quickly than in an economy relying on the competitive market.

It is, of course, no valid objection to this statement that war planning in the proper sense is a very recent growth, whereas war itself is one of the oldest phenomena of human history. We can wage a war with an unplanned economy, just as we can do so with poor strategy or arms—and even win it if the opponent's organizational, mental, or material equipment is still poorer. But a nation that plans its war economy will be vastly superior to one that does not, other conditions being equal.

While there is a special necessity for planning in wartime, there is also one basic feature of a war economy which makes it easier to plan. This feature is the definiteness of the ultimate purpose. In war, the merits of a measure are entirely dependent on its contribution to the defeat of the enemy—a goal complex enough in itself, yet not so complex as the satisfaction of consumers in peacetime. Because there is less room for choice between purposes, physical calculations are the main content of planning for war, and value planning, a method of calculating and testing relative desirabilities, is not used in reaching the fundamental decisions.

But planning in wartime has also its special difficulties. One is the uncertainty and briefness of the time for which the plan is to be established. Nobody knows at the beginning of a war how long it is going to last. Since the early nineteenth century, no war has lasted longer than six years—which is a long period to endure, but not a long period in which to plan, carry out, and utilize a major expansion or redirection of industry. Moreover, the industrial requirements of warfare are almost never realized in the beginning of a war. It seems to be the rule in modern war (at least in those countries that are reluctant to believe in the inevitability of war) that hardly a start is made in working out blueprints for industrial wartime expansion until the conflict is well under way. Thus not many years remain for the planning effort, and this naturally detracts from the technical opportunities as well as from the systematic character of war planning.

Furthermore, the requirement of rapid change, which is the principal reason for the necessity of war planning, makes it impossible to practice foresight as systematically as in peacetime planning. Within a year the portion of the national income allotted to armament may have to be raised from 3 or 4 per cent to over 50 per cent. Enemy action may deprive the planning country of a part of its production or transportation facilities and thereby make it necessary to carry out major adjustments within a few months. As a consequence of experience gathered by the military and naval staffs, it may become imperative to shift production from battleships to airplane carriers within the shortest possible time. For the war planner, the ability of quick improvisation is at least as important as careful consideration of future possibilities.

Thus the potentialities and some of the requirements of war planning are smaller than those of peace planning. War planning is a crude type of economic planning, aiming more at speed than at accuracy and relying on the moral and physical power of the government to force upon the individual citizen the acceptance of hardships which peacetime planning would try to avoid through foresight and careful calculation. Yet in spite of all these differences, a machinery built for planning in peacetime can be made to serve the purposes of war, and a country which has developed a planned system before the war has a great advantage over one that must improvise planning as it enters the struggle. The guess may be ventured that the astounding strength of resistance that the Soviet Union displayed in the war with Germany was primarily due to her established organization and highly developed technique of planning, which is far more comprehensive than that of Hitler's Germany ever was. It cannot be emphasized too strongly that the system of government, of collective ownership, and of planning, developed by the Soviet Union, are three different things, historically interrelated of course, but not logically or practically dependent on one another. The greater the weight that we attribute to dictatorship as a liability, the more important planning must appear to us as an asset, if we are to explain how the achievements of the Soviet state became possible.[1]

In wartime the execution of a plan is facilitated by the atmosphere of coöperation which the national emergency inspires,

[1] Planning had to compensate for many other factors detrimental to the Russian war effort. Perhaps the most important one was the relative inexperience of many Russian factory workers, who had been drawn from the rural population during the last decade before the war.

but it may be made more difficult by the fear of a postwar slump. When executives of private corporations are forced to expand their plants to meet the requirements of the army, they cannot be expected to disregard the question of the way in which this additional capacity may be utilized later. It is only human that this anxiety should somewhat influence their attitude toward expansion projects when they are called upon to advise the government in the capacity of industrial experts or asked to carry out the expansion plans proposed by government agencies in their factories. Appeal to patriotism, compulsion, or financial arrangements favorable to the corporations may solve part of the problem, but a complete solution can only come from an employment guarantee for the postwar period.

This is the reason why, under a system of private enterprise, war planning and postwar planning cannot be entirely separated. If the economy were fully socialized, there would still be strong reasons for planning for postwar readjustment since otherwise the standard of living might be greatly depressed, but the war effort itself would not depend on what was going to be done after the war was over. In an economic system based on the profit motive, it is inevitable that the potentiality of disaster for private industries will detract from their energetic response to a war-production program. The most effective remedy is a postwar plan which will ensure the substitution of peacetime demand for war demand.

Planning for the transition from war to peace requires fewer modifications of the pattern of "normal" planning than the establishment and administration of a war plan. It is planning for the satisfaction of consumers' desires, with a wide diversity of purpose. Value calculation is restored to its important role. Yet postwar planning shares with war planning the necessity of a sudden change of great proportions, and although the end of the postwar planning period can be chosen on the basis of technical and organizational expediency, the initiating moment is uncertain, and the conditions of that moment—particularly the productive capacity available at the cessation of hostilities—are partly unknown.

These difficulties, together with prejudices and political obstacles, have prevented the establishment of a genuine plan for industrial reconversion from war to peace. In spite of much talk and the drawing up of some indefinite programs, the transition from war to peace in the industrial field was carried out in the United States essentially by the methods of an unplanned capitalist economy. The government, it is true, has tried for some time to minimize fluctuations by price control. The policy of the OPA was not merely directed against inflation but also against rapid exhaustion of consumers' wartime savings through excessively high prices. But even before the OPA was emasculated by the legislation of 1946, it could only hope to prolong but not to perpetuate the prosperity of the war and postwar periods. Mere price control, even if supplemented by an allocation system for some types of resource, is not planning, since no serious attempt is made to calculate in advance for a definite period the prospective changes in the economy in quantitative terms. In the absence of a planning machinery, the OPA was frequently unable to avoid major mistakes in its estimates. These errors do not prove that economic developments are unforeseeable. They only confirm the truism that economic events are interdependent and that it is therefore impossible to estimate with any approximation to accuracy—for example, the supply of butter at a given price—unless a full picture of the whole economy is drawn.

Although we are paying for our failure to plan by a great deal of confusion, we have so far not incurred a major disaster—neither runaway inflation nor a postwar slump of production and employment. With the exception of a relatively small number, the discharged soldiers and munition workers have been absorbed into the peacetime economy. This favorable experience has already kindled unwarranted optimism. Yet, what has happened so far was only what most economists had expected. War savings plus urgent consumers' desires for many commodities were bound to produce a very considerable effective demand in the first two or three years after the war. Of course, during the war nobody knew with certainty that this new peacetime demand would offer so complete a substitute for war orders and army "employment" as it actually did, but the widespread impression that economists predicted a slump immediately upon the cessation of hostilities is wrong.[2]

Some day the war savings will have disappeared and the urgency of the desires for consumer goods will be greatly reduced. That day may not yet be the beginning of the depression, but from then on the economy will be deprived of the special stimulus which is now keeping economic activity high. Without this stimulus, a depression will come sooner or later. There is nothing in any of the theories about depressions that would permit us to assume that the mechanism which has in the past caused successive peaks and troughs has now ceased

---

[2] The following passage from the first edition of this book, written early in 1943, was probably characteristic of the majority opinion among professional economists during the war:

"It is not likely that these factors [uncertainties paralyzing entrepreneurs' initiative] will produce a great slump within a year or two after the armistice.... There is good reason to assume that at first political and economic pessimism will be overcome by the great demand for consumer goods originating from accumulated savings in combination with a great urge to expand consumption after wartime restrictions have disappeared" (p. 110).

to be effective. It is highly improbable, to say the least, that the undulatory movement, to which every industrial economy is subject according to an experience of two hundred years, should suddenly and for no visible reason come to a standstill.

When the depression comes there is reason to believe that it will be severe, because the uncertainties of the economic and political situation are likely to prevent a quick restoration of confidence. Taxes will continue to be heavy and their full burden will only be felt when business declines. A reduction of the national income will cause the public debt to appear still more formidable than today. International frictions are likely to cause occasional war scares which will be a particularly strong deterrent to long-range investment plans because of the extreme destructiveness of the weapons which the last conflict has left as its technical heritage. Private property will be menaced or will have been nationalized in a large part of the world. The power of the Soviet Union will be great and her prestige will be increased by the depression in capitalistic countries, since her own economy will again be depression proof, as it was during the 1930's. The general public will not carefully distinguish between the Russian form of government and the Russian technique of planning, and once more the argument will be widely accepted that communism alone is able to save the world from economic collapse. Entrepreneurs will be more frightened than ever and probably still less inclined to invest money on long term than they were after 1929. Even the great technological promise of the future, the potentialities of atomic fission for energy production, may intensify the downward trend of the economy because the opportunities for new investment may be temporarily overshadowed by the menace to existing assets, such as coal mines and power dams.

All these factors will create a tendency toward a very serious depression, but there will be counteracting forces. Perhaps the greatest of these will be the housing shortage which will undoubtedly continue for a considerable time and which will force many individuals to mobilize all the purchasing power they can possibly muster to pay for dwellings.[3] Moreover, public policy will not remain passive. If no better techniques are available at the outbreak of the crisis, public works programs will be put into operation, and economic assistance for reconstruction in Europe and Asia may well be intensified to provide increased export outlets for American agriculture and industry. Bold programs of this kind, if deficit-financed, can turn a depression into prosperity for precisely the same reason why a war can achieve this reversal of a downward trend. For good and for bad reasons, however, Congress and the administration will hardly carry deficit financing to the point at which it could create full prosperity. They will probably confine themselves to a lesser degree of "reflation," sufficient to mitigate but not to terminate the depression. The problems of that coming period will be essentially those of the New Deal era, except that very probably their magnitude will be larger. The necessity of finding more perfect forms of government antidepression policy than mere deficit financing will in time become evident.

ETHICAL AND OTHER CULTURAL VALUES

Even in the normal course of a peacetime economy the satisfaction of the consumers' individual desires, now or in the future, may not be the only rationale of a plan. In a democracy,

---

[3] It must be remembered, however, that the considerable housing shortage which still existed in many countries in the late 1920's as a heritage from the First World War did not afford much relief from the depression after 1929.

the educational aims, of which we have previously spoken, are based upon cultural values to which most citizens attribute greater significance as members of the community than as private individuals. Education, however, even if taken in the broadest sense, may not exhaust the practical consequences of those values. As a community we may build great churches and other monumental buildings, encourage the fine arts, protect the beauties of our country, all at greater sacrifice than we may find justified from our private point of view.

These "noneconomic" aims of planning are likely to be even more frequent in a nondemocratic society, since the ruling power may have a set of purposes in which the satisfaction of the desires of the subjects is either reduced to secondary importance or is considered significant as a means rather than an end. In many instances this is part of a despotic regime callous to human suffering, but an emphasis upon "noneconomic" ends may also be found in paternalistic governments. An illustration is furnished by the Jesuit state of Paraguay in the seventeenth century, which was similar to a planned economy. Although the Jesuits made great and successful efforts to promote the welfare of the natives and created an island of humanitarian policy among the horrors of early colonial administration, it was not their only purpose to provide the Indians with the necessities of life. To them the establishment of a church organization, amply supplied with all the material requisites of cult and power, was a goal of superior importance.

Perhaps the most fundamental distinction that we can draw between different forms of planning for "noneconomic" ends is between those types in which the deviation from the "economic" motive concerns the concrete purpose of the plan—namely, the kinds of goods to be produced, as in the Jesuit state or war planning—and other types in which the deviation is concerned with the function of planning—namely, types in which planning as a means of coördination is preferred, for "noneconomic" reasons, to other means by which production activities can be coördinated. Thus one primarily concerned with ethics may desire planning not merely because it will secure maximum production and therefore provide a better life for all, but also because of ethical objections to the alternative method of coördination—competition. This deviation from the "economic" motive is so important that it must be given somewhat extensive consideration.

Planning, as a system of central direction of economic life, eliminates competition from some functions in the body economic and changes its form in others. The penalty for incompetence is still loss of position, and the planning board, in setting prices and awarding guarantee contracts, still puts a premium on efficiency in diminishing cost of production and on initiating valuable innovations. But planning greatly restricts the area of guesswork in economic life and thereby diminishes its power as a competitive weapon, and the penalty that awaits one who guesses incorrectly is of lesser severity. For the entrepreneur or employee who loses his position because he has made a mistake, or even because he is not fit for his job, a new place will more easily be found, since the search for new opportunities of using man power is made a more systematic endeavor. Thus from an ethical point of view, a planned economy may seem more satisfactory than the present system. It creates at least a possibility that economic relationships may more closely conform to the idea of the brotherhood of man, and that gain and loss may more often depend on personal merits or faults.

The general character of a planned economy may not be the only reason why an economic philosopher who is primarily motivated by ethical considerations approves of planning. He will perhaps consider it equally important that planning facilitates specific reforms in which he is interested. This preference may still concern the function rather than the purpose of planning, as it certainly does in the most important instance, namely, when planning is preferred to competition because it opens a way to the reduction or abolition of economic inequality. This reform may be desired for a variety of reasons, ethical, religious, political, yet in practice none of the other motives will be strong in a person who does not consider equality an ethical value. Planning, of course, is quite consistent with any degree of inequality, but a planned system can be so organized that the economic processes do not produce the amount of inequality to which we are accustomed, and it can function effectively on the basis of a more equal distribution of income and property.

As long as industry is privately owned there must be profit, for the basic argument for a system that leaves enterprise in private hands rests on the assumption that an owner will have greater interest in its effective management than a government appointee, and he will have this interest only if most of the resulting gain is his. But planning reduces the importance of the entrepreneur's decisions and even more his risk. With less danger of loss the entrepreneur need not have as much prospect of gain as he had when he was still a commercial or industrial adventurer. Taxes and price policy can be used as instruments to reduce the profit margin to the amount necessary in a planned system, if this is the will of the community. Since profits are a major source of inequality, their reduction would

be a step toward a more equalitarian society. Other functions
of economic inequality, such as procurement of sufficient savings and of customers for newly invented (and thus highly
priced) goods can be fulfilled by provisions in the plan.

Up to a limit which may be hard to define but which nevertheless exists, reduction of inequality of income is compatible
with maximum production under a plan. Beyond that limit,
a further approach to equality will diminish the quantity of
goods and services at the disposal of consumers, but the plan
will make it possible to foresee in detail the effects of the measure and to counteract them to a great extent. This can be done
by shifting the initiative for expansion to the planning board
and—if this is not considered too high a price—by introducing
compulsory features in the machinery of plan execution. At
no time need an approach to equalitarianism have the paralyzing effects which have been observed in unplanned economies.

In the 1920's and 1930's, most countries collected much
higher taxes from incomes in the upper brackets than even
radical reformers had considered possible previous to 1914. Although the paralyzing effects fell short of expectation, one
need not be a pessimist or a reactionary to believe that tax rates
of 50 per cent and above will make a system of unregulated
capitalism sickly.[4] If this kind of taxation is combined with a

---

[4] The wartime experience with extremely high tax rates, particularly in England,
does not contradict this statement. It is true that practically no British entrepreneur
had a chance to earn more than $15,000 or $20,000 annually, and for the majority
of industrial leaders even this income, net after taxes, was out of reach. It is equally
true that production nevertheless went on with full speed. But, first of all, capitalism
in wartime England was not unregulated, and second, patriotic motives played an
important part in war production. Producers, however, cannot be expected to provide
a nation with necessities and amenities in so-called normal times merely from motives
of patriotism. Since the British Labour Government does not intend to nationalize
the bulk of manufacturing industry but plans to preserve the function of the private
entrepreneur in many fields, business and personal income taxes will have to be
reduced to percentages which leave the businessman an adequate incentive.

wage policy seriously reducing profit opportunities, and if it coincides with economic instability involving great risks, an economy which relies entirely on entrepreneurs' initiative cannot be expected to function effectively. This is not to say that the protracted depression of the 1930's was a product of governmental measures, but there is reason to believe that the stagnation of economic life in England in the 1920's was largely due to the crippling of profit chances by heavy taxation and other equalitarian tendencies in public policy.[5] If a plan had existed that relieved the entrepreneur of a large part of his risk, and, moreover, created another source of initiative for industrial expansion, there might have been "distressed areas" in Great Britain (due to the world-wide deterioration of marketing conditions and problems of mobility in the textile and coal-mining industries), but expansion of industries in general would have greatly reduced unemployment. It is also probable that recovery in the 1930's would have come sooner and would have been more complete if either a national plan had diminished the risks or lesser taxes had left greater expectation of gain to the individual businessman. Certainly there is nothing more utopian (in the worst sense of the term) than the belief that a profit system can function well without the prospect of substantial profits.

The movement toward greater economic equality became as irresistible as a tidal wave, once political democracy was established. It is logically inconsistent to recognize the responsibility and the value of every person as a citizen and keep him de-

---

[5] It is true that tax rates similar to those in England existed in Germany, together with other unfavorable conditions, without producing the same paralysis of industrial energy. But there is an explanation for this. An entrepreneurial class of unusually strong vitality, as in Germany during the Republican period, may maintain its expansive force against paralyzing tendencies to which another might succumb.

pendent for his very livelihood on the arbitrary decisions of others. It is practically impossible to prevent the masses from using the vote to gain as much economic improvement for themselves as they possibly can, and it is always likely that they hope to achieve such improvement by leveling down the higher position of the privileged few. Since the beginning of the nineteenth century we have always had to face the problem of how an essentially aristocratic order of economic life, in which inequality had a definite function, could be reconciled with political democracy.

Planning helps to solve that problem in two ways. The first we already know; planning makes it easier to prevent or at least to counteract the undesirable effects of equalitarian measures. But planning also diminishes the urgency with which equality is desired, by gratifying some of the motives which are behind this desire. The underprivileged do not merely object to the existence of people who can consume many more goods than they do; they object even more to the power of the privileged to decide on who should retain a job in times of industrial distress and on who should be promoted above the rank of the common worker. If stabilization can be achieved so that there will be no more periods in which jobs are scarce, and if a man or woman of average ability can always find an opportunity with another employer if his current employer is prejudiced against him, more than half of the problem of equality is solved.

The power which members of the entrepreneurial or managerial class can exert over other individuals has been the main grievance of the average person in his attitude toward social questions. But the intellectual vanguard of the underprivileged has also been deeply concerned with the decisions that the privileged group can make in matters vital to society as a whole. The power to make such decisions will be greatly diminished in a planned system operating under a democratic constitution. Planning by a government based upon the consent of the governed is the only way for a modern people to establish full control over its own economic affairs. If there is any method of making the existence of private enterprise compatible with political democracy, that method must surely include planning.

The values safeguarded by a planned system may be derived from any kind of cultural ideal. Some people think that society is sounder if it is based on independent small businessmen and farmers, even at the price of a loss in efficiency. A plan will show (or, at any rate, supply the data for calculating) how conditions would have to be changed to make the survival of small business possible and what the cost will be. It is quite possible that after analyzing the problem we might arrive at the conclusion that the sacrifice would be too great, and that the contemplated change should not be undertaken. Yet whatever our decision may be, it is desirable that we make it upon correct anticipation of the consequences, and a system of planning, as an apparatus of foresight, is most likely to give us that possibility.

The same principle applies to the use of planning for the attainment of national self-sufficiency. A plan can be made for the purpose of producing within her own boundaries all the commodities that a country needs, so far as natural obstacles—for instance, lack of indispensable mineral deposits or adverse climate—do not make this physically impossible. But a plan will also show the cost of such an undertaking, which, as a rule, will entirely outweigh all possible advantages, except, perhaps, to a supernationalist who is willing to pay an extremely high price for an increase in the significance of national frontiers.[6]

To summarize: a national plan can be used to forecast the effects and to determine the means not only for an effort to produce the maximum amount of the goods which are most desired by the consumers, but also, as an alternative, to produce the particular commodities preferred by the planning agency in spite of divergent preferences of consumers. Finally, the plan may modify the economic processes themselves by substituting another type of business unit or business organization for the one that is promising the greatest results in terms of goods, if the attainment of other goals is considered more important. Economic planning, therefore, is a technique which all economic policy can use, and often will have to use, to attain its goal with any degree of certainty. Necessary as it is to distinguish between government intervention and economic planning, it is also true that all government intervention, regardless of aims, is technically inferior so long as it does not use planning. Therefore, all economic policy tends to develop into planning as the defects of unplanned government action become visible.

We may like or dislike the collectivist aspect of planning. For the rest, we can take a positive or negative attitude toward planning on essentially the same grounds on which we can reject or accept the use of any type of machinery. We may judge it superior and therefore wish to use it for our own purposes. If we see it used by others, whose purposes we reject, we may well wish that they had never been able to adopt that technique. In an extreme instance, we might wish that the

---

[6] A program of self-sufficiency in some key products may, of course, be justifiable in the interest of national defense, even if the country is far from being guided by motives of extreme nationalism. See pp. 171–172.

technique of planning had not been developed, so that it might not have been possible to use it for noxious purposes. Evidently, whether we think the development of planning is a blessing or a curse depends to some extent on the likelihood of its use for purposes which we approve or for those which we reject. This is in consonance with reason, but does not detract from the necessity of distinguishing between opposition to planning as such and to the ends which planning serves in a particular instance. Moreover, if we believe, as there is good reason to believe, that the basic values which most of us cherish can be protected only by an adequate use of planning, then we shall have to accept the risk that the same technique may be applied by others with opposite aims, and we shall have to struggle with them for the most efficient use of that indispensable tool.

V. National Planning
and International
Economic Relations

THERE IS a widespread belief that national planning is difficult or impossible if economic relations between the planning country and the rest of the world are permitted,
because changes in foreign trade, which cannot be anticipated,
may upset the calculations of the planning board. The policies
of governments which were either committed to planning or
at least tried to move in that direction have furnished some evidence that economic isolation was an actual result, if not a
deliberate purpose, of planning activities. Soviet Russia has
always had a foreign trade monopoly which was used to make
her self-sufficient in important industries. Moreover, many of
the measures of economic policy which fall short of full economic planning but represent attempts at partial planning
were of an undoubtedly protectionist character. We need only
think of the agricultural marketing schemes in England in
the early 1930's, which were largely intended to restrict the importation of foodstuffs,[1] or of the International Steel Cartel,
established in the 1920's, or of the many restrictive schemes for
raw materials that originated during the Great Depression and
even before. When the United States, in 1933, wanted to regu-

---

[1] The United States marketing schemes, established through the Triple A and so-
called pro-rate agreements, are mainly intended to restrict production at home,
which in this country is far more important for the price level than importation
from abroad.

late the domestic price level, it was considered necessary to make economic relations with the rest of the world more difficult by changing the value of the dollar without immediate restabilization on another level. Undoubtedly there is more than mere accident behind these facts, but they do not prove that there is an insoluble connection between planning and economic isolationism.

The devaluation of the dollar, and perhaps more clearly the sterling devaluation of 1931, illustrates one typical situation in which a government has to choose between domestic regulation and undisturbed international relations. A nation's money cannot be kept safely stable in terms of two standards at the same time, unless these two standards are coördinated. Therefore, there is no way to maintain the purchasing power of the dollar and also its value in terms of francs or sterling, if these monies are not in their turn stabilized in terms of commodities. If money is either losing or gaining value in terms of goods throughout the world, and if a government, realizing the grave social evils that accompany any major change in the purchasing power of money, wants to put a stop to this process in its own country, it must either increase or decrease the quantity of money within its jurisdiction and thereby upset the currency ratios. If international currency ratios are unstable, exchange of goods must necessarily suffer. Concerted action of all governments would, of course, be an alternative, but a particular government may often be faced with the necessity of acting independently if international coöperation is not forthcoming. Yet it is not often that such a choice becomes necessary. Violent fluctuations in the purchasing power of money are not frequent, and the minor changes do not seriously affect currency ratios. Moreover, even in times of major change, such as generally occurs during a severe depression, a country with considerable gold reserves may return to the lower predepression level of internal money value while maintaining the ratio of her own currency to others unchanged for a long time. The United States, even in 1933, held more than one-third of the world's monetary gold. This was the reason why many experts, both American and foreign, believed that the devaluation of the dollar was unnecessary, even on the assumption that the New Deal would bring far greater changes in the domestic price level than it really did and that the rest of the world would continue a passive policy, which it did not do.

It is easy to think of other types of conflict between maintenance of international economic relations and interference with some phases of economic life at home. We cannot rationally tax a commodity unless we prevent the influx of untaxed foreign goods of the same kind or—if the commodity is being exported—take measures to refund the tax on the quantities which are sold abroad. We cannot direct capital toward a particular investment unless we make sure that the finished goods which will eventually result from it cannot be undersold by importers, and thus a tariff may be a necessary complementary measure. The practical importance of this point is increased by the probability that investment, if consciously directed, will be made to flow into channels where it meets foreign competition, for there are two main motives for such a policy: to create new domestic industries in which the country wishes to be independent of foreign importations and to create new employment. If the goal is more self-sufficiency, the need for protection is evident, except where great natural advantages, hitherto unused, can be exploited; and if the desire is to increase the number of jobs, the most obvious way is also to expand the production of goods which are not produced to the extent that they are consumed in the country.[2]

The problem looks very different when we proceed from unplanned intervention or partial planning to full planning. As our examples show, the protectionist character of partial planning usually results from the difficulty, for the government, of directing economic activities toward fields where they will not come into conflict with tendencies originating beyond the boundaries of the country. In a system of full planning the scope of government action is much wider, and therefore the chances are far greater that conflicts between goals in the domestic field and the interest in the maintenance of foreign trade can be avoided.

Full planning not only fails to give the support to protectionism which must be expected from less comprehensive forms of government intervention, it also greatly weakens the strength of protectionist tendencies—it strikes at their very roots. All protectionist policy is based on the assumption that there are not enough opportunities in a country to employ its resources. At least in a democratic state, no other argument for high tariffs is nearly so effective as the contention that imports from abroad destroy the livelihood of people at home. The argu-

[2] The most obvious way is, of course, not necessarily an effective way in the final instance. There is every reason to believe that in the long run the total volume of employment cannot be increased by building up high-cost industries behind walls of tariff protection, because the resulting price increases will force the cost level of all industries higher and simultaneously cause the markets to shrink. But in a prolonged depression the introduction of a new industry with high labor requirements may lead to the employment of resources which would otherwise remain unused and thus give the same stimulus to economic activities as public works, which are also often unproductive in themselves. This small element of truth in the idea that protection contributes to employment becomes a politically powerful factor because it supports popular errors about the blessings of producing all our needs in our own country. Moreover, the adverse effects of attempted self-sufficiency upon the labor market can only be revealed by theoretical reasoning, which most people find difficult to understand and in which they have little confidence.

ment for free trade is based upon the theorem that a nation must economize its resources and that it always has an opportunity to use additional production factors. Nobody would support protection if it were certain that every worker or entrepreneur who loses his job or his market through foreign competition would immediately regain a new and better place in the economy. Nobody, or almost nobody, would advocate free trade if the men and the capital which might be driven out of the industry by foreign competition were condemned to remain idle.

For more than one hundred and fifty years the overwhelming majority of economists have agreed among themselves that it is unwise for a country to produce within its own boundaries what can be more cheaply bought abroad, yet the world moved away from protectionism for only a few decades in the nineteenth century, and soon returned to it with great fervor. A combination of economic, psychological, and political facts is responsible for this conspicuous failure of the best minds in economic science to influence events by their advice and their exhortations. Under the system of essentially unregulated capitalism, the assumptions of the free trade economists were partly unrealistic, and to an even greater extent the facts which justified them were concealed from the eyes of the public by false appearances. Finally, even when the real facts were known and supported the free trade argument, the protectionist interest was more powerful as a pressure group than the believers in the international division of labor. In all three respects, full planning will change the situation.

Society must economize on its resources and not on opportunities to use them for the production of goods. This proposition, on which the classical economists and all their intellectual heirs based their argument, is correct in the long run, but there are always periods in which it does not fit reality. In a severe depression there are no jobs for most of those who are displaced by foreign competition. Capital, which is driven out from some industries because they have higher costs than their foreign rivals, may also remain idle. It is true that even at the very depth of the depression there is usually sufficient demand to employ the most productive units of labor and equipment, so that the community must still economize on the most efficient resources, but the general situation is thereby not greatly altered. Stabilization is the first requisite of a change in the public mind that would win the support of the masses for true international collaboration.

The false appearances which in our present economic system deceive people about the necessity of using production factors in the most economical way result, in large measure, from the general prevalence of sellers' over buyers' viewpoints—which, in its turn, follows from the experience that in an economy without inflationary symptoms it is generally easier to buy than to sell. In a well-ordered society most producers will have some reserve capacity which they can very profitably use if they find enough customers, and every day they cannot use it is a lost opportunity; but if the buyers have any reserve dollars, they are under no pressure to use them quickly. Money, in contradistinction to the working capacity of men and machines, can be stored without loss; moreover, whereas often machines and even labor can only be used for one specific purpose, money can be spent on an immense variety of objects and therefore does not depend on any one particular type of use. These facts have nothing to do with the relative scarcity of resources and of employment opportunities, but they create a fear on the part of the producers of being left without an adequate market, not counterbalanced by an equal fear on the part of consumers of being left without adequate opportunities for buying.

That resources are scarce in relation to their use is proved by consumers' competition, which is just as real in our economy as competition among producers. If consumers were fully conscious of competing with one another, they would feel that they have just as much reason to be anxious about their opportunities to buy as producers have to be concerned about their opportunities to sell; they would realize, each of them, that they are pulling a corner of a blanket which is too short to cover them all and therefore they would vigorously oppose the belief that it is longer than needed. Yet in an unplanned economy consumers' competition works largely behind the consciousness of men. In economic textbooks it is a very important concept, but it does not take an equally prominent place in the daily experience of individuals, and it becomes a palpable reality only in that minority of relationships in which buyers face each other in bidding for desired goods. Just as a great many people who have intellectually understood the basic facts of astronomy cannot get away from the impression that the sun "rises" and "sets," thus many people cannot be thoroughly convinced, although they may be superficially persuaded, that the economic welfare of a country depends on opportunities for consuming and not for selling. So long as their daily experience is not changed, they will always feel that it is only common sense to assume that underselling of domestic goods by foreign industries creates unemployment, just as in the fifteenth century many people considered it a dictate of common sense that, if the earth was really a globe, the "antipodes" must fall into the empty space of the universe.

A plan makes consumers' competition evident. In working out the scheme, the planning board will very frequently have to explain that some desires cannot be satisfied because the resources which they would require are needed for another and more urgent purpose. Everybody who studies the plan will easily realize that there would be more opportunities of increasing production in a great variety of fields if more labor, capital, and gifts of nature were available. There will be an agency—the planning board—responsible for the full utilization of resources, to which everyone can report (through sub-agencies, of course) if some or all of his working power or his equipment is unemployed, with the definite prospect that an adequate way of utilization will be found. Thus the plan will diminish the fear of unemployment in two ways: first, by decreasing the amount of joblessness to a relatively insignificant figure, and second, by strengthening the counteracting forces, through a continual demonstration of the importance of greater productivity. Production will appear as that which it has always been fundamentally, namely, production for use.

This is a prerequisite for a rational economic policy in a democratic country. Under an absolutist regime we might perhaps be satisfied with the guidance of an unseen hand that leads men to goals very different from those which they believe themselves to be pursuing; for instance, to a promotion of the consumer interest while they think they are only serving their own interests as producers. But when all have a voice in the common affairs, the results of individual action are not all that matters. The ideas behind such action are also important, since if they are in error, they may induce the individuals as citizens to support a course of action wrong for the community. Because unplanned capitalism overemphasizes the sellers' point of view, even the propagandist genius of Cobden and Bright could obtain only a temporary success. Because an economic plan makes it perfectly clear that we have scarcity of resources and not of opportunity to utilize them, it makes possible a policy which calculates the cost of any privilege that a group of producers may demand and thereby greatly decreases the probability that any such privilege will be granted. The disappearance of fallacies which give the seller's point of view undue weight will in itself strengthen the political forces on which a rational economic policy can be based. However, the weakness of these forces in the present economy is not wholly due to wrong ideas which mislead the general public, but also to the greater ability of those interested in protection and similar privileges to form pressure groups. The producers who have to gain from a tariff know it and act accordingly. The consumers who are to foot the bill rarely know their loss in advance—is any consumer aware in how many ways a tariff on steel can affect his purse?—and they are slow to oppose the protectionist demand. Moreover, as a seller, each person is concerned with just one commodity (or a group of related commodities), and knows that his economic position depends on the marketing possibilities of this particular kind; as a consumer, however, each person is interested in a very large number of goods, and he does not feel too dependent on any one particular commodity. Consequently, the producers' actions are concentrated and the consumers' actions diffused and therefore relatively ineffective.

The national economic plan will show the consumers the price of protection before the tariff is adopted, and it will bring home to them that they must not think in terms of protection of this or that specific article but rather of a depreciation of their money income through a rise in prices of all the consumers' goods which the tariff covers.

The planning board, if adequately organized, will be a natural guardian of consumers. The board is constantly faced with the question of how to produce the maximum amount of the most satisfying goods with existing resources, and it cannot fail to realize that exchange of products with other countries is one of the most effective means to this end. The advantages for all concerned of concentrating on the production of goods with the lowest costs will no longer be a fact ignored in practice although a commonplace to economists, since a public agency of dominating importance will find this rule a guide to the better fulfillment of its tasks. It is difficult to overrate the importance of such an agency as a rallying point for the political forces that can support a rational economic policy.

The planning board can play this role only if it is built upon right principles of organization. A good many writers entertain the idea that planning should be undertaken by representatives of the individual industries, assembled into a kind of national economic council.[3] Proposals that would make such councils a form of "business self-government" have probably no chance of success, because most citizens of democratic countries would find it intolerable to lay such great powers in the hands of a comparatively small group of business managers. But if representatives of labor are added to those of management, the council gains a far more democratic aspect.

Such broadening, however, would remove only one objec-

---

[3] The following criticism refers, of course, only to bodies of vocational representation, and it was almost exclusively in this sense that the term "economic council" was used until very recently. The Employment Act of 1946, however, applies the term to a body of experts, which actually constitutes a planning board. For a discussion of this Act, see below, pp. 220 ff.

tion to the economic councils. Even when they are not palpably undemocratic, they are not an adequate representation of the different economic interests according to their real weight, because they are still composed of representatives who think of themselves as sellers of individual commodities. These bodies are not likely to abolish economic privileges; they are likely to become a sort of exchange where the various interests trade votes for the mutual granting of privileges. The experience we have had with bodies of government by vocational corporations, from the *Reichskohlenrat* ("Federal Coal Industry Council," in pre-Hitler Germany) to the National Industrial Recovery Administration, bears out this expectation.[4] The planning board must receive its directives from a democratically elected legislative body, with geographic rather than vocational constituencies,[5] so that each member depends for his election on the votes of people of divers occupations and not merely of those engaged in one particular branch of produc-

---

[4] The case against national economic councils is very much the same as that against industry authorities, if the latter are proposed as instrumentalities for the execution of the plan. (See above, pp. 193–194.) Since monopoly and tariff protection are two types of economic privilege, it is not surprising that both are favored by the same fault in organization. For valuable information on economic councils, see the study by Lewis L. Lorwin, *Advisory Economic Councils,* Brookings Institution, Pamphlet Series, No. 9 (Washington, 1931). For a searching analysis, amply documented, of the movement for business self-government, see Robert Brady, "Manufacturing *Spitzenverbände," Political Science Quarterly,* vol. 56 (1941).

[5] It is a widespread mistake to believe that the psychological and political effects of horizontal divisions in modern society—into workers and capitalists, or workers, middle class, and big business—are necessarily more dangerous than those of the vertical divisions, that is, into groups engaged in different branches of production. Naturally, if group consciousness of any kind is not balanced by awareness of the interests common to all groups, it may disrupt society. But class consciousness is not so conducive to narrowmindedness as the state of mind that may adequately be termed guild consciousness; if we think of ourselves as members of a particular class, we inevitably take into account the interdependence of various vocational interests, for instance, of the different kinds of labor. Whatever the merits or demerits of Marxism in other respects, it has rendered a great service to economic progress by successfully combating the guild spirit among the workers.

tion. The legislative body must pass on the plan as it passes on the fiscal budget, in order to exert control over the experts on the planning board.

In the present economic order the desire for economic security is, on the whole, greater than the desire for economic improvement. The case for free trade in a capitalistic economy is based upon a dynamic view of economic life, upon the assumption that it is worth while to take chances with our present livelihood if we have a fair prospect of improving our position. But this was not the attitude of the masses even in the nineteenth century, and is far less so in the twentieth. Those who have nothing to live on for even a short time without a job and who have therefore to expect an extremely severe economic penalty if they become temporarily superfluous in production are not inclined to gamble with their positions. The sentiment of "safety first" prevails in their minds. The possibility that a rearrangement of economic activities through intensified international division of labor would increase real incomes has not enough attraction for them as long as they do not clearly see the particular place they can occupy after the change.[6] A tariff seems to be (although in fact it is frequently not) the best way to protect what they have, and they use it to "freeze" economic conditions as far as possible.

---

[6] The sentiment of "safety first" is prevalent so long as matters are decided by economic calculation. Under the influence of emotional impulses the underprivileged often accept great economic hazards, as no one who has studied the labor movement can fail to realize. The people in the lower stratum of society, forced by necessity to watch their steps with greatest caution in the ordinary pursuit of their vocational activities, wish to throw off this yoke with great vehemence when fear of humiliation, desire for power, or similar motives take hold of their imagination. There is no doubt that the enthusiasm with which all nations threw themselves into the war in 1914 was, at least in part, a revolt of the adventurous spirit in the common man against the routine of the life in shops and offices. The lack of enthusiasm in 1939 was largely due to the unwillingness of people who had been through the experience of the Great Depression to take risks which they thought might be avoidable.

An economic plan, if it fulfills its purpose, will remove the fear of unemployment from the worker, and the entrepreneurs will feel much more optimistic of the chance of being reëstablished in economic life after a possible displacement. In addition, it will give the average man a definite idea of his share in the general improvement that will result from an intensified international division of labor. The worker can read in the plan the increase in wages made possible by concentration of productive endeavors upon the most favorable opportunities, and members of other social groups will at least be able to form a much more reliable judgment about the probable rise of their incomes than they could ever gain in an unplanned system.

With the risk greatly reduced and the gain far more obvious, people will be willing to accept the possibility of economic change through international trade to a far greater extent than they do now. This is not to say that in a planned economy we can expect a complete triumph of the "dynamic" attitude over the desire to keep things as they are. Reluctance to leave conditions to which we have become accustomed is a fundamental trait which can probably not be uprooted by any modification of the economic order—perhaps it should not be uprooted. But the blind fear of losing what we have, which is so strong in unplanned capitalism in at least its present phase of development, will disappear.

Planning experience will not only show that international exchange of commodities is an excellent means of improving the standard of living, but will also confirm the other theorem of economic science, that isolation is a very questionable way of achieving economic security. Although it removes some sources of instability, it also removes the stabilizing influence of foreign trade. If a crop failure occurs in a planning country which has trade relations with other countries, the deficiency can be covered through adjustments in the plan which provide for greater exportations of other goods in order to buy more foodstuffs. But if the planning country has cut itself off from the rest of the world, the effects will be far more severe, for then it cannot draw on the stocks of other countries to replenish its own granaries.

Striving for self-sufficiency is irrational only when based on alleged economic advantages. As a means to achieve certain "noneconomic" ends, for instance, military security, it may be a perfectly adequate policy, and planning may be used as a technique for its execution. This was so in Soviet Russia, particularly under the first and third Five Year Plans.[7] However, the Soviet Union was forced to cut some of her economic ties with the outside world not merely because of her desire to build industries of military importance (even if, from an economic point of view, they should have been located elsewhere), but also through the tempo of the industrialization process. The great speed with which the Soviet factories were built made it necessary for Russia to import large amounts of machinery and various materials. If there had been perfect mobility of capital, Russia would have obtained proportionately large loans and could have financed these imports while keeping

---

[7] Naturally, the adequacy of the means is no argument for the ends. Although no one in the western world will deny that the Soviet Union had every reason to make herself industrially as strong as possible, even at great sacrifice, it is quite another question whether the particular dangers against which the Soviets were arming during the first Five Year Plan—namely, an imminent attack by England and possibly by France—were real. If they were illusory, there was no justification for the exaggerated speed with which the country was industrialized—and in the agrarian sector, collectivized—in the late 1920's and early 1930's. This speed more than likely detracted from the efficiency of industrialization and consequently from the strength with which the Soviet Union entered the armed conflict ten years later.

the rest of her balance of payments normal. The channels through which capital can move across frontiers proved to be too narrow for the immense needs of Russia. Although she did obtain large sums as measured by the standards of historical experience in international loans, she could not borrow enough to pay for the industrial equipment in addition to the foreign goods which her consumers had bought in former years. Consequently, the Soviet Union had to cut down very severely on importation of consumers' goods and at the same time had to force her exportations to a point that caused producers in other countries to cry out about "Soviet dumping." As long as the methods of international transfer of capital have not been developed much more efficiently, every country which adopts a program of very rapid industrialization will temporarily have to ration foreign currency through exchange controls, import quotas, or a foreign trade monopoly, and probably to subsidize exports. Since a nonplanning country can hardly undertake such a rapid industrialization process, the need for that type of foreign trade policy will only occur in a planned economy, but it is by no means a necessary concomitant of planning. Moreover, although the means temporarily applied are the same which are used for economic isolationism, the goal is very different. The Soviet Union is not trying to isolate herself economically; on the contrary, there is little doubt that she will play an increasingly important role in world trade if her political relations with the western world remain friendly. The Russian example does not support the proposition that full planning is conducive to protectionism.

Our discussion, so far, suggests the conclusion that in a world in which planning is general, economic barriers between nations would either be low or would not exist at all. But what technique would countries have to apply in such a world in order to regulate the terms of international exchange of commodities? And will this technique, or any other suitable technique, be available, even when only one or two countries possess a machinery for full planning, while the rest live under a system similar to the present one? If this question had to be answered in the negative, a country with a planned economy would still have to try to be self-sufficient until the day when the whole world adopts full planning.

The uncertainties which arise, in the absence of planning abroad, from unforeseeable fluctuations in imports and exports, are unlikely to reach proportions which would jeopardize the success of the plan in the country where it is in operation. Even in a nonplanning country, we know more about the movement of goods across the frontier than about many other economic processes. It is true that foreign trade reports, like all other statistics, refer to the past, but they permit the recognition of trends, and in foreign trade, trends rarely undergo abrupt changes. There are some instances when countries have rapidly and unexpectedly increased their production of a particular commodity for sale abroad—as, for instance, Brazil when she raised her production of cotton by more than 200 per cent between 1930 and 1936—but this is exceptional. The First World War interfered with international trade more than any previous event in modern history and most of all with the commercial relations of Germany, which was cut off from the rest of the world almost entirely for four years. Yet after the war, the bulk of German exports went to the same countries to which they had gone before; the structure of her foreign trade did not undergo any change comparable to the magnitude of the disturbance.

Between 1913 and 1929 there lies not only the First World War, but also the peace treaty and German inflation, which both deeply affected Germany's internal economy. Yet if we eliminate those countries whose territories were greatly changed by the war, and Russia, where internal conditions went through extreme changes, the distribution of Germany's exports among the various countries of destination was strikingly similar, as the following table shows.

DISTRIBUTION OF GERMAN EXPORTS
(in per cent)

	1929	1913
Great Britain and Ireland	9.9	14.2
Netherlands	10.1	6.9
United States of America	7.4	7.1
France	6.9	7.8
Switzerland	4.7	5.3
Italy	4.5	3.9
Belgium	4.5	5.5
Denmark	3.6	2.8
Sweden	3.5	2.3

Source: *Statistisches Jahrbuch für das Deutsche Reich,* 1914 and 1930.

The most conspicuous change, namely, the decrease in British and increase in Dutch imports from Germany, is probably no true change at all in the final destination of German exports; it means that Holland was partly substituted for England as an intermediary in Germany's commercial relations with the colonial world.

There was also some uniformity in the kinds of commodities exported. The tabulation on page 175 gives the value of certain German exports in terms of the percentage of total exports.[8]

---

[8] Owing to differences in statistical classification between the prewar and the postwar period, the comparison is not entirely accurate. One large item, Germany's chemical exports (7.1 per cent in 1929), has been left out entirely because of the difficulty in finding a comparable figure for 1913.

In spite of this remarkable evidence of stability in international trade relations, major disturbances in world politics or world production will, of course, deeply affect world trade. Just as the war, while it lasted, interrupted the exchange of commodities or entirely changed its character, so did the Great Depression exert a tremendous influence on commerce. Exports and imports cannot remain stable in an unstable world, yet they are not themselves sources of instability. Since even

VALUE OF GERMAN EXPORTS
(in per cent)

	1929	1913
Iron goods, exclusive of machinery . . .	14.5	13.2
Machinery	9.2	7.4
Cloth	8.0	9.1
Coal and coke	6.4	6.6

Source: *Statistisches Jahrbuch,* 1914 and 1930.

after an economic earthquake like the First World War the old trade relations tended to restore themselves, there is little reason to fear that a planning country will encounter major difficulties because of unexpected changes in its opportunities to buy or to sell abroad within the few years of a plan period. Perhaps a reservation should be made for monoculture countries, which may suffer greatly if a substitute product appears on the market, although there is hardly any instance where such an appearance has been so sudden as not to permit time for adjustment, if such adjustment was at all physically possible. But no country with diversified foreign trade encounters a substantial risk of having to abandon its plans because of changes in another country, and it need not build walls around its territory to avert this alleged danger.

A planning country has even a fair chance to shift the remaining minor risks to its partners in trade, because of the strength of its position in commercial negotiations. If, under the present economic system, the United States offers Argentina a reduction of the tariff on beef, this does not necessarily mean that the meat importers in the United States are going to buy substantially more beef from Argentine cattle ranchers. It means only that the government has made it easier for those importers to purchase Argentine beef, and there may still be circumstances which will prevent them from taking much advantage of this opportunity. If, however, the United States had a national economic plan, the trade agreement would be followed by the insertion in the plan of increased consumption figures for beef, and even without a formal purchasing contract this would almost amount to certainty for the Argentine producers that they could sell more of their produce in the United States.

A trade concession made by a planned economy in good faith means, therefore, far more than a seemingly identical concession made by an unplanned economy. (If the concession is not made in good faith, a planned economy has possibilities of nullifying the effects of any reductions in the tariff, but if the plan is published in all its details, the fraud would soon become obvious.) During the Great Depression, attempts were made by nonplanning countries to supplement their trade concessions with guarantees that a stipulated quantity of imported goods could be sold. The successes of the Soviet Union in her negotiations with Germany and other countries had shown how greatly every exporting country valued the assurance that it would be able to sell a definite quantity; and since all countries tried to limit imports as much as possible without losing too much of their export markets, it seemed an excellent device to offer little in quantity but to make the concession more valuable by adding the guarantee that within these narrow limits sales would actually take place.[9] The widespread substitution of quota restrictions for tariff protection seemed to facilitate the sales guarantee. When the government of the importing country (A) had already formed an opinion of the quantity of foreign product from country B that the domestic market could receive without too great a depression of prices, it seemed a relatively small step to change the permission to import a certain quantity from B into a real purchase by A. The development of exchange regulations, which made it necessary to connect the supply of foreign currency with the granting of quotas, reduced the difference even further. Yet the difficulties of assuring the sale of a definite quantity on an essentially unplanned market proved to be so great that not much came of the whole idea previous to 1933. Then the Nazi regime increased the degree of internal regulation in Germany and also made at least some effort at systematic anticipation of economic developments, thereby creating the presuppositions for a wide-

---

[9] A good example can be found in the commercial treaty between Germany and Poland, signed in March, 1930. One section of this treaty, which was intended to terminate a "tariff war" of several years' duration, provided that 200,000 hogs could be annually exported from Poland to Germany, and that these would go directly to sausage factories. The factories, through the *Reichsverband der deutschen Industrie* ("National Federation of German Industries"), gave some sort of pledge that they would purchase the full quantity. (See *Der deutsche Volkswirt* of March 21, 1930.) The particulars of this interesting arrangement between the sausage factories and the two governments have unfortunately not been published. The treaty was not ratified.

In the middle of the 1930's, the Netherlands obligated themselves in commercial agreements to have their import monopoly agencies—established as an emergency protection for domestic producers—buy stipulated quantities of commodities from various other countries. Their treaty with the United States contained a commitment to buy in this country a quantity of wheat flour equivalent to not less than 5 per cent of the annual total wheat flour consumption in the Netherlands (and also a quantity of milling wheat equivalent to not less than 5 per cent of the annual total consumption of foreign milling wheat in the Netherlands). See Margaret S. Gordon, *Barriers to World Trade. A Study of Recent Commercial Policy* (New York: Macmillan, 1941), p. 311.

spread use of sales guarantees in German negotiations of trade agreements with foreign countries.

These events give some indication of what might happen in commercial relationships between countries with a planned and an unplanned economy. The planning country will give its partner assurance that it will take definite quantities from the latter, and it will naturally try to obtain as much certainty for itself as possible. There will thus be pressure upon the non-planning countries to guarantee purchases. They may meet this by granting additional advantages in order to outweigh the risk that the tariff concessions may not result in a proportionate increase of actual sales, but this way is very expensive for countries without a plan. Therefore, they will tend to fall back on sales guarantees, but they cannot put them into effect without a considerable amount of domestic regulation, and the latter calls for systematic anticipation of its effects—economic planning. In this way national economic planning, if established in one country, will have a tendency to spread to other countries for which commercial relations with the planning state are essential.

In commercial agreements between two countries with full planning, provisions about tariffs will be reduced to minor importance. There will not be the same tendency as today to make tariffs excessively high. Consequently, exporting countries will not need the same safeguards against protectionism. Moreover, a low tariff would be of little significance if the plan made no provision for the use of imported commodities. The main purpose of commercial negotiations between planning countries will be the exchange of information on intended expansion or contraction of industries, and the resulting treaties will contain definite commitments on supply and purchase.

Country *A* will inform country *B* that it is going to invest money in the production of, say, automobiles, and that therefore after some period the purchases of automobiles from country *B* will decrease or cease entirely; that *A* would be glad to expand its chinaware industry if *B* were willing to increase its importation of that commodity; that *A* expects to consume more butter, electric bulbs, and newsprint which might well be imported from *B;* and that *A* will not be in a position to supply *B* with as much dried fruit as it did in the past, because it expects an increase of domestic demand for that commodity. Country *B,* if it thinks it worth while, may try to induce *A* to continue trade relations on the former basis by offering lower prices for automobiles and higher prices for dried fruit or by making other concessions. These negotiations may be just as much a display of shrewdness and hard bargaining as trade negotiations between countries today, but the aims of the parties will be different. Since the plan reveals to each of them that it is necessary to economize on resources and not on opportunities of employment, they will look upon exporting not as something desirable in itself, but as a means to obtain imports. Therefore, they will not seek their advantage in getting rid of as many goods as possible through foreign trade but in receiving as many commodities as possible of the desired groups for as few commodities as possible of the groups that each country can spare. Competition for export opportunities will not cease, but will be dominated by the idea that resources are limited and will, therefore, be keen only when export offers a chance to secure larger-than-average compensation through imports.

If all important countries have planned economies, they will probably set up a system of international planning, by creating some sort of international agency for the drafting of schemes for development. This body may or may not be also charged with executive functions in relation to the schemes. If the future political organization of the world has the character of a close federation, the international planning commission may well be given executive powers; in a loose organization the individual states will probably reserve this responsibility for themselves, aside perhaps from establishing an arbitration court to decide whenever one country feels that another is not doing its part under the common scheme. In any event, the international agency should visualize the economic problems of the world as if no boundary lines existed. Since frontiers do exist, this can only be a first approach, and before a workable international plan is presented, all sorts of concessions will have to be made to such interests as national defense; yet there is great value in having the first draft conceived without regard to political divisions. The international agency would endeavor to find out where every commodity could be produced with the least social cost and where investment of capital would be most promising. There may be great tasks of economic development which surpass the resources and even the ordinary borrowing capacity of any nation, and it may well be desirable that for a time the economic strength of all nations, as far as it is not needed to satisfy current consumers' wants, be concentrated upon such an effort. It will be the duty of the international agency to suggest undertakings of that kind and to submit proposals for the mobilization of resources and for the organization of the common effort.

Nations which have realized the advantages of planning can hardly fail eventually to create such an instrument, since it will contribute much to the effectiveness of their economic efforts. Yet international planning—that is, planning by an international agency[10]—is only a useful implement to, and not a presupposition of, successful national planning.

It would be a mistake to assume that an international agency is as essential in coördinating the plans of individual nations as a national planning board is in coördinating the activities of individuals. The shortcomings of an unplanned national economy result from the inability of any one person to know the intentions of the others and therefore to foresee the conditions on which the success of his own plans depends. If national planning is general, every nation will know what the others intend to do, for national plans could not be kept secret even if it were desired, and there will rarely be any such wish. With a reasonable degree of common sense, technical economic knowledge, and conciliatory spirit, the necessary modifications of the national plans can be obtained through mutual understanding. National planning, therefore, need not wait for a development of the international spirit that would make international planning possible. There will even be some advantages in having national planning established for a considerable time before an attempt is made to plan internationally, so that national plans may offer a solid foundation for world-wide schemes.

Exceptional conditions may necessitate a deviation from this sequence. It is still uncertain to what extent national planning will be introduced in the near future, but there are already definite indications that international planning will be attempted. The Economic and Social Council of the United Nations will hardly be able to fulfill its tasks without trying to assemble at

---

[10] Occasionally the term international planning is used in so broad a sense that it includes any attention paid to international relations by planning countries. In my opinion, the term should be reserved for an arrangement in which a plan-making agency, if not a plan-executing agency, exists as an international instrument.

least the rudiments of an international plan. Henry Wallace once suggested that the principle of the "ever-normal granary" be applied to world production of agricultural goods and raw materials. He, like others, thinks that the controls created in wartime for production and commerce should be continued and made to serve the needs of peace. Most of these ideas are still vague and many of them quite impracticable, but they suggest a question which must certainly be discussed: Is it possible to plan on an international scale without an established system of comprehensive national planning?

The argument for a negative answer to this question is obvious. International exchange of goods depends on domestic production in individual countries. If we have no machinery to anticipate the development of production in individual countries, we cannot hope to know in advance the future of international commerce or even to estimate with any degree of certainty the effects of our own foreign trade policies. A postwar reconstruction agency in charge of the distribution of capital throughout the world might work on the presumption that industries which were doing tolerably well during the 1930's are worth rebuilding, and it might thus reconstruct the Coventrys and Bremens of the Old World. But even in the field of postwar reconstruction proper this principle offers only a limited amount of guidance. How many of the English textile factories should be rebuilt, considering the distressed condition of the textile industry even previous to 1929? What should be done with the rubber plantations of the Netherlands East Indies, if the United States, and perhaps Britain too, establish their own synthetic-rubber industries? If we knew how many more suits and dresses people are going to wear in years to come or how many more automobiles will be operated in such lands as China or the less motorized countries of Europe, we could answer these questions, but that knowledge requires national planning in the potential customer countries. Thus, at best, an international planning agency charged with post-war reconstruction would have to leave some very urgent problems unsolved, so long as the individual countries do not plan.

What would international planning, unsupported by national planning, be able to achieve for the postwar emergency? We may take some suggestions for an answer from an analysis of the past. In the first phase of the Great Depression, an international planning board might have called attention to the dangers resulting from the large amount of international short-term loans, and might thus have mitigated the severity of the credit crisis which came in 1931. It might have urged the lenders to realize that the whole credit situation in the debtor country must be taken into account, that, in order to have a safe creditor position, a creditor cannot protect himself by lending only to personally reliable borrowers, since a general collapse might impair the ability of the Central Bank in the debtor country to provide the foreign currency for the repayment of the debts. Generally speaking, an international agency, gathering whatever information exists about the individual countries and forming an opinion as far as the material warrants, may discover some mistakes which banks or industrialists are making because their information is even more incomplete than that of the international agency. That may be useful enough to justify the establishment of such agencies, even if we cannot overcome the obstacles in the way of national planning. Then, however, we shall not have taken any decisive step toward greater economic security and must wish that the international agencies will know of their limitations.

So long as there is no national planning in the individual countries, there is no clear dividing line in economic forecasting between guesswork (often disguised as intuition) and genuine calculation, and therefore optimism or pessimism and all sorts of wishful thinking may distort the judgment of responsible men. An agency equipped with international authority but unable to check its guesses by any accurate means must confine itself to the correction of obvious errors in international transfer of capital and in trade policy and forego all ambitions to direct world production. Such a restriction of tasks is not only necessary to avoid mistakes, but also to prevent deliberate misuse of an international institution—or the suspicion of such misuse, which is nearly as dangerous. Since, in the absence of national plans, the path of economic reason is not clear for an international planning agency, it is difficult for public opinion to recognize it if the agency leaves that path to follow the dictates of special interests. It is equally difficult for the agency to prove that it has tried its best to stay on the path and has resisted the temptation to dispense special favors. If we remember how the nations in the Great Depression revolted against the gold standard, which was not a machinery subject to deliberate misuse but only a coördinating mechanism of a neutral character, we must expect a great deal of mistrust and resentment against an international planning commission, so long as the latter cannot be fully controlled by the individual nations, which is only possible if these nations have plans for their domestic economies.

The attempts at international planning and some related activities of international agencies will very likely furnish another stimulus for the development of national plans. Perhaps the best example is the International Bank for Reconstruction and Development, created by the agreements of Bretton Woods. For the development of international planning proper, the Bank is probably of less importance than the Economic and Social Council, since only specific needs of individual countries will lead to applications for loans which the Bank has to consider. The financial resources of the Bank are so limited that it will not be able to mobilize a substantial part of existing physical resources. Consequently, the Board of Governors and the executive officers of the institution will have little reason to develop anything like a global plan showing which resources should be used for which needs. But in deciding on loan applications the Bank will often have to request the applying country to submit very complete data about its prospective development—data which will contain the essential elements of a national plan. This is true, at any rate, if the Articles of Agreement, constituting the charter of the Bank, will be administered with respect not merely for the wording of the provisions but also for the underlying intentions.

In making or guaranteeing a loan, the Bank shall pay due regard to the prospects that the borrower ... will be in a position to meet its obligations under the loan; and the Bank shall act prudently in the interests both of the particular member in whose territories the project is located and of the members as a whole.[11]

In the nineteenth century a like provision would have merely obligated the Bank to ask for reasonable guarantees that the government of the borrowing country would keep its budget balanced over the average of the years until the loan was repaid, and that it would not arbitrarily deviate from the gold standard. If, furthermore, careful examination had revealed no

---

[11] Articles of Agreement, International Bank for Reconstruction and Development. Article III, Section 4, no. (V).

probability of an adverse change of the country's trade balance, the Bank would certainly have felt entitled to grant the loan, for in a period of rapid and almost continuous growth of population, production, and commerce only irresponsible action or exceptionally unfavorable events were in any way likely to prevent the repayment. Today, prudence requires greater precautions. The world has lost its expectation of uninterrupted growth, and all sorts of catastrophes are within the limits of plausibility, if not probability. Will the borrower country be able to produce a surplus of foreign exchange sufficient for the payment of installments and interest? The answer to this question, even as a mere statement of probability, involves a searching quantitative analysis of the country's position and prospects.

Another provision, if it is taken seriously, will also make such an analysis necessary. "Loans made or guaranteed by the Bank shall, except in special circumstances, be for the purpose of specific projects of reconstruction or development."[12] This rule is strengthened by a sentence in the following section: "The Bank shall make arrangements to ensure that the proceeds of any loan are used only for the purposes for which the loan was granted, with due attention to considerations of economy and efficiency . . ."[13] It will be simple enough to make certain that, in a formal sense, the money is spent only for the declared purpose of the loan. If China, for instance, is granted a loan to build railroads, the government will have to show that all the proceeds of the loan are put at the disposal of the agency in charge of the railroad project. Presumably, the international loan will be granted only in the amount necessary to pay for equipment and materials which will have to be im-

---

[12] *Ibid.*, no. (VII).   [13] *Ibid.*, Art. III, Sect. 5 (b).

ported: the governments represented at Bretton Woods seemed to have in mind that the Bank should not try to assist the governments of underdeveloped or war-devastated countries in the mobilization of domestic resources for construction projects but merely in the financing of purchases abroad for these purposes. The Bank will therefore probably insist on evidence that an amount of foreign currency, equal to the proceeds of the loan, is spent on imports of producer goods for the project. Reasonable certainty about these points can be obtained by customary auditing procedures.

No allocation of money in the bookkeeping sense, however, provides a conclusive answer to the question: Was it the loan that made the execution of the railroad project possible, or would the government have built the railroads in any event, and through the loan was merely relieved from the necessity of economies in other fields? If the latter alternative is correct, the sense, although not the letter, of the charter provisions has been violated. Perhaps these provisions should not be applied in their full strictness. It may well be justifiable to spare a country rigid economies, for example, in foreign purchases for consumption, which would otherwise be necessary to make a vitally needed construction project possible. Many economists and students of international relations will applaud if the Bank or the contracting governments decide to revise the charter provisions by way of a lenient interpretation, if not by actual amendment. In any event, however, the Bank should know whether the granting of the loan makes railroad construction or increased consumption possible. There is no justification for being satisfied with evidence of a merely formal character, without penetrating to the actual effects of the loan.

The effects of a loan can be judged only by comparing the

prospective development of the economy in the event that the loan is refused with the prospective development in the event that the loan is granted. To proceed rationally, the Bank would have to ask the loan-seeking government to submit a comprehensive development plan for its country. As a matter of good faith, if not for other reasons, the government would have to take measures for directing the economic life of the country, as far as reasonably possible, into the channels which the plan showed as desirable and which the creditors approved. Although in the highly developed, industrialized countries the fear of depression, and next to it the need for a rational and peaceful decision of struggles between social groups, will furnish the greatest inducement to national planning, it is quite possible that the desire for international loans, greatly stimulated by population pressures, will play the same role in some of the underdeveloped countries.

The only reason why this is not a certainty lies in the psychological obstacles to consistent action. It is never entirely safe to conclude that a certain thing must be done because, if it were not, an institution which has been founded previously could not work efficiently or even without major defects. Men have great ability in avoiding the implications of their actions for a long time, whenever these implications seem undesirable. Undoubtedly, the bank experts who will be on the Board of Governors of the International Bank are no enthusiasts for planning. However, the logic of history, although it does not make certain that men always draw the logical conclusions from that which they have previously done, puts penalties on inconsistency, and there is a considerable chance that men will overcome their prejudices and their wishful thinking because they realize that the opposite course would cost them too much.

VI.
Partial Planning

IN THE UNITED STATES, as in a number of other countries where economic life is in principle governed by competition, measures were taken in special fields to correct the results of the competitive struggle by collective control based on foresight. Some of these measures have had a limited success. All have had the very beneficial consequence of calling attention to the potentialities of planning and of developing the beginnings of a planning technique. The more their limitations are realized, the stronger will be the urge to proceed from partial to full planning. For this reason, it is appropriate here to survey the most important types of partial planning and to show why none of these undertakings can fully achieve its purpose unless it is part of a complete national plan.

In a discussion of partial planning, the question may be raised of who should plan. Full planning will not be tolerated by a modern nation except as an activity of the national government. Should another agency, for instance a committee of entrepreneurs or of entrepreneurs and labor representatives, constitute itself as a planning board, it would hold the life of the country in its hands, provided it could obtain the powers necessary to secure all the relevant information for planmaking and could execute the plan when it is compiled. These functions and powers must not rest with a private body, which can never be made fully responsible to the people at large.[1] Partial planning, however, may well be undertaken by private groups whose members, through the right of ownership, possess power to determine how certain resources shall be used. Although planning by cartels and similar bodies is possible and has considerable practical importance, it is not closely related to our main topic, which is the theory of full planning. The purpose of this chapter, to show the relationship of partial to full planning, requires only the discussion of partial planning as undertaken by the government.

---

[1] In the United States, the agency which so far has come closest to assuming the functions of a planning board is a private one: the Committee for Economic Development. This Committee was established in August, 1942, by a group of business leaders who were convinced that the attainment and maintenance of high employment after the war dare not be left to chance. "To seize the opportunities for unprecedented peacetime prosperity in the postwar era and to avoid the real perils of mass unemployment or mass government employment, they believed that individual employers, while in no degree relaxing their efforts toward military victory, must begin to plan promptly, realistically and boldly for rapid reconversion and vigorous expansion after the war." ("A Note on the Committee for Economic Development and Its Research Program," published as an appendix to *Jobs and Markets,* see p. 127.) The Committee recognized that "to plan for the future, the businessman needs particularly some measure for estimating postwar demand for his individual product." (*Op. cit.,* p. 128.) The Committee tried to satisfy this need by a "postwar market analysis, conducted with the coöperation of many trade associations and leading industrial firms and covering more than 500 finished goods products." (*Ibid.*) The findings were presented in a report, *American Industry Looks Ahead,* published in August, 1945. The character of this study is similar to that of *Markets After the War,* an earlier publication by Morris S. Livingston, for which the Committee had also acted as a sort of cosponsor with the Department of Commerce (see above, p. 74). Livingston's study, however, is an analysis by a statistical expert, whereas in *American Industry Looks Ahead* the estimates are made by the leaders of American industry, with the research staff confined to the function of reviewing and supplementary analysis of the material. The Committee is also fully aware of the importance of public policy for the businessman's decisions and for the success or failure of his actions. The exploration of the most desirable course of government action is one of the main tasks of the Committee's Research Division. The study *Jobs and Markets,* with the subtitle: "How to Prevent Inflation and Depression in the Transition" (Authors: Melvin G. de Chazeau, Albert G. Hart, Gardiner C. Means, Howard B. Myers, Herbert Stein, and Theodore O. Yntema [New York and London: McGraw-Hill, 1946]), was a product of these efforts.

The full discharge of the tasks which the Committee has assumed would require

PHYSICAL PLANNING

Most types of government partial planning are concerned with the physical effects of present economic actions. Probably the oldest type of physical planning is planning for the use of land. As long as there have been inhabited places, where more than a few families live together, it has been realized that the construction of buildings could not be left entirely to the whim of the individual. This follows from two basic facts. First, it is a characteristic of land that the use that an owner makes of his own unit influences the way in which the neighboring unit can be used. Second, in all but very primitive economies, build-

---

the compilation of a national plan. This plan would have to be far more comprehensive than the market analysis contained in *American Industry Looks Ahead*. Of course, the Committee has no power to compel anyone to give information or to comply with the plan, if one were established, although its 2,900 local committees, working under a Field Development Division, form a machinery through which considerable influence can be exerted upon the business community.

At present any fears that this influence might be misused seem unjustified. The present leaders of the Committee represent, on the whole, the most progressive section of American business. In their selection of experts and in the tone and content of their publications they have never shown any partiality for conservatism, and their past and present actions give no reason to suspect that they would ever intentionally use pressure methods to defend the status quo, or to pursue any aim contrary to the majority opinion of the American people. It is therefore inconceivable that the Committee, under its present leadership, would ever strive for the position of a supergovernment. The Committee must be highly commended for its attempt to develop a kind of guidance for industry which at this particular juncture could not be provided by the government because Congress and public opinion would not yet support such an extension of governmental responsibilities. If the Committee feels, as it most probably does, that the charting of the future course of the economy should be in the hands of a business organization rather than in the hands of the government, such a preference is very understandable in businessmen. The fact remains, however, that the Committee is doing a kind of work that should eventually be taken over by the government, because, if fully developed, it would be tantamount to directing the country's economy. That job, even if carried out on the basis of moral authority without any compulsion, would involve power over the nation's life, and a private agency assuming that task, however excellent its intentions, would, through its activity, narrowly limit the government's freedom of action even in the strictly political sphere. Such a state of affairs would be intolerable in a democracy.

ings are durable, and the effects of mistakes cannot be corrected for a long time, except with excessive loss.

Physical planning for the use of urban land can do much to prevent mistakes which might otherwise seriously affect the life of the community for a long time. When new buildings are erected, the width of streets should be determined not merely by the present amount of traffic but by the probably greater amount that can be foreseen for the next decades. When a new residential district is opened, assurance should be given that the immediate neighborhood will be kept free from factories creating noise or smoke and that, if the surrounding land is opened for settlement at a later time, enough parks, schools, and traffic lanes will be provided for accessibility and a sound community life. Otherwise, people might hesitate to move into the new homes.

Yet, although it is possible to avoid obvious mistakes, no one can, even in these relatively simple problems, determine the optimal solutions with any degree of certainty through mere physical planning. The extent of any future need for which land may be used depends on economic conditions. It is true that, whatever the general industrial situation, we shall need larger airfields in the vicinity of our big cities, since, for technical reasons, aviation is undoubtedly bound to make progress, and even in a greatly deteriorated economic situation society would not entirely forego the advantages of these technical improvements. It is safe to assume also that the big cities will need still wider streets and more parking space, since trucks and automobiles are likely to become technically still more perfect, thereby less expensive to operate and more easily utilized. Thus people will seek the most advantageous location for dwelling as well as for production purposes, even if this requires more hauling of goods and more personal travel. Yet aviation will grow more rapidly if people have much money for travel, and street traffic will be far greater if prosperity increases the amount of goods and the number of workers that are to be moved than if depression exerts a diminishing influence on both. The need of a city for new residential and factory districts depends not only on the general economic development, but also on the fate of particular industries that are likely to be established there.

There are similar problems relating to rural land. Some unquestionable mistakes mere physical planning can avoid. Some of the wasteful practices in American agriculture and forest exploitation would not have been justified by any economic conditions, and an advance calculation of their physical effects might have aroused public opinion to preventive measures much earlier. Yet to determine how much of each crop the United States needs depends on her foreign trade policy, on the purchasing power of her urban population, on the development of agriculture in countries with competitive production, and on a number of other factors outside the realm of merely physical considerations.

Even in such a seemingly unambiguous activity as reforestation of cut-over areas only gross malpractices can be ruled out by physical planning alone. Any more accurate determination of the line between what ought and what ought not to be done depends (aside from other factors such as the probable imports of timber, the prospects of the woodworking industry, etc.) on the rate of time preference. If this rate is low, it will justify great present effort to produce timber for the future, even though timber does not mature for seventy or eighty years. With a high time preference only the most suitable forest land, readily accessible and likely to bear the most valuable trees, should be reforested.

The limitations of strictly physical planning are equally important in resources other than land, for instance, sources of energy or mineral deposits. Up to a point physical planning can improve methods by pointing out the long-range physical effects, but to determine the amount of conservation and the degree of restriction that should be imposed on present exploitative practices, economic decisions are required which cannot be supplied by purely physical considerations. These decisions must be based on a survey of all production and consumption and an estimate of their development which requires calculation in value units as well as in physical quantities.

REGIONAL PLANNING

There are types of partial planning that are not of a merely physical character. The planned sector of the economy may be not the sum total of the processes by which a given physical resource is utilized but the economy of a given region or of a given social sector. Regional planning, it is true, need not be economic. It is sometimes confined to the investigation of the physical effects which the exploitation of one resource may exert upon that of another; for instance, the utilization of water on land used for agriculture and settlement. But regional planning can be economic, that is, it can include decisions, reached through value calculation, on the relative desirability of technical processes among which the community must choose. This implies that the planning agency tries to anticipate distribution of income, the way in which it is spent by the people in the region, and the ways in which these people earn their living. The outstanding example of regional economic planning is the Tennessee Valley Project, as originally conceived. Although subsequently the degree of guidance offered to the local population was so greatly reduced that the TVA became more nearly a regular power-dam project, the broader aspects did not disappear entirely.

It is not an accident that regional economic planning was first developed around a water-power project. The question of how an ample supply of electricity can best be used touches upon the economic life of society in nearly all its phases. Moreover, the construction of a power dam is related to problems of irrigation and thereby of agricultural land use, and since in the TVA and other projects, places of habitation had to be submerged in newly created artificial lakes, questions of resettlement and city planning were necessarily raised. Neither consumption of electric power nor the proper mode of dwelling nor agricultural or industrial production for the local market can be effectively planned without calculation of the income of all social groups in the region. Regional planning, therefore, if centered around a large power-dam project, necessarily becomes planning in terms of dollars as well as of kilowatt hours, tons of grain, acres of land, and number of dwelling units.

Although regional planning of the TVA type has overcome the limitations of merely physical planning, other limitations obviously remain. How much of a particular product the people of, say, the Tennessee River Basin, can buy depends on the marketing conditions for their own products in the rest of the country, and on the prices that they are charged for essentials in other parts of the United States. The regional planning board may have some indirect influence on these factors. It may, for instance, secure low prices for electrical appliances from producers outside the region, as the TVA tried to do,[2] and it may try to find new markets for the commodities which the region has to sell, or may organize price-maintenance organizations if there are no legal or material obstacles. Yet these efforts can have only a limited effect, and what is even worse, the regional planning agency lacks means to discover in time tendencies that might be dangerous to its plans, if these tendencies originate outside the planned sector. A deepening of the depression could have wrought havoc with many aspects of the scheme which the Tennessee Valley Authority developed for the people in the region, and even more so if the scheme had been as comprehensive as was at first planned. If a similar regional plan were established in the Pacific Northwest, an unexpected reduction in the operations of the sawmills, caused perhaps by shifting of some industries from wood to plastics or from brick-and-wood to steel-and-concrete construction, might vitiate the assumptions of the regional planning board concerning the purchasing power of the population of Washington and Oregon.

What has been stated about the possibility of national without international planning has no analogy in the relationship of regional to national planning. It rarely happens that foreign trade plays as large a part in the economy of any nation as the exchange of goods and services with the rest of the United States does in the economy of the Tennessee or Columbia river basins. A national economy, kept together not only by a common customs line but also by a common credit and currency system, is a unit with which, so far, nothing in the international sphere can compare. Whereas movement over the national borders is controllable, it is in the nature of a na-

---

[2] The attempt was made in 1934 through the Electric Home and Farm, Inc., a TVA subsidiary.

tional economy that goods should move free and unregistered from and to points within the frontiers, as from Nashville to New York and from Seattle to New Orleans.[3]

PLANNING FOR SOCIAL GROUPS

Planning for a social rather than a geographical sector in the country has not in reality developed beyond an embryonic stage, but there have been elaborate suggestions for one such type of planning—namely, a production system in which the unemployed work for the satisfaction of their own needs. The most complete of these "production-for-use" schemes in the United States is Upton Sinclair's "Epic" plan.[4] The outlines are simple. The state takes over, with compensation, unused plants where the unemployed can produce their own clothing, shoes, furniture, and household equipment. Farms foreclosed for overdue taxes can in the same way be used for production of food. Through a careful calculation the agency in charge of the scheme must find out how much of each kind of good is needed. This unemployed sector is then able to satisfy the main needs of its members by itself, but must still receive some supplies and services from the outside, at least electricity, both for factory and household use, and railroad transportation. There are two ways of providing means of payment for these purchases. Either the unemployed sector must be permitted to sell some of its products to the outside world, or it must receive subsidies from the government which would still leave the Treasury far better off than it would be with an ordinary

---

[3] This postulate is not completely satisfied, because of interstate trade barriers. But the latter are, of course, not comparable in significance to international customs lines.

[4] Upton Sinclair, *The Epic Plan for California* (New York: Farrar and Rinehart, 1934). In 1931 the late Dr. Emil Lederer, then professor at the University of Berlin, submitted a basically similar scheme, which, for a time, was even favorably looked upon by the Reichsbank as preventing the popularity of inflationary projects.

relief system. Some sort of special scrip or bookmoney would have to be used to distribute the products within the emergency sector according to labor performed, but it would be necessary to prevent the uncontrolled exchange of this special money for regular money, otherwise demand for goods within the emergency sector would be undeterminable.

It is to be regretted that no serious attempt has ever been made to put a production-for-use scheme to a real test. It is impossible to say whether or not the experiment would have been successful, but the hopes of Sinclair and the fears of his opponents were equally exaggerated. The Epic plan could not possibly have undermined the capitalistic order. The plants that are out of use in a depression are, with relatively few exceptions, the less efficient plants, and the average unemployed worker is not so efficient as the average employed worker.

Moreover, production would have to be carried on in plants dispersed over a whole region (in Sinclair's scheme, the State of California) and not originally destined to be operated as a sort of unified concern. A shoe factory near San Diego might depend on its leather supply from a factory near the Oregon border, and unnecessary transportation costs would be the consequence. Certainly the wages which could be paid in the sector of emergency work would be lower than those in the "normal" sector, and most people employed in emergency work would be on the lookout for "normal" jobs. The greatest danger of the scheme would have been the temptation to misinterpret it as a test of the potentialities of planning. Its shortcomings would then have been taken as a confirmation of a complacent attitude that opposes any change in the social order because it takes for granted that nothing better than the existing order can ever be constructed.

Technical failure of the production-for-use scheme might well result from uncontrollable influences which events in the emergency sector would exert upon the "normal" sector or vice versa. If goods produced in the emergency sector are not offered in the same proportions as consumers desire them—if there is, for instance, a relative oversupply of clothing and an undersupply of food—people will try to sell their clothing at secondhand stores or directly to consumers and use the proceeds for the purchase of food. Thus normally paid labor in the textile and clothing industries would be undersold by labor on an emergency schedule of wages, and new unemployment would be the inevitable consequence. It is hard to imagine that, with the very limited choice of plants available, the production in the emergency sector could be entirely balanced. This does not necessarily mean that production for use is impossible. The advantages of the emergency scheme may be great enough to outweigh some serious inconveniences and even some displacement of labor in "normal" industries; yet the danger of creating too much disturbance in the unplanned sector imposes limitations on the emergency scheme. If available facilities permit a large production of textiles, but not a compensatory production of food, the danger that large quantities of dresses and suits might be sold or bartered for food which is still more urgently desired will necessitate a curtailment of clothing production in the emergency sector long before all clothing workers are employed or all want for clothing satisfied.

Events in the "normal" sector might easily disturb the mechanism of emergency work. In the first place, every improvement of employment conditions in normal industry will attract workers who have so far been employed in the emergency sector. If these represented ordinary, unskilled labor, there would be no great damage, but most likely it will be the best of the emergency workers, the men and women with some training, who will first be absorbed into regular work. This will deprive the emergency sector of the most efficient part of its man power and will force it to depend still more on sub-marginal labor. It does not even take a change in the general business situation to affect the operation of the emergency scheme. If technical improvement in the "normal" sector makes possible a decline in the price of some commodities which pay an important role in emergency production, say clothing, the emergency workers will be tempted to use part of their cash allowance or permitted dollar earnings for the purchase of this article rather than to take it from the emergency sector. Such a change in the spending pattern can be prevented only by cumbersome and obnoxious control measures. The difficulties arise not merely because developments in the "normal" sector might affect the emergency scheme, but because in the absence of any machinery for planning in the "normal" sector, developments in this sector cannot be foreseen and cannot probably be even recognized in their beginnings, so that timely adjustment in the emergency sector is impossible. Moreover, adaptation of plants to changing conditions requires investment, and since the emergency scheme is only a stopgap, substantial investment is out of the question.

This is not an exhaustive study of partial planning, but the point which is most important for the purpose of this essay has probably been sufficiently illustrated: that the greatest difficulties and weaknesses of all partial planning result from the connection between the planned and the unplanned sector. It is impossible to prevent the measures taken in the planned sector from affecting the rest of the economy and vice versa, yet it is equally impossible for the planning agency to undertake any systematic anticipation of these effects because it has insufficient knowledge of developments in the unplanned sector.

CREDIT PLANNING

In the introductory analysis of the purpose of planning, we mentioned planning for the supply and use of credit as one of the suggested alternatives to planning of production. The aims of credit planning are not exactly analogous to those of other types of partial planning. The intention here is not merely to correct some maladjustment in the credit sphere itself—as land planning is intended to remedy malpractices in agriculture or urban building—but to stabilize the whole economy through the steering mechanism of credit regulation. Thus the purpose of credit planning is the same as that of full national planning. If it could really achieve this purpose, it would represent a most useful short cut, enabling us to avoid a great many difficulties.

The case for credit planning as a substitute for production planning is based on the function of credit in providing the community with money. There are three basic ways in which the circulation of money can be increased: first, production of precious metal when the latter is a means of payment; second, public spending of new paper or bookmoney created on the government's own authority; and third, lending newly created money.[5] The last way is on the whole the most important. Every textbook on money and banking shows the processes

[5] Instances in which the government borrows from the Central Bank may be regarded as a hybrid form between types two and three. Technically, the government is granted a loan when it exchanges its own certificates of indebtedness for the notes or for the bookmoney of the Central Bank. Actually, the Central Bank has received its powers from the legislative branch of the government; of the earnings, a substantial part, if not the whole, flows into the public treasury; and, most important, the Central Bank rarely finds it possible, even if it possesses the legal right, to refuse

through which various forms of loans result in an augmentation of the means of exchange. The simplest form is increased purchase of commercial paper by the Central Bank of Issue. This purchase means, of course, a loan, for the bill of exchange is created when the buyer of merchandise is not able to pay cash, whereas the seller needs cash. Therefore, the bill is given to a bank which advances the amount. In the typical transaction, the bank would not be willing to grant the advance if it were not certain that the Central Bank of Issue would, if necessary, relieve it from its creditor position by purchasing the bill.

It has long been recognized that private banks also have power to create money, although this power is not stipulated in any law and extends only to bookmoney. If they lend the major part of every deposit that is made with them, as private banks attempt to do in the course of their business, a great increase of the available means of payment is involved, since the depositor can draw on his deposit to its full amount and the borrower can draw on that part which was granted him as a loan. Moreover, a large part of the loan is sure to revert to the banking system in the form of new deposits, with which the same operation will be repeated. The businessmen who receive the loans pay wages, salaries, rent, and dividends, and earn profits, and in this way the money which the banks have created finds its way into the consumers' pockets. An increase in bank loans, therefore, produces an increase in purchasing power. For this reason many economists believe that credit policy can be used as a regulating instrument to turn the undulatory movement of business life into a straight-line trend.

---

a request for funds from the government. Therefore the procedure closely resembles an intragovernmental operation. The following discussion will make it clear why this hybrid form, even more than the pure type three, is particularly significant for the purpose of our analysis.

The only agency which would be able to undertake this regulation is the Central Bank of Issue, with the backing of the government. However, since the Central Bank is not the only producer of credit, there is the question of whether it has enough power over the private banks to keep them in line with its own policy. In the nineteenth century, there might have been justified doubts on this point, but in the meantime the hands of the Central Bank, as the agency which creates cash and usually administers the bulk if not the totality of the gold and foreign exchange reserves, have been very much strengthened not merely by new laws but also by the course of economic events. Central Bank control of private credit institutions is now not merely assured by technical means, such as changes in rediscount rates and reserve requirements, but most of all by the knowledge of the private banks that situations may arise in which their existence will depend on assistance by the Central Bank. No prudent bank manager will therefore give the Central Bank an unfavorable impression of his own conduct of business—and that means in most instances that he will refrain from counteracting the intentions of the Central Bank.

In spite of the strength of its position, however, the Central Bank meets formidable obstacles in trying to regulate business activities through credit policy. Although the Central Bank may force private banks to expand or restrict their loan offers, it cannot force customers of these banks to borrow. In times of prosperity the willingness of people to incur debts depends to a considerable extent on the rate of interest, hence the Central Bank can control the volume of loans by raising or lowering its own rediscount rates, changing the reserve ratios, and using moral pressure on the banks as a supplementary means. Yet once a collapse of economic activity has occurred, interest-rate policy loses at least a large part of its effectiveness, and the other instruments of an "easy money policy" become wholly ineffective. Even at zero interest, people will not borrow if they are pessimistic about the prospects of all investments.[6]

[6] This statement should be carefully distinguished from the proposition that the interest rate can never have any serious influence upon the business situation because it is allegedly not a major factor in entrepreneurial decisions. The Harvard Graduate School of Business has unfortunately been led into an attempt to sustain this proposition by an inquiry, in which businessmen were asked to state the factors influencing their decisions about expansion and contraction of operations. As one would expect, only a minority mentioned the interest rate as such a factor, and none as a controlling factor. (See the report by J. Franklin Ebersole, *American Economic Review*, March, 1938, Supplement, p. 74.) This has been interpreted as showing that "effective demand" is a more powerful factor in determining the business situation than the interest rate. (See, for instance, J. A. Estey, *Business Cycles* [New York: Prentice-Hall, 1941], pp. 294–295.)

This interpretation mistakes the issue. The problem is not one of choice between effective demand and the interest rate as determining factors, but of the influence which the interest rate exerts upon effective demand. No inquiry can disprove the fact that anyone who contemplates constructing an office building, a power dam, a large mine shaft, or a subway will be greatly influenced in his decision by a difference of, for example, 1 per cent in the interest rate which he has to pay for his capital. All his construction cost is eventually turned into interest charges; if he could borrow at zero rate for an unlimited time, the building or plant would cost him nothing, whatever the prices of material or labor. Nor can there be a doubt that large construction projects are a determining factor in the business situation. Yet the suppliers of steel, concrete, and machinery, the sellers of food, clothing, and recreation to newly employed workers, will be right in stating that their decisions are influenced by chances to sell, and not by opportunities to borrow. They may not be at all aware that their chances to sell have been improved by someone else's chances to borrow at low rates. Unless the inquirer includes in his investigation the firm which actually orders construction work, he would not likely be told by anyone that the interest rate is the controlling factor. Even the ordering firm may not make a statement to this effect. Aside from other limitations on an entrepreneur's insight into the factors determining his decisions, the extent to which his attention is fixed upon the rate of interest depends not only on the objective importance of this factor for his business, but also on the range within which he expects the rate to change. Unless the inquirer and his informant agree on the range that should be taken into consideration, the answer means little.

J. R. Hicks (*Value and Capital*, pp. 225–226) expresses the opinion that considerations of risk frequently overshadow the influence of changes in the rate of interest precisely with respect to those long-term projects which otherwise would be most strongly affected. "Interest is too weak for it to have much influence on the near future; risk is too strong to enable interest to have much influence on the far future; what place is left for interest between these opposing perils?" He believes,

Therefore in a protracted depression the government must step in as a borrower and invest the newly created money in public works.

---

however, that "a space will probably be left between the extremes where interest is ineffective, within which it can have a significant influence . . ." The space is likely to be considerably larger than Hicks seems to assume. In come important types of investment the length of the period is not a risk-increasing but a risk-reducing factor, at least for the kind of risk which influences entrepreneurs' decisions. Few businessmen will make their decisions in any degree dependent on considerations of general insecurity in human affairs, or will consider the possibility that such revolutionary inventions as atomic fission may upset economic calculations. Only possibilities which are within the range of experience are usually taken into account, unpredictable price changes having top rank. But it is far more difficult to foresee the change in product prices between now and a year from now, than to make a reasonable estimate of the average price for the next ten or twenty years. In the course of a long period, the effects of the peaks and of the troughs are likely to cancel out. Only the long period average of prospective prices is a controlling factor in large construction projects.

The risk argument for the relative ineffectiveness of interest changes can be found in even more elaborate form in E. F. M. Durbin, *The Problem of Credit Policy* (New York: John Wiley, 1935), pp. 82–83. Durbin assumes that industrial investment generally, not merely long-term investment, is fraught with so many uncertainties that the entrepreneur will not be much influenced by moderate or even substantial changes in the rate of interest. If he believes that the earning prospects are even slightly improved he will disregard any but an excessive change in the rate, and even a small increase in pessimism about earning chances may already be too large to be offset by a rate reduction within the normal range. But if Dr. Durbin's assumptions were correct, entrepreneurs' attitudes would cause the safety margin between the cost of loan capital and earnings in industry to be very large, and, as a consequence, the average earnings of risk capital would have to be high above the rate of interest—much higher, it seems to me, than the actual difference between stock dividends (plus rises in stock prices due to undistributed profits) and interest on bonds.

Moreover, aside from the hazardous types of investment on which Durbin concentrates his attention (especially labor-saving devices), there are other types which carry only a moderate amount of risk and still are very important for the capital market. The least risk is involved in the construction of homes for one's own use, but even the building of apartment houses is, in many localities, not distinctly more risky than the purchase of first-rate industrial bonds. Undoubtedly the movement of mortgage interest is of primary importance for this kind of construction activity. The hazards of investment in office buildings, power dams, and many traffic enterprises are greater, but hardly great enough to overshadow possible changes in the rate of interest in anyone's mind. The changes likely to be produced in home and apartment-house building and in the construction of office buildings by fluctuations in the rate of interest would suffice to give the rate very substantial influence upon the market conditions for labor.

This experiment has never been carried far enough to permit definite conclusions. In many countries the policy was started in the 1930's, and in some—the United States, Germany, and Sweden—on a large scale. Whenever it was tried, it diminished unemployment. But the final test of the method can be found only in its ability to carry the economy to the point where no new public investment is needed to maintain prosperity.[7] Sweden probably came closer to that point than any other country, but there is reason to believe that the relatively prosperous state of the Swedish economy in the late 1930's was as much a product of the European armament boom as of domestic policies. In Germany, no attempt was made to put the full employment economy on a self-paying basis, for there government expenditure was not primarily a means to stimulate economic activities but to carry through the process of rearmament. In the United States, there was an attempt in 1937 to keep government expenditure within the amount covered by current revenue; the effect was a relapse into depression. It is possible to argue that the attempt was premature or that previous injections of government money into the economy had been too small. But we must at least conclude from the 1937 failure that the effectiveness of a policy of "pump priming" depends on the development of a technique, still to be

---

[7] This statement is somewhat controversial. Alvin Hansen, in *Fiscal Policy and the Business Cycle,* chap. xii, has distinguished with great clarity between "pump priming" and mere "compensation" by public spending. When "pump priming" is intended, the purpose is achieved only if the economy is eventually enabled to carry on without further "shots" of new public money. The concept of compensation, however, involves merely that public spending, in excess of tax revenue, should be substituted for private spending which is not forthcoming to a sufficient extent. When only the latter is intended, the policy may be considered successful though private investment is not stimulated. Hansen and others favor deficit spending even if it is only of a compensatory nature. Mere compensatory spending leads inevitably to a continually growing public debt, and the arguments against a policy involving such growth are presented later in this chapter.

devised, for ascertaining the amount of additional money that must be put in circulation and the period of time through which this policy must be continued.

In retrospect, it is surprising that this need was not generally realized at the time. In 1933 and 1934, the effectiveness of monetary injections in producing recovery did not require much explanation, nor was there reason to discuss the dose. At that time the economy needed money as arid land needs water—the more the better. In 1937—to retain the analogy—the question was: Could irrigation be stopped safely? How could this be answered except after an investigation of how deeply the soil had already been soaked? But no effort was made to estimate the prospective expenditure by individuals for purposes of consumption and investment. Nor could such an effort have been successful without a production plan. The right moment for stopping monetary injections and the right decision as to a complete or partial stoppage will never be found except by accident, unless our economy is better equipped with sources of information and steering machinery than at present.

But why is it important to determine the right moment for stopping public "pump priming" or compensatory expenditure? Why can we not continue the process until its desired effects become indubitable? If we thereby run into a little inflation, will it not be easy to correct that mistake by taking the excess money out of circulation again? What permanent harm can come from too much deficit financing?

Many contemporary economists are inclined to minimize the dangers. They believe that it will still be time to stop when the figures show that the employment goal has been reached. The position of this school—which has recently chosen the term Functional Finance to designate its approach—implies that planning is superfluous because our capacity to regulate the quantity of money is an always effective weapon against depression and inflation—an instrument which we only have to use resolutely to stop a slump as soon as it appears or—in reverse—to forestall any serious effects of an overdose of the antidepression remedy.[8]

The controversy over monetary antidepression policies has suffered from an undue concentration on the question of the public debt. Although for the conduct of financial policy it is

[8] As we would expect, the different groups which share the Functional Finance approach to the problem of full employment entertain this belief in the efficacy of purely monetary policies in different degrees. The most optimistic position is probably that of Dr. Lerner. On the other hand, the research staff of the Committee for Economic Development, in the study *Jobs and Markets,* sees considerable difficulty in the correct timing of monetary injections and deflationary measures. "The key to successful policy will be timing. The difficulties in correcting a major excess or deficiency of demand, after it has gathered momentum, are much greater than in arresting or reversing small departures from the 'right' level. The developing situation must be centrally appraised in its various aspects and the signals called for policy action. Monetary policy, tax policy, and expenditure policy must be made to work together in the interest of a smooth transition" (p. 125). To assure correct timing, the authors suggest, first, developing "built-in flexibility" in the tax system, that is, placing principal emphasis on taxes which "tend automatically to reduce excesses and deficiencies of demand. When incomes are high and demand is likely to be excessive, they dampen demand by taking in taxes a larger share of incomes. When incomes are low and demand is likely to be deficient, they take a smaller share. The effect is prompt and requires no legislative or administrative action" (p. 119). As an example of high "built-in flexibility," the authors mention the pay-as-you-go income tax, and as an example of the opposite, most excise taxes. Various changes in financial and credit organization are proposed by the authors to increase "built-in flexibility." (Reprinted from *Jobs and Markets* by the Committee for Economic Development Research Staff, by permission of McGraw-Hill Book Co., Inc., copyright 1946.)

As a second principal means to assure promptness of the desired inflationary and deflationary effects, *Jobs and Markets* suggests administrative preparedness for deliberate adjustments. The proposed measures range from "a large shelf of public works projects" to the appointment of a special administrator of the stabilization program, who can give his whole attention to the task of watching the signs of an approaching inflation or slump, so as to be ready for immediate action.

The "central appraisal" of a "developing situation" will not be complete and thorough unless it is based upon a quantitative analysis of the prospects of all the individual branches of production, in other words: upon a production plan. Promptness in the application of monetary means is not the only requirement; it is also necessary to know how much money should be injected into or drained from the

very important to know from what point on or under what circumstances public borrowing may become dangerous, this question holds no key position in the problem of deficit financing as a full employment policy.

The funds which the government wishes to spend in excess of tax revenue may be procured by direct creation of new money instead of by borrowing. This method, to be sure, seems the apex of unorthodoxy to some people, yet if we are really convinced that an increase in purchasing power is necessary, there are no more important objections to a creation of new bookmoney, or even to the use of the printing press, by the government directly than there are to a policy which achieves the same purpose in an indirect fashion, via the issuance of government bonds and the subsequent expansion of bank credit. The techniques which the government may use to create money directly are well known. The issuance of noninterest bearing government securities, not redeemable at any definite date but at the discretion of the government, to the Federal Reserve Banks in return for an identical amount of bookmoney or bank notes is perhaps preferable to any other method because it would retain a psychologically desirable resemblance to more conventional procedures.[9]

---

economy, otherwise the economy may be thrown out of gear by an overdose of the remedy, or precious time will be lost in trying out the right amount. If a production plan is established, its execution cannot be secured by monetary means alone: some such arrangement as a sales guarantee system will be necessary to make certain that the estimates of production which will supply the basis for the monetary decisions will actually come true. The research economists of the Committee for Economic Development have conducted the kind of economic analysis which will be required for a production plan and have tried to connect it with monetary policy, but they have stopped short of the necessary decision to place the main reliance in the plan and in the direct methods to secure its execution, and to forego the hope for semi-automatic stabilization through changes in the monetary and fiscal mechanisms.

[9] This method has been suggested by Fellner, *Monetary Policies and Full Employment*, pp. 221 ff., where a very clear discussion of the whole problem can be found. Securities with an indefinite life and with no interest yield are not certificates of

Let us assume that the government, whenever the first symptoms of an impending slump become noticeable, will use this or some other method to increase money in circulation until the danger is removed. If it then appears that an overdose of the remedy has been given or whenever inflationary tendencies originate from other causes, the government will raise taxes and destroy or "sterilize" part of the proceeds so as to reduce the amount of money. Both injection and drainage of money, however, have other effects besides their influence on the price level. The injection of money into the economy can hardly be carried out without temporarily depressing the rate of interest.[10] This lowering of interest through new loanable money will have the well-known effects of "forced saving"—an expansion of the capital sector in the long run and a sharp rise in prices in the short run. With the problem arising out of the latter we shall deal below. The increase of capital equipment beyond the "natural" amount—that is, the amount justified on the basis of a "natural" rate of interest— might not be a reason for serious worry if the adjustment to this "artificially" enlarged capital sector could be planned. This, however, is impossible without a general plan of production and consumption; in an unplanned system, the oversized long-range investments are very likely to become a cause of trouble.[11]

---

indebtedness in an economic sense, and the method is therefore one of money creation rather than of money borrowing. These so-called securities would be merely memoranda to the effect that money in circulation has been increased and that at some future date it may prove necessary to offset that increase by deflationary measures.

[10] Some of the money will find its way into loanable funds and will temporarily be used as such. The effect of this increase in supply upon the rate of interest is likely to be very noticeable in the first phase of the operation. It will fade out if and when the improved prospects of marketing products and the higher prices of capital goods cause a compensating increase in demand for loanable funds.

[11] The whole question of distortions in the economic system, caused by policies

Moreover, an attempt to maintain full employment by monetary means alone will give pressure groups a chance to raise prices without any definite limit. Eventually, the government will be forced to choose between accepting this continuously progressing inflation or abandoning its original policy by permitting a depression. Even before the injection of money has produced a state of full employment, sellers of some commodities and services who bargain under less than perfect competition will demand and obtain higher prices. At first these will be sellers of "bottleneck" goods (and of "bottleneck" labor). With the progress of employment all sellers, except those working under perfect competition, will be able to raise such demands and have them satisfied. The available quantity of money will then become inadequate to sustain the price level and the government will either have to issue more money or let the prices drop, which will mean a slump of production and employment.[12]

varying the amount of money, has been neglected in recent discussions. Perhaps this neglect was caused by the influence of Keynes's arguments against the usual form of the "forced saving" theory (see *General Theory*, pp. 81 ff., esp. pp. 82–83). To this writer, the Keynesian arguments seem unconvincing. There is no room here for a full discussion of the problem which would require an analysis of the distorting effects of reducing as well as of increasing the money.

[12] The danger is obvious at this time (winter of 1946–1947). Wartime controls have been abolished or made ineffective in the United States. Purchasing power in the hands of consumers is still large enough to buy many commodities at present prices, but at times purchasing power has shown signs of considerable slackening. Simultaneously, new wage demands have already been brought forth and are being based on the last increases in the cost of living, which have indeed not yet been compensated by additions to wage earners' incomes. Also, it seems at least likely that entrepreneurs in monopolistic or semimonopolistic positions are still trying to widen their margin of profit. If prices are again increased by higher wages or monopoly profits, new workers' demands for the adjustment of wages to living costs and by efforts of property owners to adjust the yield of real assets to the depreciated value of money will result. Within the existing institutional framework the movement can come to a stop only when the money available is no longer sufficient to sustain the price level. The collapse of the price level will undoubtedly initiate a depression. If the government refuses to let the depression take its course enough money must be

This point has not been overlooked in the discussion of monetary antidepression policies, but it is usually treated as a difficulty inherent in full employment as such rather than in its maintenance by monetary regulation alone.[13] Cyclical unemployment of men and machines, so the argument runs, has an important function: to discipline the producers, to interrupt the inflationary spiral, and thereby to protect the value of money which must be maintained not merely in fairness to the saver but also for stable economic relations between nations. The argument is correct: depressions do have this very important function in our economic system. The function cannot be dispensed with, but it can be fulfilled in another way.

In a previous chapter of this book it has been stated that planning creates some essential presuppositions of rational and effective arbitration of labor disputes, by enabling the arbitrators to calculate the correct economic wage. The argument applies not merely to wage disputes but to the whole problem of income distribution. Planning makes it possible

---

provided to prevent the price drop. If this is known to be the government policy, pressure groups will again raise their prices, and the government will be forced to finance that continual increase unless, in the end, it prefers to accept a slump.

The advocates of "free private enterprise" who have insisted on the abolition of the OPA, instead of helping to remedy its undeniable shortcomings, have not served their own cause well. Once it is proved that the price movements on the unregulated market force upon the community the choice between inflation and depression, the demand for over-all planning will become much stronger. This moment could have been postponed if price controls had prevented an early exhaustion of purchasing power reserves.

[13] See for example, William H. Beveridge, *Full Employment in a Free Society* (New York: W. W. Norton, 1945), pp. 199 ff., 203 f. and *passim;* Fellner, *op. cit.,* pp. xii, 235; Alfred Braunthal, "Wage Policy and Full Employment," in *Planning and Paying for Full Employment,* pp. 143 ff. (his exposition of the problem is far more convincing than his optimism about the forces that will bring a solution); Barbara Wootton, *Freedom under Planning,* chap. vii (discussed in the text above).

to determine the prices that should exist by considering the needs and the resources of the economy. Thereby planning sets standards by which to judge the claims of various social groups for price increases. The standards are, of course, not self-enforcing; the methods of their enforcement, such as price ceilings in sales guarantee contracts, antimonopoly laws, and so on, have been discussed before. Yet the setting of standards is an indispensable prerequisite of any successful attempt to give to each group that which it ought to receive. Planning, therefore, cannot only prevent depressions, but it can also make provision for the fulfillment, by less wasteful means, of the anti-inflationary function which under unplanned capitalism was fulfilled by the periodic paralysis of economic life.

In the present organization of our economy depressions achieve one other essential result—although at far too high a price—the weeding out of high-cost units of production. In every prosperity period the economic penalty on inefficiency is largely suspended, especially in monopolistic or semimonopolistic industries. If we had a permanent good weather economy, without a special mechanism for squeezing out the inefficient, too many uneconomical practices would continue indefinitely. Here again planning offers a possibility of obtaining the results without the suffering of an industrial paralysis. The planning board can and must operate as an agency for the protection of the consumers, not only from monopolistic exploitation but also from the consequences of producers' inertia. In negotiating the sales guarantee contract, the board will naturally try to concentrate production in those units in which consumers' needs can be most cheaply satisfied. But the board should do more than give preference to existing low-cost capacity: It should in every way encourage low-cost producers to expand their production so that high-cost units can eventually be dispensed with. It should also apply auxiliary means: facilitate the exchange of "know-how" and the common use of patents and strive for a reform of the patent laws, to bring this legislation closer to a happy medium between the just claims of the inventor (and of the firm or individual who has invested money in research) and the consumers' interest in technical progress.

To sum up: increase and decrease of money in circulation are likely to produce structural changes in the economy, which must be calculated in advance if adjustments are to be made and disturbances are to be avoided. Moreover, if the government is committed to the maintenance of full employment, at a price level which is largely determined by producers operating under imperfect competition, it would have to underwrite price rises which very probably would follow one another in continuous succession, and the result would be the disintegration of the monetary system. Only through a plan can the government determine the correct dosing and timing of money injections, anticipate the structural changes which are likely to be produced, and lay the basis for a price policy which will maintain the value of money. Pure monetary regulation, not supported by a production plan, should never be more than a stopgap.

The defects of all pure monetary regulation are inherent even in the most ingenious scheme of that kind—proposed by Frank D. Graham. He suggested that a special government agency declare itself ready to purchase "liens" on standard storable goods, such as automobiles, washing machines, and many types of industrial machinery. This procedure would enable and induce the entrepreneur to continue production, in spite of a decline in the absorptive capacity of the market, and as a consequence any tendency toward a depression would soon be arrested: the employers in the durable-goods industries whose products come under the scheme would continue to pay wages out of the money they receive for the liens, and thus the purchasing power of their workers would be maintained. The temporarily unsalable products would be stored under government supervision, until economic conditions have sufficiently improved to permit the sale. The price which the government will pay for the lien is intended to cover merely the out-of-pocket expenses of the entrepreneur, on the theory that the overhead costs will continue in any event and have, therefore, no influence upon the entrepreneurs' decisions. The entrepreneur is bound by a "first-in-first-out" rule, that is, he cannot sell merchandise produced later than the one mortgaged to the government without first possessing the latter stock by paying back the lien, unless the government consents to a change of sequence. In this way the government advances are to be protected from "freezing" and an undue accumulation of mortgaged goods is to be prevented.

If the scheme were to work out as intended, it would be quite automatic in its operation. In the event of a decline of economic activity, some commodities would prove unsalable and would be mortgaged to the government. The government purchase of liens would then cause an increase of money in circulation—the liens would be bought with newly created money—and this injection of purchasing power is expected to restore prosperity. Since the money injectors are to be established only in limited fields of industry—standard storable goods—it might be doubted that enough money will be poured into the economy to offset depression tendencies under all conditions.[14] Furthermore, in spite of Dr. Graham's efforts to prove the opposite, the danger that goods under lien may become obsolete seems to involve a major obstacle to the successful operation of the scheme. There might be hope, however, for the correction of this and other faults if there were greater promise of success in the principle of automatically operated valves for the injection and drainage of money into and from the economy.

Suppose the system is in operation, and symptoms of a beginning depression are noticed. Prices will drop and many entrepreneurs, unable to recover even their variable costs from the proceeds, will sell liens to the government. As a consequence of the influx of money, conditions will improve. Now everyone will wish to take advantage of the incipient prosperity. As market conditions continue to improve, all economic pressure groups will insist on higher and higher prices. Not all the effects of this price rise will be unfavorable to the operation of the scheme. The costs of the mortgaged goods will appear low in comparison with the prices of new ones and this differential may help to liquidate stocks under lien and limit the losses from obsolescence. The moment will come, however, when sales of all commodities will slacken because the supply of money has become inadequate in view of the price level. Then goods under lien will again accumulate, money will flow back into the economy, and a new turn in the inflationary spiral will have been made. An automatic mechanism providing for an ever-sufficient money supply, but not containing any devices of price control, will quite naturally lead into the same kind of impasse as a deliberate policy

---

[14] It should be noted, however, that Dr. Graham does not think of durable industrial commodities alone, but also tries to fit raw materials into his scheme. See his article in *Planning and Paying for Full Employment*, p. 53.

which is directed toward the same goal and also fails to regulate prices. The automatic character may accelerate the development and thereby speed the decline of the value of money.

Although the advocates of economic stabilization through
monetary policies alone cannot offer a convincing program for
the achievement of their principal purpose, they have greatly
contributed to both the development of ideas and techniques
of financial policy. The principle of Functional Finance, as
defined by Abba P. Lerner, is incontestable. Of course, the
"financial activities of the government should be judged not
by any traditional canons of fiscal propriety but by considering the effects of each act and deciding whether these effects
are desired or not."[15] But the desirability of an effect may not
be self-evident. Systematic anticipation of economic development over a number of years will often be necessary to decide
how much of a stimulating or of a restricting effect is desirable
at a given moment. Lerner is not at all opposed to the compilation of an economic plan for the purpose of determining
the right time and the right magnitude of every financial
measure. He warns against "dogmatism"[16] in elaborating full
employment policies, that is, against the belief that adher-
ence to one solution necessarily precludes the recognition that
other approaches may also be useful. In discussing various
proposals for securing full employment, he writes: "If we
have a plan or policy which is prepared to meet all eventualities, we can leave the matter open without harm. The important thing is that we should not gamble our future prosperity
on any one of the underlying theories but be prepared to
meet all eventualities."[17] Some other spokesmen for Functional
Finance are equally free from any prejudice against planning

---

[15] "An Integrated Full Employment Policy," pp. 163–164.
[16] Ibid., p. 202.   [17] Ibid., p. 196.

in the sense in which it has been defined here. This is very fortunate. Much harm could be done if the advocates of Functional Finance and those of production planning were to attack each other with that sectarian zeal which in the past has so often been characteristic of different schools of reformers. But broadmindedness alone, however necessary, will not solve the problem. Lerner's sympathy with planning hardly goes beyond the recognition that it can do no harm, that it represents a sort of safety device in the event that the financial mechanism may for some unforeseeable reason fail to function properly, and that the experience in planning will lead to a considerable advance of economic science. All this is true, but if no more could be said for the necessity of planning, the chances of inducing the community to the strong effort required for success would be slim. We have to decide whether, as even most of the sympathizers with planning within the Functional Finance School seem to believe, the right answer to the question of timing and dosing of monetary injections and drainage measures can be read from the current employment figures or whether a systematic anticipation, in quantitative terms, of the prospective development of production and consumption is necessary.

No believer in the necessity of planning, however, will deprecate the importance of monetary policies. No plan could be properly carried out if the amount of money was either decidedly too small or decidedly too great. The techniques of varying the amount of money in circulation must therefore be carefully studied by the planners, and the only reason why these techniques have not been more thoroughly discussed in this essay is the elucidation which has already achieved in this field, largely by economists of the Functional Finance School.

"National Budgets"

Some of the authors who followed more or less the ideas of the Functional Finance School have found it necessary to investigate the problem of timing and dosing monetary injection and drainage measures. In working out techniques for this purpose, they have made proposals which could not be carried out without the establishment of a national plan for production and consumption.

This development became apparent with the publication of Sir William Beveridge's book: *Full Employment in a Free Society*.[18] He suggested that a new type of budget was needed: one comprising not merely fiscal revenue and fiscal expenditure, but also the output of industry and agriculture and the outlay of business and private individuals. Instead of striving for a balance of revenue and expenditure of the treasury, the new budget policy should aim at an amount of public outlay which, together with the private outlay that will be spontaneously forthcoming, suffices for the purchase of the whole output of production at full employment. Following Beveridge's idea, Nicholas Kaldor, in an appendix to *Full Employment in a Free Society,* has calculated actual figures of such a budget for Britain as they might be in 1948. He has also shown that there are several alternative ways for the government to maintain a sufficient amount of outlay, for instance, reduction of private consumption accompanied by the maintenance of

[18] Beveridge, *Full Employment in a Free Society.* There is no need here to trace the origin of the idea of the National Budgets to individual writers. Anyone interested in the origin and growth of the idea will find the literature references given by Jacob Mosak and Albert G. Hart in the course of their controversy in the *American Economic Review* very useful. See *American Economic Review*, Vol. XXV, No. 4 (Sept., 1945), Vol. XXXVI, No. 1 (March, 1936), Vol. XXXVI, No. 4, part 1 (Sept., 1946).

high public and private investment on the one hand or a policy of favoring consumption at the expense of investment on the other. Several American economists have engaged in the building of similar "models."

The ideas disseminated by the "model builders" produced action in the United States Senate and led to the most promising step on the road to planning yet taken in any western country. Under the leadership of Senators Murray, Wagner, Thomas of Utah, and O'Mahoney, a group in the upper house introduced a Full Employment Bill, which was also endorsed by President Truman.[19] After declaring that "all Americans able and desiring to work are entitled to an opportunity for useful, remunerative, regular, and full time employment,"[20] the bill provided for the annual compilation of a "National Production and Employment Budget." This Budget was to be submitted to Congress by the President at the beginning of each regular session and to contain the following statements:

(1) for the ensuing fiscal year and such longer period as the President may deem appropriate, an estimate of the number of employment opportunities needed for full employment, the production of goods and services at full employment, and the volume of investment and expenditure needed for the purchase of such goods and services;

(2) current and foreseeable trends in the number of employment opportunities, the production of goods and services, not taking into account the effects of the general program provided for in paragraph (3) hereof; and

(3) a general program.... for assuring continuing full employment, together with such recommendations for legislation as he may deem necessary or desirable. Such program shall include whatever measures

---

[19] The bill, S. 380, was introduced on January 22, 1945. It was kept pending during most of 1945 and then adopted by the Senate with some modifications. It was passed by the House in January, 1946, after having been greatly weakened.

[20] The quotations are from the version adopted by the Senate.

he may deem necessary to prevent inflationary or deflationary disloca-
tions or monopolistic practices from interfering with the assurance of
continuing full employment.

Thus the President of the United States was to be obliged
to state first the volume of economic operations that would be
necessary for full employment, then the volume that would
be forthcoming without government interference by special
measures, and finally a program of action that would close the
gap, if any, between the necessary and the probable output and
employment. Obviously, the obligation could not be fulfilled
without calculating the exact pattern of spending and production, and that would have meant preparing a plan.

Some critics of the Full Employment Bill pointed out that
the measure would not provide a single new job. Indeed, the
proposed law would have merely created a mechanism for the
procurement of information and of programs of action, but
left it to Congress and the President to draw their conclusions
from the information and to consider, adopt, or modify the
programs. Yet, precisely this innovation would have been of
crucial importance. All previous antidepression activities had
in the last instance been frustrated by the lack of a plan, which
it is never possible to improvise. By making sure that a plan
would always exist, the bill would have struck at the roots of
the evil. Of course, without energy and determination all policies will fail, but neither can blind energy achieve its purpose.

The Full Employment Bill was emasculated in the House of
Representatives. For the National Production and Employment Budget, the final Act substituted an Economic Report,
which is to compare the probable with the desirable "levels"
of output and employment and to make proposals for bringing the former up to the latter in the event of a threatening

deficiency. Under favorable circumstances the difference between "Budget" and "Report" would be merely verbal. If the President and the Congress were agreed to compile a full-fledged plan, they could find the authorization in the Act. But Congress, as presently constituted, will not wish for the creation of a comprehensive plan, and there is nothing in the Act that would compel an unwilling legislature to make it possible for the President to have such a plan worked out. The statistical work involved in real planning would require substantial appropriations which in the present situation will hardly be forthcoming.

Only in one respect is the final version superior to the original bill. The Murray Bill, as submitted to the Senate, directed that "the National Budget shall be prepared in the Executive Office of the President under the general direction and supervision of the President." No special body that could take upon itself the functions of a planning board was envisaged, although the President could, of course, have ordered the setting up of a special division or bureau within his executive office. The Bill also provided for a Joint Committee on the National Budget, to be composed of members of Congress, for the purpose of reviewing the National Budget as submitted by the President and reporting to the Congress about its essential features and merits. The new Act provides for an Economic Council to consist of experts, appointed by the President with the consent of the Senate, like other high-ranking officials. The requirement of senatorial consent may at times be a handicap in selecting the best-qualified persons—best qualified not merely by knowledge and experience but also by belief in their task—but when legislative prejudice against planning has been overcome, the requirement will probably prove useful as a safeguard against the possibility that the important office may fall to individuals lacking either in competence or integrity. In any event, the establishment of an expert body charged with the continual analysis of the United States economy is a step toward planning. The experts will now have greater authority than if they had been put in their places merely by directive of the President, and the Joint Committee will now be less tempted to concern itself with the preparation of the Report—a task for which it is not fit—and will be more easily induced to confine itself to the examination of the Report when it has been submitted. In this way a clearer line of demarcation will be drawn between the technical functions of the experts and the political functions of the legislature.

Considering the problems which the United States will have to face in the near future, the dangers of a postwar slump for its economy, its social structure, and its position as a world power, the enactment of a Full Employment Bill with mandatory instructions for planning would seem the least Congress ought to have done to build antidepression defenses. The American people, however, has not yet been sufficiently educated to the necessity of planning. The public had not yet understood the extent in which government intervention is needed to achieve economic security—the object of nearly everyone's intense desire. In view of the failure of the public mind to keep pace with the needs of the hour, the emasculation of the original bill may, perhaps, have been a blessing in disguise. Great social and economic reforms cannot be introduced surreptitiously. Sometimes, it is true, important changes are accomplished by the enactment of measures which only gradually reveal their full implications, but in planning it is desirable that the people at large accept the consequences more consciously than they would have been ready to do in 1946, when the change would have been merely the work of a few enlightened Senators.

PLANNING AND ECONOMIC POLICY

Although partial planning varies from traditional forms of economic policy, since it involves a systematic quantitative estimate of the effects to be expected from present measures, its fundamental weakness is a weakness of all forms of government intervention which are not based upon a total plan of production and consumption. Economic history is full of examples in which the imposition of a tariff or other measures of economic policy had important effects which were not foreseen by its authors; a total plan would have revealed them in advance. The most urgent need in contemporary economic policy is coördination. Credit policy, welfare policy in fields like social insurance and housing, foreign trade policy, agricultural policy, and taxation all have extremely important effects upon one another. Yet even if each official in charge of any one of these fields had the most universal economic education and the broadest vision, he could not precalculate the net effect of his own measures upon the other fields without a comprehensive plan established by all government departments in coöperation.

Thus the purpose of full national planning is not merely to correct the evils of laissez faire, but also to substitute order and reason for confusion and anarchy in the economic measures of the government. The critics of government intervention since the First World War were right in many of their specific arguments. They charged with good reason that government agencies, pursuing one particular aim, disturbed the price mechanism without taking into account the full effects of such disturbances, and left it to the businessman to bear the consequences. If private enterprise continues its fight against government intervention (except in forms like the tariff), it will not achieve its aim, but its resistance may perhaps be successful enough to preserve, for a long time to come, the state of confusion and planlessness which now characterizes the economic policies of most, if not all, governments.

VII. Economic Planning
and Democracy

IN THE FOREGOING PAGES our discussion was guided by the desire to combine a high degree of economic security for the individual with maximum guarantees of personal liberty. There is little need to offer elaborate arguments for the thesis that this combination alone can give man a happy life, so far as happiness depends on social organization. Obviously, it detracts from a man's happiness if his livelihood is in constant jeopardy, and there is little point in calling him a free citizen, whatever his political rights, if jobs are scarce and he must have the good will of his employer in order to be able to feed his children tomorrow and pay his rent next week. Nor are the prospects for his happiness any brighter or his freedom any more real if he is perfectly secure in his job but does not know whether or not he is going to be taken from his home the next night and put to death or thrown into a concentration camp.

Of the two evils, political despotism and economic insecurity, the former is the more hopeless case. Since the masses were given political rights, they have always tried to use these rights for their economic benefit. Although they have made many mistakes in the course of these attempts, they did build protection against the worst hardships of the competitive struggle. Thus the man who possesses rights of free citizenship has a weapon with which to work for economic security, but he who is fed by a dictator as long as he obeys orders does not find any means in the economic system to fight for political freedom; on the contrary, the threat of being put outside the pale of economic security is an additional weapon against a rebel. Also, the means by which economic security is achieved and which involve control of individual economic activities may make it more difficult for anyone to escape from the rules which the regime has established.

This is a starting point for many attacks on planning, and one point must certainly be conceded to the attackers. Like any other measure which makes government more efficient, planning will mean as great a setback from a humanitarian point of view if it is used by a government not dependent on the consent of the governed as it will be a step forward in the hands of a government of the people. If we have a despot above us whom we cannot drive from his seat of power, the best we can hope for is that he will encounter technical difficulties which will frustrate his plans and leave loopholes in his organization of power through which we can obtain some measure of freedom. But if we possess a government of our own, which we consider an instrument for the pursuit of our common purposes, we should wish it to be as efficient as possible. Why should we not be able to preserve political institutions that will prevent misuse of the planning apparatus?

It is, of course, impossible to foresee every political contingency of the future, and if democracy is destroyed, the machinery of planning might fall into the hands of despotic rulers and thus be alienated from its original humanitarian purpose. But in such an eventuality it is not likely to matter much whether or not the machinery was previously constructed. If dictators succeed in attaining power they will, in all probability, not have to rely on any apparatus they find ready for use but will be perfectly able to build their own machinery. On the other hand, their coming to power is far less likely if democracy offers as much economic security as it offers freedom. The evidence of the past decades shows that for modern man the temptation to trade freedom for security is tremendous, and not even for real security, but for a condition in which income seems safe while other values and life itself are put in continuous danger. Therefore, it is poor policy to permit the foundation of democracy to be undermined by economic insecurity in the hope that the absence of institutions which would protect the individual from the hazards of competition may make it more difficult for a future tyrant to pacify the people.

Yet some of those who question the possibility for democratic government to survive in a system of economic planning do not so much fear that the state may be captured by an absolutistic ruler as they are afraid of the tendency of any government machinery, even in a state with free political institutions, to substitute its own ends for those of the electorate and to use its position for the increase and perpetuation of its power. The individual citizen, so the argument runs, will be too dependent on the good will of the officeholders to use his rights according to his own judgment and interest. To obtain the favors which he needs for a satisfactory life, he has to comply with the wishes of those who steer the machinery of government. Consequently, he will have no real freedom, and even if the technical instruments of democracy, such as elections, habeas corpus, and so on, are maintained, these institutions will be void of meaning, because through economic pressure upon political dissenters the opposition will be more effectively crushed than it might ever be through government by decree or even through arbitrary arrests.

If the danger that economic pressure may render the rights of citizenship meaningless were really great enough to justify the sacrifice of economic security, this would mean a serious argument against planning but a far more serious one against the present economic system. After all, the masses of people are very much exposed to economic pressure by their employers, and it is not merely a theoretical possibility that this pressure can be used to prevent employees from expressing their preferences for political ideas or organizations which the employers dislike. Yet history has shown that, in spite of their dependency, the workers have built great political and economic organizations which the employers at first fought tooth and nail. They were able to do that because even the early age of capitalism had brought them not only the new serfdom of the factory, but also some shreds of political liberty. Even citizenship rights as restricted and precarious as those which the workers enjoyed in the various countries of Europe during the greater part of the nineteenth century sufficed to overcome a tremendous economic pressure. The idea that the citizen of a planning country, in the full possession of democratic rights, will permit a class of bureaucrats—or, for that matter, anybody else—to tell him how to vote, what papers to read, what meetings to attend, or how to organize for political action, overestimates the amount of patience that can be expected or underrates the effectiveness of legal and political safeguards if applied with a determined will.

Nor do other experiences, sometimes quoted in support of the proposition that any increase in the economic powers of government is a threat to democracy, really substantiate that claim of the opponents of planning. In the struggle over the American work relief program, it was one of the arguments of the opposition that a WPA worker was too dependent on the government to exercise rights of citizenship freely. There was a great deal of talk after the elections of 1940 that "it was impossible to beat that many millions of relief money." In the use of this slogan two different factual allegations were confused. That workers might fear that they would be dismissed from WPA pay rolls, or not taken on, because of their political affiliations, their presumable vote, their campaign utterances or activities, their known contributions to one party chest or failure to contribute to another, is one thing; that these workers would be likely to support an administration which maintained a work relief system and thus enabled them to earn wages instead of a dole, is something entirely different. The former is not only a violation of decency, but, if it occurs on anything like a large scale, destroys the essence of democracy. Fortunately, there is every indication that attempts of this nature were relatively rare and mostly defeated their own purpose because they furnished stronger arguments to the opposition than could be outweighed by their intended effects. The second assumption, on the contrary, was one of the major causes of the Democratic victories in 1936 and 1940, particularly since the maintenance of the WPA was desired not only by the persons already on relief jobs, but also by those still in regular employment who considered themselves subject to the risk of losing their jobs. For workers to elect representatives who will give them protection from unemployment is certainly as legitimate, and as compatible with the functioning of a democracy, as for entrepreneurs to elect those who promise them a tariff or for the land hungry to "vote themselves a farm."

If it were really true that no safeguards are of much avail once the government is equipped with ability to do harm, we would indeed have much reason to tremble, for our governments are already in the possession of powers that might well make our lives miserable if they were not effectively controlled. Yet all of us, even the strongest advocates of laissez faire, show considerable confidence that these powers, to which we are accustomed, will not be seriously misused. Although we know that not all our police officers are beyond the temptation of considering private interests and sentiments in conflict with their duties, we do not live in constant fear that we shall be suddenly dragged from our home or business by some policeman under a pretext or that the police will abandon our home to burglars because we have incurred their disfavor. Nor do we fear that the chief of the fire department will refuse to send his men and equipment to our home in case of fire if we happen to be on bad terms with him. Most of us trust even the public agencies in tax matters to the extent that we do not expect them to discriminate against us willfully because we have offended the tax collector or some important person on the city council who may have something to say about the property tax. In all this there is no unrealistic belief that human passions do not play their part in social life. But experience has developed a confidence that the institutions of civilized society make it extremely difficult and dangerous for any public official to indulge in gross misuse of public power, and arbitrary acts and injustices of minor significance must be accepted as a risk inseparable from life in contact with others.

There is no reason why equally effective safeguards should not protect the individual from any serious discrimination by the planning board or its subagencies. The board will not be able to refuse to conclude sales-guarantee contracts, as described in previous chapters, with any firm that is ready to enter into such contracts, except for good and sufficient reason. It will not be able to deny access to jobs, or training facilities for jobs, to any qualified person. The claim of every entrepreneur and worker to equitable treatment by the planning agencies may well be made enforceable through the ordinary courts or special judicial or semijudicial agencies. Also, the force of public opinion, controlling through an unfettered press and thorough legislative investigation and discussion, will work as a powerful check on any public official who may be tempted to dispense favors to his friends or to penalize his enemies. It is the absence of these guarantees in Soviet Russia, as previously in the fascist countries, and not the existence of a Five Year Plan that puts the individual in that country at the mercy of government representatives.

Again, let us remember that there is not much logical consistency in an attitude of callousness toward the reality of discrimination by employers and oversensitiveness toward the possibility of discrimination by public officials. Very often a person cannot get a particular job, regardless of qualification, because the color of his skin or the form of his nose does not please the employer. Often, too, people have learned by experience that they must try to please the boss, or the manager, or the foreman, yielding not only to his personal wishes but also to his prejudices of all sorts, if they want either to hold their jobs or to obtain promotion. We might all like to be as independent of others as the pioneers were, but, in fact, most of us are not. Planning will not restore that full independence which only a personal isolationist could have, yet it will give a much greater measure of freedom to the average person, because it will assure conditions under which demand for labor is not substantially smaller than supply of labor, and where, therefore, a person can give up a position with reasonable assurance of finding another one that is suitable.

However, aside from this problem of interference with individual freedom, there is the other question of whether the planning board might not impose the personal preferences of its members upon the people by arbitrarily determining what ought to be produced and how it should be produced. This danger has been mentioned earlier in this essay, yet it is necessary in this context to summarize once more the safeguards by which it may be averted.

First of all, everything that safeguards rationality also protects our freedom to determine the purposes of production. In the political sphere, we speak of government by laws, in contradistinction to government by men, as a guarantee of freedom. This term is perhaps not the best that can be found, but it expresses something very true. If arbitrary action is to be prevented, the first necessity is to define it in a way which makes it recognizable in practice. The law must not only state the general purpose of government action, but must indicate specifically to what tests any individual measure is to be subjected to find out if it is in accordance with the stated purpose. The general law, by which the planning board is bound, should stipulate that the consumers must be given what they wish to have within the limits of available resources, unless their collective will, expressed by the representative institutions of a democracy, approves deviations in favor of educational aims, social needs, or of a greater sacrifice of present to future needs. But this law could not be administered without a system of accounting which enables us to determine if, in each case, the best possible use is made of existing resources. The use of money and the addition of value planning to physical planning are, therefore, not only necessary to assure efficiency—they also afford protection for our rights as individuals.

In his philippic against planning,[1] Friedrich A. Hayek has disregarded this function of the rules of rationality and also of the rule of consumers' sovereignty. He argues that the adoption of planning means the sacrifice of the Rule of Law, that is, of the principle "that government in all its actions is bound by rules fixed and announced beforehand."[2] Hayek is right in placing great value on the maintenance of this principle. The coercive power of government should not be used in an incalculable way—not even by a legislative majority.[3] Therefore the

---

[1] Friedrich A. Hayek, *The Road to Serfdom* (Chicago: University of Chicago Press, 1944).

[2] *Ibid.*, p. 72.

[3] Herman Finer, in his *Road to Reaction* (Boston: Little, Brown, 1936, chap. iv., esp. p. 60), defends the absolute sovereignty of the majority. He affirms that a majority has even the right to vote a dictator into power. I do not believe, however, that Professor Finer himself would accept all the consequences of this view. Suppose a dictator, voted into power by a majority, would start killing his opponents: Finer would certainly not blame these opponents if they did not meekly wait for the ax but started a revolt, even if the majority continued to applaud the dictator and his executions, as majorities have sometimes done. Presumably, Dr. Finer would not even criticize people for a revolt against a ruler, who, after being voted into power by a majority, took away the people's right to elect representatives in the future. What, then, does it mean to say that "the majority would be right" in voting a dictator into power? Probably not more than this: it is technically impossible to make legal provisions for invalidating a majority decision, even if it reduces democracy *ad absurdum*. That much can be granted. We have many instances in which fundamental justice cannot be written into the statute books for technical reasons, since legal concepts, as all other human tools, have their irremovable imperfections, but justice remains justice whether or not it can be administered in a given instance by our judicial machinery. Nor can a solution be found in distinguishing between ethics or morals and law. In an ultimate sense, no act is illegal against which the holiness of the law, as an ethical argument, cannot be invoked. A majority decision which renounces the people's right to change their minds does not deserve to be respected. It is a mistake to believe that civilization is possible without the concept of a "higher law" or democracy without the concept of inalienable rights, which neither a majority nor even the individual himself can give away. In fairness to Dr. Finer and the long list

twin rules, basic to democratic planning, the principle that available resources should be used for the best possible satisfaction of consumers' preferences, and the other principle that they should be used as efficiently as possible, are vitally important for two reasons: first, for the sake of the goals which they establish, and second, because they are rules of conduct for the government and thereby make governmental policies calculable.

It is difficult to see how Hayek could have overlooked the second point and its importance as a refutation of his own "Rule of Law" argument against planning. For years he had been conducting a controversy with various socialist writers on the methods of spelling out the rules of consumers' sovereignty (or consumers' free choice, the difference being of minor importance in this context) and of efficiency of production in a planned system. Although he maintained that this effort could never produce any set of clear, unambiguous and workable directives, he must at least have recognized that the overwhelming majority of noncommunist "planners" were deeply concerned with the establishment of the Rule of Law. The only place in his *Road to Serfdom* where he takes cognizance of this discussion is a footnote in which he refers to "some academic socialists," who "under the spur of criticism

---

of his intellectual ancestors who defended the unlimited right of majorities, it is necessary to recall the frequent misuse of the minority rights argument. Very often the intention was not "to keep open the way for the future" (a good expression of Finer's, p. 60), that is, to maintain the right to subsequent elections and that process of free exchange of opinions which alone makes majority rule useful as a tool of progress, but to protect the special advantages, economic or otherwise, of a privileged minority—advantages having no relationship to basic human rights or to the essentials of the democratic process. The outstanding American defender of the limitation of majority rule, John C. Calhoun, used the argument for the defense of slavery. (For a lucid presentation of the controversy in the period 1820 to 1850, see the chapter "Minorities and Majorities" in Arthur M. Schlesinger's *Age of Jackson*, Boston: Little, Brown, 1946.)

and animated by the fear of extinction of freedom in a centrally planned society, have devised a new kind of 'competitive socialism' which they hope will avoid the difficulties and dangers of central planning. . . ."[4] No reader can possibly understand from this footnote either the bearing which this whole discussion has upon the problem of the Rule of Law, or the true significance of this group of "academic socialists" whose ideas are far more characteristic of the tendencies among the "planners" than the quotations from Harold Laski and Karl Mannheim, which Hayek uses to support his own interpretation of what the planners wish to do to the rest of mankind.[5] Hayek's belief that he has proved the impossibility of translating consumers' preferences and the requirements of efficiency into clear rules of conduct for the managers of production does not give him the right to speak as if the proponents of planning had never discussed any basic rules to restrain the government from imposing an arbitrary scheme upon an unwilling population. That the socialists and planners have been aware of the problem which Hayek discusses in his chapter on the Rule of Law could not legitimately be treated as a matter of minor

---

[4] Hayek, *op. cit.,* p. 40.

[5] *Ibid.,* pp. 62–63, 132, 199 for Laski; pp. 21, 72, 158 for Mannheim. Laski is an eminent political scientist and Mannheim was one of the original thinkers in sociology. The question of whether Hayek is right or wrong in regarding them—as he obviously does—as spreaders of totalitarian germs may remain open here. In any event, the problems of economic planning are in the frontier region of analytical economic science. There is excellent reason for obtaining the opinion of social scientists from other fields on these problems, just as in discussing atomic fission, we might be interested in learning the opinion of an outstanding biochemist; but we would presumably be even more anxious to hear the specialists on nuclear physics. By the same token, if someone wishes to know how consumers' preferences and the requirements of production efficiency can be made the basic law of a planned system, to override or preclude arbitrary decisions by government agencies, he has to look primarily for the opinions of the economists among the proponents of planning—opinions which Hayek has all but ignored in his *Road to Serfdom.*

importance.[6] This fact proves that the Rule of Law itself is not an object of controversy between the majority of noncommunist advocates of planning in the western countries and the "antiplanners." Only the techniques by which the Rule of Law can be made effective are at issue.

Hayek's discussion of the Rule of Law and some other passages of his book contain an unqualified praise of formal law and formal ethics. "Like formal law, the rules of individualist ethics . . . are general and absolute; they prescribe or prohibit a general type of action irrespective of whether in any particu-

---

[6] The heat of the controversy over Hayek's book has in large measure been due to the impression which he gave to his opponents: that he conducted his argument without the minimum degree of generosity which is absolutely essential to a fruitful debate, because it is impossible to get to the core of the matter if one party insists on putting the worst possible construction on all parts of its opponent's position. The refusal of generosity in debate proved all the more exasperating because of a form of presentation which appeared subtle in a high degree. When Hayek relegated the decisive point in the planners' position on the Rule of Law problem—the point which he had debated with his opponents in numerous articles for more than a decade—to a footnote of vague content, he should have known that this was worse than not mentioning the point at all. Hayek may have thought that it was impossible to explain the connection between the problem of pricing in a planned order and the Rule of Law problem to readers untrained in economics, but he should at least have told them that there was such a connection. In a popular presentation the author may simplify but he must not omit essentials.

An equally antagonizing example of Hayek's method in polemics was his attempt to identify socialism or planning with the German spirit and his own brand of economic individualism with British tradition. Even with better support from facts it might not have been the kind of argument a scholar would find it pleasant to use in the midst of a war against Germany, since he would not wish to take advantage of nationalist prejudice; still, with incontrovertible evidence on his side, he might feel obliged to call public attention to this side of the matter. But Hayek could easily have escaped from the dilemma, since the thesis is utterly doubtful. The greatest propagandist for socialism in the early nineteenth century was Robert Owen, and Ricardo had socialist disciples decades before Marx wrote the *Communist Manifesto*. Most important, the first great modern mass movement of prevailingly socialist character, Chartism, was an English movement. On the other hand, Hayek himself, in criticizing the Vansittardists, emphasizes the existence of a liberal tradition in Germany, represented by such men as Alexander von Humboldt. Then why discuss the problem in terms of the British versus the German spirit?

In the fall of 1946, after a stay of several months in the United States, Dr. Hayek stated in rather vigorous terms that he was unhappy over the enthusiastic welcome which reactionaries had given to his book. He expressed hope for collaboration with

lar instance the ultimate purpose is good or bad."[7] Why should
such law exist at all, and why should such ethics be regarded
as praiseworthy or even as acceptable? Most certainly, when
we are judging a human deed, the goodness or badness of the
ultimate purpose matters very much. Although some types of
action have always bad effects, which goodness of the purpose
may or may not be able to outweigh—this problem will be discussed below—other actions are as such ethically indifferent
and should per se neither be approved nor disapproved by the
law. In these instances it is the purpose which makes the action
legitimate or illegitimate. No code of rational law or ethics can
therefore be written in disregard of human intent. Hayek's
implied thesis that law and ethics are on a higher level when
they are more formal amounts to a glorification of early phases
of human development at the expense of civilization. On a
primitive level of religious development it is generally assumed
that the approval of the gods depends on certain outward performances, which must therefore be regarded as commendable, and that other outward performances bring about the
wrath of the gods and thereby are proved to be wicked.
Granted that some remnants of these magic creeds survive in
our code of morals, it seems highly unfair to the philosophers

---

those planners who upheld the liberal tradition, referring especially to Barbara
Wootton. (See *New Leader,* August 24, 1946, p. 9.) Although even in the *Road
to Serfdom* Hayek had occasionally recognized the existence of liberal tendencies
within the socialist and planning movements (e.g., pp. 144, 168), he had minimized
their significance, and his whole book seemed to be an appeal to all liberals to
avoid ideological contact with all socialists, planners, and other advocates of government intervention in order not to be infected with the germ of collectivism. If a
statement recommending some sort of collaboration between liberals and socialists or
planners had been made in the book, the impression that Hayek was driven by a
fanatical desire not merely to refute but to ostracize the thoughts he criticized would
not have originated, and the controversy between Hayek and the planners might have
produced less heat and more light.

[7] Hayek, *op. cit.,* p. 146.

of individualism to burden them with the responsibility for such remnants from mankind's adolescence.

Although the degree of formality in law is certainly no criterion of its high level of development, but rather the opposite, all law has to be formal to some extent, otherwise it could not be administered. In our modern codes, we do not treat—as most primitive law did—all kinds of homicide alike. The person who inadvertently causes a fatal accident to someone else is not regarded as a murderer. The policeman who shoots an escaping dangerous criminal is, as a rule, not prosecuted at all. Nor is the soldier who kills in war, although our legal order—in contradistinction to that of earlier ages—normally protects the foreigner as well as the citizens. In all these cases we consider the good intention, or the lack of bad intention, utterly relevant, but even in our law all does not depend on purpose. In spite of recognizing that under some extraordinary circumstances someone's life has to be taken to save values which society rates higher even than human life, we have not enacted a blanket rule covering all such cases: We have merely granted standardized exceptions from the general prohibition of homicide. This arrangement appears unsatisfactory to the logical mind, yet it is unavoidable. Any blanket rule would be interpreted differently by different judges, it would become impossible to know what is permitted and what is forbidden, and the resulting evils would be worse than the shortcomings of the present system. Law cannot dispense with formal rules, but their formality makes it inevitable that every rule covers some situations which, according to its ethical rationale, it ought not to cover, and fails to cover others, which should come under its scope. Hence originate the tragic conflicts between formal and substantive justice.

It is one of the most important tasks of policy to keep the conflict of formal law with substantive justice—and with other vital human purposes—within reasonable limits. In this endeavor, two principal means have to be applied. First, we should give our laws only that degree of formality that is indispensable for effective administration. In civil, in penal, and in public law a great deal of recognition can be given to the intent of the author of a deed or of the parties concerned. Actually, in lawmaking as in ethics, progress has largely consisted of an increased consideration for intent (and this progress has been rightly regarded as a triumph of individualism). Hayek's ideal of law, if his own description can be taken at face value, would bear closer resemblance to the Roman law of the Twelve Tables or the law of the Teutonic tribes at the time of the Great Migration than to Justinian's law or any modern code.

The other means to reduce the conflict between formal law and substantive justice is change in the conditions to which the law applies. What Anatole France[8] wrote about the law in its majestic equality forbidding the poor and the rich alike to sleep under bridges, to beg in the streets, and to steal their bread, should make it inadmissible for any author to ignore the limitations of formal law: but the Frenchman's irony would lose its point if extreme poverty were abolished. Therefore the task of preserving and enforcing formal law cannot be dissociated from the problems of social reform. All formal law gives a measure of protection to the *status quo*, because it lays a ban on the use of some of the means by which existing conditions might be changed. If the *status quo* is extremely bad, and if other means for its improvement seem unlikely to be available or effective, men will rebel and break the rules of

---

[8] *The Red Lily, Modern Library Edition* (New York: Boni and Liveright, 1917), p. 75.

formal law, and who can say that they should not do so? All anti-interventionists tend to overlook this vital point, and Hayek is no exception.

By sometimes confessing inability to condemn a violation of formal law, for the sake of still more important values, we do, of course, not mean to deny that every violation of the law is an evil: we merely assert that in the particular case "the end justifies the means." Hayek maintains that only "in collectivist ethics" is the justification of means by the ends regarded as admissible; "in individualist ethics" this principle is "regarded as the denial of all morals." But Hayek himself concedes that "we may sometimes be forced to choose between different evils,"[9] which means precisely that the end can justify the means: choosing the lesser evil is the same as undertaking an action, which is bad in itself, because it is made legitimate by its effect, preventing a greater evil.[10] Differences in philosophy and outlook upon life cause divisions of opinion on what ends can justify what means, although the most important dividing line hardly runs between individualists and collectivists, as Hayek uses these terms.[11] The principle, however, that means

---

[9] *Op. cit.*, pp. 146–147.

[10] Hayek tries to draw a dividing line between his position and that of the collectivists by stressing that even lesser evils "remain evils." But every person who is not morally insane—collectivist or individualist, democrat or totalitarian—would concede that much. Lenin, for instance, would not have denied that shooting bourgeois "remained an evil," only he regarded it as a lesser one if compared with the effects of not taking reprisals.

[11] Every person with a normal moral yardstick can name a few acts which he believes he would not commit under any conceivable circumstances. We must be very careful, however, not to mistake a limited scope of imagination for moral sensitivity. Previous to the present war, few of us would have foreseen how far we would go in approving horrible means for the purpose of defeating the fascist powers. We found that in the presence of a purpose of overriding importance we could not limit our choice of means as much as we had formerly assumed. The intensity of belief, not the individualist or collectivist character of the convictions involved, is the decisive factor in drawing the line between means which we think can be justified by vital

may be justified by their ends must in essence be accepted by everyone, because we cannot live without doing many things that are "wrong in themselves" but necessary for the sake of higher values.

The fundamental problem of formal law, its potential disharmony with vital human purposes, has an important bearing upon democratic planning. A democratic constitution is a body of formal law rules, and planning, aside from other relationships to democracy, is intended to be a means for the betterment of existing conditions and by achieving this purpose to prevent people from breaking the framework of rules. This is the positive relationship; there is also a negative one. The essence of political democracy is the prohibition of certain acts regardless of the purpose for which they may be undertaken. However good our own cause, we must submit to the arbitrament of the polls; we must not suppress newspapers, even if they uphold views that we regard as very bad; generally, we must not substitute violence or fraud for argument, even if it appears inadequate to prevent an evil. This democratic system, as all formal law, is based on the premise that no single purpose is more important than the maintenance of the framework of rules and this premise naturally applies to all purposes served by planning.[12] In the overwhelming majority of situations, the

---

ends and those which cannot. Probably the best treatment of this whole question is found in Max Weber's discussion of the conflict between *Gesinnungsethik* and *Verantwortungsethik* (see *Politik als Beruf*, in his *Gesammelte Politische Schriften*, München: Drei Masken Verlag, 1921, p. 448.

[12] This proposition is tantamount to stating that formal law must be maintained only if the common good does not require its violation. This is a very dangerous truth, for obvious reasons, but we cannot object to the validity of a proposition on the ground that it may be misapplied. The concept of the common good as the ultimate yardstick by which to judge courses of action is not, as Dr. Hayek believes (see *Road to Serfdom*, p. 147), a characteristic of collectivist beliefs. Whoever thinks that he can dispense with that yardstick is committing an error. If a new Hitler were

premise is valid, for obedience to the formal law of democracy is even more important than obedience to penal or civil law. The community can continue a peaceful existence even if a murderer or thief goes unpunished, or when A obtains an unlawful gain at B's expense, but when a precedent is established showing that the arbitrament of the polls will not be obeyed, or that elections will not be reasonably honest, civil war may well follow.[13] In an extremity, it is true, planning may appear to us as an indispensable condition for the survival of the community, we may feel that we have to introduce it at any risk, even if this action requires the breaking of the rules of democracy. Such a situation would be an enormous calamity. Fortunately, although the possibility cannot be ruled out in theoretical considerations, the likelihood that an immediate introduction of planning will be both a suitable and an indispensable means to save values greater than those of democracy, and at the same time its establishment will be impossible within the democratic framework, is so exceedingly small as to be negligible for practical purposes. Aside from all other

---

elected, in an entirely constitutional manner, to the position of chief of state in a great nation, where he would have access to atomic weapons and instruments of biological warfare, we would all feel that he should be shot before he could set the world afire. We would not feel that in wishing for that deed, perhaps in helping perform it, and in applauding it when it was done, we would violate any commands of morality, although we would certainly violate formal law. Here again we are meeting the problem of the justification of a means by its end. The sanctity of the formal law itself can only be based upon the idea of the common good. Therefore a violation of formal law, although an evil, is justified if there is no other way of safeguarding the common good.

[13] In the past civilizations have flourished under autocratic types of government, which sometimes have even tolerated a limited amount of freedom of thought, yet it is hard to see how in this age of ours people can live in a civilized fashion except under a democratic constitution. Before modern rationalism caused people to question tradition and divine right, a ruling individual or group could sometimes feel safe enough to forego the harsher methods of repression and even to permit a good deal of liberty. Today, every autocrat feels unsafe and therefore by necessity resorts to strict censorship, firing squads, and concentration camps.

reasons, undemocratic procedures are likely to make planning a curse rather than a blessing and even to spoil its technical effectiveness.

But even if the planners obey the law of democracy, what about the antiplanners? May not some group feel that the prevention of planning is of absolutely paramount importance and therefore regard itself as entitled to break the laws of democracy if the *status quo* of economic organization cannot be preserved by other means? Although Hayek is wrong in believing that a planned economy could not be democratic, is there any chance for planning to be established through democratic processes?

The conditions under which social change may be achievable without violent conflict have been discussed in innumerable controversies. Even a brief review of these discussions would require more space than is available here. Not more can be done than to summarize the conclusions which, according to a widely accepted view and in the opinion of this writer, should be drawn from the debates and from recent experience. Social change can be carried out within the democratic framework only if no individual step in the period of transition appears irrevocable, unless approved by so great a majority that opposition by force is obviously hopeless. If the individual step puts society on a one-way road toward a completely different form of organization, the party of the *status quo* will regard this as the end of the world and will wish to rebel. Many people will be frightened by the idea of an irrevocable change and will therefore join the defenders of the existing economic order, thus enabling the latter to engage in a life-and-death struggle with some chance of success. Only if the change can be split into steps small enough to be retraced, if the majority so desires, can the opposition be effectively told: If the results prove you right, you will win a majority and can undo what we have done. Therefore you do not have even a good pretext for trying to stop us by force.

Can this rule of gradualism be observed in the establishment of a planned system? Planning cannot be introduced piecemeal: There must come a day when the first plan for the national economy is put into operation. Can antiplanners be expected to acquiesce in this step?

We may take it for granted, of course, that there will always be some people who would start a civil war rather than accept planning, but if planning is introduced as an experiment from which society can withdraw if it proves unsuccessful, the minority that will oppose it at all costs can be reduced to an insignificant number. A person who would have suggested resistance by force against the Full Employment Bill, if it had been enacted in its original version, might have found applause among a small circle of people who used to call Franklin D. Roosevelt "public enemy no. 1," but among all others, including the great majority of the conservatives, such a suggestion would have been laughed out of court. Nor would the situation in all likelihood have been different if a system of voluntary inducements to comply with the plan, operating through sales-guarantee contracts or otherwise, had been written into the law.

For a peaceful transition it is important that a national plan can be superimposed on the private enterprise system. Should planning not prove successful, the machinery of planmaking and plan execution can be removed without bringing the process of production to a stop. This possibility will be a consolation for the skeptics and thereby will help to isolate the diehards. If it were necessary to dismantle the basic structure of the economy before planning could be established, we would have to wait until an overwhelming majority for such a policy could be found. That would probably be true only after an economic catastrophe, and then it might be too late to prevent the disintegration of democracy.

But if it is recognized that a system of planning can be introduced without an irrevocable commitment to its completion, is not this possibility of reconsidering the original decision very dangerous? May not a planning policy, based on democratic institutions, be so easily reversible as to be lacking in the necessary stability? This is one of the problems with which Barbara Wootton is struggling. "...economic planning demands continuity, and political freedom appears to imply instability. Nothing can alter the fact that we cannot both make effective long term plans, and continually exercise the right to change our minds about anything at any time."[14] Not only planning, however, but most kinds of government activity would become impossible if the average voter exercised his right to change his mind without restraint. The voters have the indisputable right to elect a militaristic Congress, which would establish an enormous army, and two years later a pacifist Congress which would abolish it, and to swing back to militarism after two more years. In the same fashion, the post office, or the income tax, or the diplomatic service could be abolished, reëstablished, and abolished again. If the voters were sufficiently fickleminded, not even matters regulated by the Constitution of the United States would be exempt from successive changes in opposite directions. The fate of Prohibition shows that. Even the high wall which the Fifth Article

---

[14] Wootton, *Freedom under Planning*, p. 131.

has built around all constitutional provisions has little strength of resistance to the force of strong popular sentiment.

Actually, however, institutions in democratic countries have been fairly stable. There have been regrettable instances in which long-range plans were reversed without good reason. Barbara Wootton mentions the inconsistency of British housing policies during the 1920's. It would be easy to supply equally pertinent American examples, for instance, from the fate of the OPA. All these changes, however, occurred in fields in which government activity was relatively new and experimentation therefore seemed legitimate, whatever objections any one of us might raise against the individual step. Full planning, too, will have to pass through a period of trial, in which a repeal of the basic laws, a return to an unplanned system is entirely possible. This possibility will even have to be stressed to relieve some of the strain which this transition to planning will impose on the democratic framework of our society, as every major change of policy inevitably does. It would, of course, be undesirable to have planning abolished after its first introduction, and to let society go through some further experience with an unplanned system before a planned economy can be finally established. Such an event is less likely if planning is inaugurated at a moment when public opinion is already so deeply convinced of the necessity to plan that it will not be swayed from that conviction by the unavoidable initial difficulties of the new system. But historical roundabout ways are sometimes unavoidable, and if we must have a period of wavering before the course will be finally set toward the new goal, it would be a small price to pay for the peacefulness of a great act of social reorganization. Once the machinery of planning has existed for a number of years, its abolition is no more likely than that of the public school system or of the federal judiciary.

Perhaps Barbara Wootton felt less concerned over the possibility that the planning system might be repealed than over changes in the voters' minds (or their representatives) with respect to particular plans. Might not Congress interfere with the operation of a plan during the planning period? Obviously, this will be an important danger only if the division of labor between the legislative body and the experts is imperfect or not firmly established.

Barbara Wootton, realizing the importance of this point, recommended the setting up of nonpolitical boards to handle the problems of planning. She hopes that in these boards, removed as they would be from party strife, a line of fundamental agreement may eventually appear that could be made the basis of a consistent policy, not exposed to attack by any one faction. The remaining issues, in her opinion, will be very largely of a technical character and capable of being settled by more thorough exploration of facts.

This opinion may be questioned with good reason. Barbara Wootton probably overestimates the achievable degree of unanimity, since political issues, such as national defense and education, must deeply affect any plan and cannot be made uncontroversial by delegating the power to decide them to a board. Furthermore, she seems to envisage a number of "extra-parliamentary authorities" for the administration of different matters rather than one planning board, and this multitude of independent boards would hardly leave us any hope for a unified plan.[15] One basic feature of Barbara Wootton's position,

---

[15] This is not the only point at which Barbara Wootton seems to think of plans rather than of a plan. If she really regarded national planning as a juxtaposition of a

however, remains unaffected: a clear dividing line must be drawn between technical questions of planning, which should be decided by independent nonpolitical experts, and all political decisions, which must be made by elected representatives. This distinction is as vital for continuity in planning as it is for the protection of the consumer. The basic political decision will be the directive to the planning board to give to the consumers what they want to have so far as these goods and services can be provided through the most efficient use of available resources. This directive will certainly never be repealed. What, then, are the areas in which a change of the opinion of the voters or of their elected representatives might upset the plan?

Such changes may concern the setting of the time preference rate or the modification of consumers' sovereignty for educational reasons or for reasons of national security. In these fields a legislature may well be tempted to make an abrupt change if it discovers the importance of some goal which was previously neglected. If Congress, in making such a decision, is fully conscious of the cost in terms of interfering with the continuity of the plan, there is no cause for an objection on principle. The legislature, however, might be so anxious to put its new policy into operation that it will fail to calculate the cost correctly. Therefore a strong case can be made for regulations forcing the legislative body to think twice before making changes in instructions to the planning board during a planning period, and to make these changes only if a large majority is convinced that the gain is worth the cost. Such regulations would have to be written into the procedural rules of Congress, but it may

---

number of partial plans, the disagreement between us would be fundamental, but she has not set forth her position on this matter unambiguously enough to make this interpretation necessary.

also be useful to put them on a firmer basis through enactment as a public law or even as a constitutional amendment.

Even if Congressional decisions do not actually interfere with the provisions of the plan, they may cause difficulties in its operation by altering its premises. Congress may, for instance, enact a new minimum wage law. By raising the cost of production and consequently the level of prices, this law may reduce the salable quantities of many goods and services, and will therefore require alterations in the plan. The right to enact such laws must remain with Congress: it cannot be delegated to the planning board without making popular control over these vital matters too remote. The solution lies in adequate timing. The planning board should be given the right to demand that any measure, which it regards as seriously affecting the plan, be postponed until the necessary adjustments in the calculation and in the arrangements for plan execution have been made. Congress should have power to override this suspensive veto, but under restrictions so severe as to be prohibitive except in generally recognized emergencies.

Of the great positive contributions which planning will make to the strength of democratic government, the first is economic security, which will diminish the temptation to accept dictatorship and, at the same time, will help to produce that sane type of mind which is essential to the functioning of democracy. The second is the possibility for the average citizen to recognize clearly the effects of governmental actions, so that responsibility for economic measures becomes real and meaningful, whereas in the present system it is largely fictitious. Any action which the government takes today is encumbered with the hazard of incalculable changes in the conditions on which success or failure depends. A tax measure, a tariff reduction, an act of social welfare policy, however well calculated, may be frustrated by an unexpected turn in the business cycle or by a slackening in the activity of some industries; however badly calculated, it may be saved by an equally unexpected event that works in the opposite direction. Yet the mechanism of democracy requires that a government be held responsible for its actions. If the true merits of a policy cannot be judged, nothing is left but a verdict based upon outward success or failure, which not only means a great waste of leaders, who are rare enough in any case, but also introduces into democracy an element of falsity and many opportunities for demagogues. Democracy can only be a sound system if economic events are precalculable to a much greater extent than today, and this can only be achieved through a system of planning.

Finally, planning will strengthen democracy by removing, or at least reducing, the contradiction between a democratic form of government and an essentially aristocratic economic constitution. It is true that human institutions are not based on logic alone, and forces of faith may sustain dogmas and organizations in spite of underlying assumptions that are illogical. But democracy, in our own days at least, has to defend its position by rational argument, and cannot afford to be blamed for lack of consistency in the application of its own rationale. If a man should not be subjected to another man's will as a citizen, if in the realm of politics power should only be exerted as a public function and a trust, why should it be different in economic life? It is perfectly possible to argue that private management of industries is in the interest of the masses, but then it must be generally recognized that this is the only reason why private enterprise is to be preferred to public ownership and management. Consequently, freedom of action should be granted to the entrepreneur not as a matter of his own right, but merely within the limits in which his management proves the best way to produce goods and services, for the satisfaction of the consumers. The system of planning, as sketched on the preceding pages, tries to achieve precisely this. It is not only based on the principle that the public interest can overrule the right of private ownership, but it also equips society with a mechanism by which the entrepreneur's freedom of action can be restricted or expanded, dependent on whether private initiative or centralized administration promises better results. If private enterprise proves itself in the future a superior tool of human welfare, it will be safer within the limits of the new system than in the old; then there can be no doubt that it is not maintained as a privilege for the owner but in the interest of the community. Not complete equality of income and economic status, but the supremacy of the nation's will over the vested interests of any property owner is a requisite of democracy.

These are the long-run aspects of the problem. What will happen within the next years? In the Russian-dominated part of the world the potentialities of planning have greatly increased. Territories of considerable economic importance have been annexed to the Soviet Union and still far more important ones have become parts of the Soviet "sphere" as nominally independent states, but with the prospect of being integrated economically as well as politically into the Russian system. Area and population in themselves mean much for the success of the Five Year Plans, since they increase the possibility of regional specialization. Where a whole country is managed as if it were one gigantic industrial enterprise, division of labor between the different regions becomes as important as it is within a factory, and no country is so large that it cannot gain by further increase in size which makes possible more intensive specialization. Moreover, some of the Soviet acquisitions and new dependencies have not merely size to contribute. Aside from such assets as Rumanian oil and Silesian coal, the additions to the Soviet sphere bring in a dowry of great advantages of location: the ice-free ports of Koenigsberg, Danzig, Fiume, Dairen, and others, the Danube, the possibility of reaching western Europe and the Atlantic Ocean from Soviet-controlled territory over short distances and convenient alternative routes. (The northwestern tip of Czechoslovakia is not more than about 150 miles from the French border.)

Therefore, from a strictly economic point of view, an observer would be tempted to forecast an even greater success for the Russian Five Year Plans than was achieved in the past, so that the reconstruction of the war-devastated areas would be speedily achieved and the scene set for a spectacular rise in the standard of living. It is merely for political reasons that this development does not seem quite certain. Although the triumph over Hitlerism has enormously enhanced the prestige of the Soviet leaders among the peoples of the Soviet Union, the war has also imposed stresses and strains upon the Soviet system, and not all of them may have disappeared with the conclusion of hostilities. Population groups numbering many hundreds of thousands, if not millions, of people were transferred from their European regions of habitation to Soviet Asia, because they were regarded as politically unreliable, and nothing is known of the success of this resettlement, nor of the magnitude of the remaining resentment. Millions of Russian soldiers have come in close contact with western populations and have been in a position to notice a much higher standard of living in Poland and the Baltic regions, not to speak of Germany, Austria, and Czechoslovakia. Will these masses be so objectively minded as to remember the low starting point of the Five Year Plans and the absorption of Russian resources by the need for national defense? And even if they do, will they not at least feel that in the future the Soviet government should give them a supply of consumer goods comparable with that of the western countries, rather than again emphasize the production of an enormous amount of capital equipment within the shortest possible time? Suppose they feel this way, will not the conflict between popular sentiment and governmental intentions become the source of much friction and loss? Finally, the head of the Russian government is approaching old age, and only experience can show whether any workable provisions for succession have been made. The implications of dictatorship are more than ever a threat to the final success of Soviet planning.

The world outside the Soviet sphere is divided into a section in which majority opinion likes to be told that the basic form of economic organization is "free competitive enterprise" and another one in which the preference is for some type of socialism unspoiled by dictatorship. The first section consists mainly of the United States, the second of non-Russian Europe, with most of Latin America, the British Dominions (except conservative South Africa), and perhaps Kuomintang China in between. The difference in basic impulses is not so great as it may seem. In the United States as in Europe people want economic security in a form compatible with individual liberty. It is even doubtful whether there is any great difference in the emphasis placed respectively on liberty and security. But many Americans are still inclined to believe that a reasonable degree of economic security can be achieved without an intensive and systematic use of governmental powers for the stabilization of economic life, and that such use should be avoided because liberty is safer if governmental functions are kept within relatively narrow limits. Europeans, on the other hand, have had the unforgettable experience that a regime which extinguished personal liberty even in its most elementary forms grew and spread with the support of private capitalists. Therefore restriction of the economic power of business and its close supervision by the government seem to most Europeans not merely compatible with personal liberty but one of its prerequisites. The Europeans have also received an object lesson in the political dangers of economic instability. In Europe, no observer with an open mind can fail to realize that Hitler, in spite of all the support he received from the capitalists, would never have come to power had it not been for the despair brought about by the Great Depression. Finally, Europeans have had enough experience with government regulation to know that governmental power can be made to respect individual liberty through democratic control—which means, of course, not merely control by the majority of a legislature but majority rule plus an independent and impartial judiciary watching over the inalienable rights of the individual.

The European nations, however, seem to be in danger of committing one very serious mistake. From England as well as from the continent we hear much of socialization, but hardly anything of serious attempts at full planning. The term planning is used very frequently, but without the idea that the economy should be guided by a single unified plan. Rather, planning is thought of as a sort of supplement to socialization. When the government has taken over an industry, the agencies in charge naturally wish to eliminate the inefficiencies which they have inherited from private ownership, and therefore they establish a special plan for that industry. These various plans may eventually grow together and, when the remaining gaps are filled, an integrated national plan may originate. There must be men and women in the British Labour Party who see that goal now, but in Britain as elsewhere the emphasis is on public ownership and not on national planning.

As a matter of time sequence, a good case could be made for giving priority to socialization. It might be argued that the state, in order to cope with possible sabotage of planning by the entrepreneurs, must have an experienced staff of industrial managers in its own service, and that this can be achieved only if a substantial sector of the economy is publicly owned. But are these fears, which might seem exaggerated in the United States but are at least not entirely unjustified in Europe, really responsible for the lag in planning? Does the cause not rather lie in a continuation, through mere inertia, of the socialist tradition which regards private ownership in the instruments of production as the source of all evils and its removal as the one basic change necessary?

Not only is the concept of full national planning relatively new and unfamiliar to the political leaders of socialist parties, but its practical application is also beset with greater technical difficulties. The nationalization of mines and factories is a simple process. Their efficient operation by the government may prove to be a somewhat more difficult problem, but eventually the government is likely to achieve at least a reasonably satisfactory level of performance. The establishment of a national plan would involve far more of an experiment. Methods would have to be tried out in the process of compiling the

national plan and putting it into execution, and a temporary
failure, without much significance for the final result, might
politically embarrass the party in power. Thus a natural tendency to work along lines to which minds have been long accustomed may be reinforced by the apprehensions of leaders
for whom the maintenance of their parliamentary majority is
a very legitimate consideration, and who, in choosing between
alternatives, will interpret party interest in terms of short-run
effects unless conclusively shown that a definite long-term interest requires a different course.

The long-term interest of the labor movement and the fulfillment of its secular task in the development of human society
do require an emphasis upon planning rather than nationalization. The transfer of factories from private to public ownership may by itself produce important economic results when
profit rates are abnormally high, as they sometimes are in
colonial enterprises or as they were in the early phase of the
Industrial Revolution. Otherwise, the value of the change, except for considerations of political necessity or social power,[16]
depends entirely on the use which the government makes of

[16] A nationalization policy may be worth while, in spite of limited material effects,
because it reduces the amount of power which one individual, as an employer, can
exert over others. Of course, nationalization will increase individual freedom only
if the government which steps into the shoes of the private entrepeneur is democratically controlled. Differences in income and wealth, even aside from employer-
employee relationships, often create conditions of dependency and infringements
upon personal dignity, in instances ranging from the creditor's power over the
debtor to the economic roots of prostitution. To the extent that nationalization makes
economic status more nearly equal it contributes to human liberty.

Although nationalization may be a suitable means of removing causes of dependence, there are usually other methods by which the same purpose can be achieved,
perhaps not quite so completely but in a degree to take much weight from the social
power argument for nationalization. Labor unions reduce the employers' power over
his employees; social insurance laws, public relief for the destitute, provisions for
emergency loans, by cushioning the effects of unemployment make it less vital for the
average person to keep in an employer's good graces.

the instruments of production. If government ownership leads to the elimination of diseconomies, and especially if nationalization proves to be a prelude to over-all planning and thereby to stabilization at full employment, it will be successful. In any other event people are likely to discover that the change has not deeply affected their lives, and they will be disappointed. Even if nationalization meant the immediate confiscation of all surplus value, the effects would not be of sufficient magnitude to mark a great historical change, for in no modern country do the earnings of the wealthy,[17] after deduction of taxes, amount to a very large part of the national income. Moreover, the nationalization procedures in democratic countries do not involve confiscation, but transfer of property with compensation, and the effects of nationalization as such upon income distribution are therefore even more limited. If nationalization was the last word instead of the first act of the reforms which the British Labour Party and Continental European socialists are now trying to introduce, the present moment would go into history as one more opportunity missed by reformers.

Many such opportunities have been missed in the past. The socialists of Germany and Austria after their coming into power in 1918, the British Labour Party in 1924 and especially in 1929, Leon Blum as the leader of the Popular Front government in the 1930's, could all have achieved much more if they had been able to recognize the most decisive tasks and to attack them with a clear program. The same is true, perhaps in a still higher degree, of the New Deal. Great were its achievements, but they could have been much greater if there had been a

---

[17] For the sake of brevity, the difference between the concepts "surplus value" and "earning of the wealthy" is neglected, since the failure to distinguish between the concepts does not affect the conclusions.

deeper realization of the relative significance of goals and a more realistic appraisal of means. The NIRA was almost entirely a waste of fine impulses, political energy, and favorable climate for reform.[18] The reformers of the interwar period have often been accused of lack of will power and of an undue readiness to compromise, but most if not all of these accusations were unjustified. With more right the reformers could have been criticized for lack of a thoroughly planned strategy, for a failure to recognize among the many troublesome questions those whose solution would produce the greatest results with the least sacrifice, and then to concentrate all the resources of political power and expert knowledge on the key spots. In the whole period from 1918 to 1939, the task of working out a comprehensive plan for the full use of all resources according to consumers' preferences should have been given priority among all problems which the reformers had to face.

But the failure to chart the right course for reform was very pardonable in that period. The concept of planning was still in its early phase of evolution. Almost by necessity, it became confused with the idea of "business self-government" and had therefore little appeal to anyone who understood that the latter term was merely a euphemism for compulsory cartels. Moreover, the real achievements of the interwar period in the field of social insurance, collective bargaining, public housing, and others created a consciousness of progress which did not make

---

[18] The structure chosen for the NIRA was greatly influenced by uncertainty about the freedom of action which the Supreme Court, in interpreting the Constitution, would allow to Congress and to the administration. Moreover, even provisions which in themselves could not do much good might well be justified as a means of encouraging industry by showing that the government was no longer passive. Although these conditions provide a partial justification for the course of action which the Roosevelt administration chose in 1933 and 1934, it still remains true that this was not the most constructive use that could have been made of the extraordinary readiness of the American people, in the early 1930's, to welcome far-reaching reforms.

it easy to see that the most decisive point had not yet been attacked. Also, in the 1930's, the improved technique of miti- gating a depression by fiscal policy was quite naturally over- estimated and wrongly taken as a final answer to the problem of stabilization. Our own epoch, however, could hardly plead attenuating circumstances if it failed to progress much farther toward the realization of economic security under freedom.

The failure, so far, of the European reformers to inaugurate over-all planning does, of course, not prove that they will not undertake this task in the near future. Especially among the intellectual leaders of the British Labour Party, the idea will almost certainly gain ground that the establishment of an integrated national plan rather than a change in the owner- ship of some industries will be the task which labor must fulfill in order not to be found wanting. The opportunity is still there, but the political mood which made the great labor victory of 1945 possible will not perpetuate itself. It must be supported by successes great enough to outweigh the natural growth of opposition against the party responsible for government under difficult circumstances. Unless the Labour government under- takes the establishment of a national plan, and succeeds in this undertaking, it will exhaust its credit with the voters probably in the not-too-distant future.

If Great Britain were to provide an example of successful national planning, the effect upon the United States would be very great. The reverse, however, is true in an even higher degree. If the United States, widely regarded as the firmest stronghold of unplanned capitalism, were induced by experi- ence to turn to systematic planning, the whole world would almost certainly follow suit. Is there any chance for such a development?

On the surface the prospects seem almost nil. Wartime government regulation, especially the OPA, has left Americans with a great desire to rely again on the "operation of the law of supply and demand" rather than on conscious regulation of the market. At the present moment, the people of the United States is not yet in the proper state of mind for an objective evaluation of its economic experience during the great conflict. This was not an experience with full planning. At no time was there even an attempt to establish a national plan, showing how much of every type of commodity could be produced and why that specific quantity would be bought. To be sure, there were rough estimates of total spending power and total production to determine the inflationary gap; also, the various government agencies, allocating material to various industries, implicitly decided what the output should be. Had they made these decisions after advance calculations and a thorough comparing of notes, instead of "muddling through" from one emergency to another and with the right hand often ignorant of what the left hand was doing, a national plan might have originated. As it was, we have lived in an economy with intense government interference, containing some elements of planning, but not in a planned economy.

The haphazard character of the wartime regulation policies was unavoidable. Full planning of the war economy was prevented not only by the difficulties inherent in that task, which have been explained in a previous chapter, but also by the failure of the United States to establish a planning machinery in peacetime, and of her lack of a governmental staff to administer complex economic regulations—high-ranking expert advisers are not adequate substitutes for skillful administrators on all levels. Perhaps the worst handicap was the slow awakening of the American people to the economic realities of modern war. Under these circumstances, the improvised machinery of economic administration could operate only in a very imperfect fashion. At times, the economic policy of the government, conducted by harassed officials facing tasks for which there were no precedents, undoubtedly resembled the throwing of monkey wrenches into gears rather than the careful steering of a complex and delicate mechanism. Yet if a machine is getting out of control, as the price mechanism on occasions threatened to do, it may be better to throw a monkey wrench into its gears than to let it proceed on a dangerous course.

Just as unavoidable as the shortcomings of the war economy, however, was the failure of the general public to distinguish between planning and makeshift intervention. The prejudice against planning was supplemented by the absence of a slump immediately following demobilization and the canceling of war orders, and the resulting comfortable belief that even without far-reaching antidepression measures the experience of the 1930's would not repeat itself. The combined effects of this optimism and of the resentment against war regulations became apparent in the election results of November, 1946, in which the voters' motives were the precise analogy of the "return to normalcy" vote of 1920.

But the illusion that the wheels can be turned back will be of short duration. The conservatives, perhaps even more than the progressives, are anxious to protect the American economy from the effects of labor disputes. This extremely urgent problem cannot be solved merely by weakening the unions as some legislators, at the time of writing, seem to believe. Even if public opinion approved of such a policy, organized labor could not be deprived of its fighting power without the utmost resistance, and the effort to force the unions into a position in which they would be incapable of organizing many strikes would probably produce an enormous strike wave before it could obtain its success—if it ever were successful. Moreover, any strong antiunion legislation is likely to consolidate the labor vote against the party responsible for such enactments, and the conservatives cannot hope for that unanimous support from all other groups which alone could sustain their majority in the face of a common front of labor opposition at future elections. What the nation wishes and needs is not a shift in the prospects of winning out in labor disputes: it is a substitution of peaceful methods for industrial warfare.

All efforts to solve the strike problem will therefore ultimately lead to a system of arbitration which is not based entirely on voluntary acceptance of awards. The implications of such a system have been explained. Wages and prices are linked, because without knowing the prices which will prevail it is impossible to determine the wages which industry can pay and which workers must have. There is no effective labor arbitration without wage planning, no wage planning without price planning, no price planning without production planning. Peaceful settlement of labor disputes is impossible under a policy of "taking government out of business."

The conservatives will face still another dilemma. During the battle against the OPA they urged that full reliance be placed upon the "law of supply and demand." Their argument was that price control would prove unnecessary because prices would drop when demand would prove incapable of taking the whole supply off the market at the existing price level. This expectation is perfectly correct—but what does it mean? The inadequacy of demand will be noticed by the sellers only if unsold stocks accumulate. This accumulation must be sufficiently persistent to force dealers and producers, who have bought merchandise or material at higher prices, to resign themselves to the inevitability of losses, and then to force the same attitude on the sellers of semifinished goods, raw materials, and tools. A substantial reduction of the price level, in other words, is not possible without the material and psychological symptoms of a depression. But no government, conservative or liberal, can afford a severe depression. Therefore, as soon as the "law of supply and demand" leads to serious price drops and consequently to a slump on the labor market, Congress and the administration will have to intervene with WPA policies—probably surpassing the original model in magnitude. This return to New Deal methods will be politically difficult for party leaders who in the past have bitterly attacked the New Deal. Specifically, the conservatives in Congress are committed to the idea of a balanced budget, which is incompatible with antidepression policies.

However the conservatives may act in the face of this dilemma, it will become clear that there is no conservative formula for the smooth solution of our problems—no formula that would spare the United States a major reorganization of her economy. It is equally important to know that there is no probability that the present trend toward the Right will lead to extreme solutions—barring a major political or economic disaster, which would substitute counsels of despair for calm thinking. The fears of disappointed liberals, who are inclined to regard the elections of 1946 as the preliminaries to a triumph of fascism in the United States, have no more justification than the apprehensions of conservatives in the 1930's who saw in Roosevelt the inaugurator of a communist revolution.

The "conservative recession" may even prove highly advantageous, not merely for the reason that it gives the American people an opportunity to explore once more the alternatives to planning and thus more firmly convince themselves of its necessity, but also because it will demonstrate the area of agreement among practically all Americans. In a previous chapter of this essay, we have rejected Hayek's idea that unanimity of opinion on the purposes of specific plans is required for planning. It is true, however, that democracy, with or without planning, cannot function unless there are some basic tenets of social life on which virtually all members of society agree. Democracy, as an order of peace destined to protect the common interests of all members of society during unavoidable conflicts, has sufficient strength only if the common interests which all recognize include not only material welfare but also some basic ideals of social living. The succession of a period of prevailing conservatism following a period of prevailing liberalism is likely to show, through the limited character of the ensuing changes, that we all have more in common with one another than we usually realize in the heat of the party struggle. In her chapter on "Political Freedom," Barbara Wootton describes very convincingly why the area of agreement so often appears much smaller than it really is: "In political controversy it is generally customary . . . for opposing parties to attack *the whole* of each other's program."[19] Therefore "political tactics demand that every disagreement should be exploited and magnified, and every agreement minimized or kept dark."[20] She stresses the need for *"discovering* agreement

[19] *Freedom under Planning,* p. 147. As mentioned above, she probably underestimates the area of disagreement which would remain even if the magnifying effect of party politics were removed.

[20] *Ibid.,* p. 151.

prior to action,"[21] and certainly this discovery is never more important than before society enters into a phase in which a great task of economic reorganization must by necessity be performed. In the course of that process our political framework will inevitably be subject to stresses and strains, and therefore we must reinforce it by calling to mind that which we have in common. No reform, however praiseworthy in itself, would give us an adequate compensation for a break in the framework of democracy, but it is just as true that democracy has to prove its vitality in securing the necessary reforms. Error, however costly, is tolerable, so long as the will and the strength to effect corrections remain. Only stagnation is intolerable.

At the present moment there seems to be a great opportunity to reduce the price which we should have to pay for avoidable roundabout ways and unnecessary hesitations. We can spare ourselves much sacrifice if we ignore the soothing words, which try to make us believe that there is no great danger of a new depression, or that we can meet it by breaking monopolies, by a public works program, by extension of the social security services, by intensification of international trade, or by any other means short of the conscious guidance of production toward the full use of resources for the satisfaction of the consumers. Many of the other measures recommended as a remedy against a postwar slump are excellent in themselves, and some are even conditions for the survival of democracy, but they alone are inadequate as a protection from the danger of a new "crisis of abundance."

In the course of this essay, the industrial use of atomic power has been mentioned as a possible cause of abundance, which

[21] *Ibid.,* p. 148.

would put the problem of planning under an entirely different aspect. The sinister side of the great discovery, however, has an equally important bearing on the subject—but a separate and voluminous book would have to be written to elaborate the economic implications of the military use of atomic fission. In such a book, most of the space would have to be given to the problem of defensive preparedness for atomic warfare. Conceivably, the threat of atomic bombing will seem so great in the near future as to force us to disperse our industries and our population over as wide an area as possible, dissolving our big cities. Such an eventuality would make any discussion of planning in preatomic terms obsolete, nor would the concepts of balanced budget or limitation of government interference with business have a sound of realism in the face of this task. If a great dispersal movement became necessary at a time when atomic power was already available for industrial use, with that enormous increase of our productive capacity which some experts expect, a great deal of heartbreak would still be unavoidable, because it will always be found where people are uprooted from their habitual ways of life indiscriminately and without regard for their personal preferences, even if the standard of living can be maintained on a high level. Infinitely worse, however, would it be if dispersal was forced upon us before our industrial resources have been multiplied by the peaceful effects of atomic fission. In this event, the United States would lose much of the accumulated fruits of labor without compensation, and the resulting drop in the standard of living could be reduced but not eliminated by wise and careful planning. Let us hope that we can use planning as a means of making economic progress greater and safer instead of merely minimizing the loss of retrogression.

INDEX OF AUTHORS

INDEX OF SUBJECTS